THE ORTHODOX PARISH IN AMERICA

THE ORTHODOX PARISH IN AMERICA:

Faithfulness to the Past and Responsibility for the Future

Edited by
Anton C. Vrame

HOLY CROSS ORTHODOX PRESS
Brookline, Massachusetts

© Copyright 2003 Holy Cross Orthodox Press
Published by Holy Cross Orthodox Press
50 Goddard Avenue
Brookline, Massachusetts 02445

ISBN 1-885652-70-4

Cover photographs courtesy of CJK Design.

LIBRARY OF CONGRESS CATALOGING–IN–PUBLICATION DATA

The Orthodox parish in America : faithfulness to the past and responsibility for the future / edited by Anton C. Vrame.
   p. cm.
Includes bibliographical references.
ISBN 1-885652-70-4 (pbk. :alk. paper)
1. Orthodox Eastern Church—United States—Government. 2. Parishes—United States. I. Vrame, Anton C.
   BX733.O78 2003
   281.9'73—dc22
                                    2003017168

CONTENTS

Editor's Note

Holy Cross Greek Orthodox School of Theology hosted the academic conference, "The Orthodox Parish in America: Faithfulness to the Past and Responsibility for the Future" from September 28 to October 1, 2000 in response to the invitation of His All Holiness Bartholomew, Ecumenical Patriarch of Constantinople, to commemorate the advent of the third Christian millennium. The conference brought together approximately 125 clergy, scholars, students and other laypeople from throughout North America to study together and reflect on the state of the parish in America. The papers presented there generated lively discussion in and out of the conference sessions. Rather than be confined to "academic papers," the conference also included workshops on practical areas of parish life as a means of bridging the large gap that often exists between theory and practice.

No conference can address all the aspects of any topic. The Holy Cross conference was no exception. There are many issues facing the parish that were not addressed in the conference and thus are not included in this volume. However, some of these have been raised in other venues worth mentioning. For example, shortly after the Holy Cross conference, over 200 women gathered nearby to discuss issues facing women in Orthodox Churches. Later in the year, the Ecumenical Patriarchate held its first-ever, worldwide Clergy-Laity Congress with the theme: "The Parish: Cell of the Church's Life – Living Reality, Contemporary Orientation and Challenges." Discussion of parish issues could be a full-time occupation; the need for the Orthodox Churches to initiate an organized and systematic effort in this area is readily apparent.

Many of the papers and a few of the workshops are presented here to continue the discussion among Church members and leaders. The issues raised in these essays are challenging, from the broad concern of how Orthodoxy deals with American pluralism to the narrower issue of how music is utilized in worship. These papers also become a "first statement" by Orthodox to the growing discipline of "congregational studies," also opening areas for further study and reflection.

Anton C. Vrame
Editor

THE ORTHODOX PARISH IN AMERICA

THOMAS HOPKO

The word *parish*, like the word *diocese*, originally meant a geographic territory. A parish was a region of a diocese. The head of an Orthodox church in a parish was the parish priest (presbyter). The head of the diocese was the bishop who served as pastor of the diocese's main parish church.

The words *parish* and *diocese*, at least today in North America, no longer signify geographic territories or regions. In America today an Orthodox "parish" is a community of Orthodox Christians containing one or more priests, perhaps with one or more deacons, and other servers of various sorts. An Orthodox "diocese" is an association of such communities headed by a bishop who may have auxiliary bishops helping him to administer his "diocesan" collection of "parishes."

A situation like this has never existed in Orthodox history until early in the twentieth century in North America. Now it exists not only in the United States and Canada but in other areas of the so-called "Orthodox diaspora" such as South America, Western Europe and Australia. It has also recently appeared in places formerly having territorial Orthodox dioceses and parishes, such as Ukraine, Russia and Estonia.

Voluntary associations

Orthodox parishes and dioceses in North America today are, sociologically speaking, voluntary associations of like-minded Orthodox Christians organized for purposes determined by their members. An Orthodox parish, and even a diocese, can exist for any number of reasons: spiritual, national, cultural, ideological, political or even personal. A parish belongs to the diocese of its choice, most often on its own terms. This is ultimately true even when a parish was originally founded through diocesan, rather than simply parochial, initiative. In some cases in North America, parishes considering themselves Orthodox have not belonged to any diocese at all; or have belonged only nominally to insure a minimal measure of legitimacy for their ecclesiastical status. When an Orthodox parish in the United States

1

or Canada experiences a dispute which leads to a division of its members into one or more "parishes," the resulting "parishes" usually end up in different "dioceses."

There are countless reasons why such a situation now exists in North America, which all demonstrate the loss of Orthodox Christian consciousness, understanding, and behavior by Orthodox Christians, including church leaders, in America and abroad. Our present task is not to deal with the reasons for the present situation. It is rather to state the essential things to be believed, understood, and done if Orthodox parishes in America today are to be in the least way Christian according to traditional Orthodox teaching and practice.

One, Holy, Catholic and Apostolic

An Orthodox parish, i.e. a local community of Orthodox Christians with a priest, has only one God-given reason for being. It exists to be the one, holy, catholic and apostolic Church of Christ. Whatever the original reasons and conditions for its founding, whatever other services and activities it may provide, whatever other desires and needs it may fulfill for its members, a community of Orthodox Christians with one or more priests, must be Christ's one holy Church. If it is not, then it is neither Christian nor Orthodox, whatever else it may be and do.

We say that a parish must be *the* Church of Christ, and not simply *a* church, because, according to the Orthodox faith, every local community of Orthodox Christians with a priest must be – and, theologically understood, actually is – the one Church of Christ. Theologically speaking, there are not many Orthodox Churches; there is only one. An Orthodox parish is this one Church or it is not an Orthodox church at all. Each parish, therefore, must be the one and only Church of Christ.

The parish must be holy because Christ's Church is holy. Everything in the parish, and everything about it, must be holy because God and Christ are holy. The parish church is holy because it is from God, about God, and for God. There can be no part of a parish not sanctified by the holiness of God and His Son Jesus Christ, "the holy one of God." There can be no aspect of a parish not inspired and empowered by God's Holy Spirit, who is the Spirit of God and of Christ. Nothing in the parish, therefore, can be "merely human" or "secular." Everything in and about a parish – its organization, structure, administration, finances and properties, as well as its theological and moral teachings and practices, and its liturgical and sacramental rites and services – must be of God. They must be determined by God, inspired by God and submitted to God for His glory and the good of His people. Everything in the parish must be "sacredly theanthropic," so to speak, if the parish is what it must be, namely, Christ's holy Church.

The Orthodox Christian parish must also be catholic. For the parish to be "catholic" means that it is full, complete and whole; lacking nothing to its mystical and sacramental being and life as Christ's holy Church. In an Orthodox Christian parish the whole fullness of God must dwell, as in Christ's body, with all the fullness of life and grace and truth, by the indwelling of the Holy Spirit.

The word *catholic* literally means full or whole or complete. It does not, in the first instance, mean universal or worldwide. Thus every local Christian community, every "parish" in the contemporary American meaning of the word, theologically, mystically and sacramentally is, in apostolic words, "Christ's body, the fullness of Him who fills all in all" (Eph 1:23). It is "the household of God, which is the church of the living God, the pillar and bulwark of the truth" (1 Tim 3:15). Everything in the parish participates in God's fullness and wholeness. Everything expresses it. Everything testifies to it. Whatever is merely human, partial, fragmentary and incomplete has no place in an Orthodox parish. Whatever, in a word, and playing on words, is merely "parochial" cannot be there. This obviously does not mean that a parish will not be particular and limited in its human empirical, cultural and sociological forms. It has to be, since it is made up of human beings. But all of a parish's particular aspects, with all of its teachings, services and activities, if they are Orthodox and Christian, will be open to the boundless fullness of God and will thereby be inclusive of everyone and everything that is good and holy and true to the measure that this is possible, given the actual people who comprise the community.

And, finally, according to the notes of Christ's Church in the Nicene creed, the Orthodox parish that is truly Christian will not only be the same Church of Christ with every other parish; one with God's unity, holy with God's holiness, and catholic with God's fullness; it will also be apostolic with God's own apostolicity which is found in the Church of Christ in all times and places.

An Orthodox parish, if it is Christ's one holy Church, will be apostolic in at least two meanings of the term. It will be apostolic because it is founded upon Christ's apostles and firmly rooted in apostolic doctrine and tradition. It will keep and live "the faith which was once and for all delivered to the saints" (Jude 3). It will preserve and pass on the apostolic "deposit" (*paratheke*) which has been guarded and developed by Orthodox Christians, particularly through their bishops, in all times and places, from apostolic times to the present (cf. 1 Tim 6:20; 2 Tim 1:12,14).

An Orthodox parish is apostolic also because it exists with God's mission, which is the mission of Jesus Christ, the Holy Spirit and the apostles of all ages, beginning with Christ's own. The Greek word *apostello*, from which the words apostle and apostolic are derived, means to *send*. So does the Latin word *mitto*, from which are derived the words mission and missionary. According to the Scriptures, Jesus the Messiah is himself "the apostle" (Heb 3:1). According to his scriptural testimony, especially in the Gospel according to St. John, Jesus speaks the words, does the work, and accomplishes the will "of the Father (or the one) who sent" him (cf. Jn 6:29,44; 7:28, 33; 17:3, 18). In the same Scriptures, the apostles, being filled with the Holy Spirit who proceeds from the Father and is sent by the Son, are themselves sent into the world by Jesus to proclaim the gospel of God's kingdom. "As the Father has sent me, even so I send you... Receive the Holy Spirit" (Jn 20:21).

An Orthodox Christian parish, however it was founded and for whatever purpose it was organized, must understand itself to be an apostolic community with a missionary purpose. Its members, especially its leaders, must be conscious of themselves as people sent by Christ from God and empowered by the Holy Spirit to bring God's unity, holiness and fullness to all human beings in this divided, sinful and fragmented world. If a parish has no awareness and consciousness of being "sent" by God to speak His words, to do His work, and to accomplish His will in this world, then it is not an Orthodox Christian parish. At best it is a bunch of decent people carrying on a bundle of benign activities for their own benefit. At worst, to use apocalyptic words, it is a "synagogue of Satan" perverting God's gospel by its "blasphemy against the Holy Spirit (which) will not be forgiven, either in this age or in the age to come" (Rev 2:9, 3:9; Mt 12:31-32; Mk 3:28).

Prophetic, priestly, and pastoral people

For an Orthodox parish to be Christ's one, holy, catholic, and apostolic Church, its members must understand themselves to be a prophetic, priestly and pastoral people. They must know that by faith and grace they are called to actualize Christ's presence and power in their midst as God's unique messianic prophet, priest, and pastor. They must see the head of their parish, the presbyter with his bishop, as the sacramentally ordained prophet, priest, and pastor who ensures that "God is with us," through Christ His Son, constituting the community as "a chosen race, a royal priesthood, a holy nation, God's own people" by the Holy Spirit (1 Pet 2:9).

As a prophetic, priestly, and pastoral people the members of an Orthodox parish must be motivated to keep God's commandments as their essential and ultimately exclusive reason for being. The life and activity of an Orthodox Christian parish, made by Christ to be a prophetic "kingdom, priests to his God and Father" (Rev 1:6), can be perfectly described by Jesus' answer to the question concerning the first and great commandment of the law of God:

And one of the scribes... asked him, "Which commandment is first of all?" Jesus answered, "The first is, 'Hear, O Israel: The Lord our God, the Lord is one; and you shall love the Lord your God with all your heart, and with all your soul, and with all your mind, and with all your strength.' The second is this, 'You shall love your neighbor as yourself.' There is no other commandment greater than these" (Mk 12:28-31).

In the Gospel according to St. Matthew, Jesus teaches that "on these two commandments (Dt 6:5 and Lev 19:18) depend all the law and the prophets (Mt 22:40). For our present purposes we can also say that on these two commandments depend the whole being and life on an Orthodox Christian parish as a community of prophetic, priestly, and pastoral people.

Heart: Liturgical worship and sacramental service

Jesus says that God must be loved first of all with all one's heart. In biblical usage, the heart is the center of a person's being. It is the ground of a person's life, the seat of a person's will, and the source of a person's activity, beginning with one's words. It is the "place where God bears witness to himself," according to St. Isaac of Syria; the place in a person, according to St. Macarius of Egypt, which contains God Himself, and Christ and the Holy Spirit, and the whole of creation, visible and invisible, spiritual and material, good and evil. A person's heart reveals what he or she really is, and really thinks, and really wants, and really does. "For where your treasure is," "Jesus tells us, "there will your heart be also" (Mt 6:21).

The heart of a parish, if it is Christ's one holy Church, will be totally given to God. In this sense, the heart of an Orthodox Christian parish will be its liturgical and sacramental worship. Worship will constitute the parish's core. It will be the parish's essential mode of self-realization. It will be its basic reason for being, the foundational purpose for its existence and life.

An Orthodox Christian parish is first and foremost a worshipping community. It exists to praise, bless and glorify God; to ceaselessly sing the thrice-holy hymn to the life-creating Trinity. Its essential purpose is to baptize people in the name of the Father and the Son and the Holy Spirit; to enable them to die in Christ and to be raised with Him to newness of life; to be sealed with the gift of the Holy Spirit; to hear God's Word, to respond to God's Gospel, to participate in the eucharistic sacrifice of Christ's Body and Blood; and to actualize God's kingdom on earth, in spirit and truth, by faith and grace, until Christ comes in glory at the close of the age.

If an Orthodox parish is not fundamentally a community of liturgical and sacramental worship, if it is merely an association which provides cultic rites to its members, often for a fee, as they desire and demand, then it is not an Orthodox Christian church. It is, as we have said, at best a center of benign and benevolent activities, some of them 'religious' and some of them 'secular,' enacted by order of its members; and at worst, it is a 'synagogue of Satan' which will not be forgiven its blasphemy against the Holy Spirit.

Soul: Spiritual life and pastoral care

An Orthodox Christian parish must also be a community of people loving God with all their souls, as God's law commands and Jesus confirms. The word *soul* (Greek *psyche*, Hebrew *nefesh*) literally means *life* and is often rendered as such in contemporary translations of the Bible into English.

Loving God with all one's soul means loving Him with all of one's thoughts, words and deeds in all of the routine thinking, talking and acting involved in everyday living. For an Orthodox Christian parish, if it is Christ's holy church, this means that the community as a whole, and each individual member of it, is personally committed to living a Christian spiritual life by struggling to keep God's commandments. "If you love me," Jesus says in St. John's Gospel, "you will keep my commandments. And I will pray the Father, and He will give you another Comforter (Grk: *parakletos*; counselor, advocate) to be with you forever, even the Spirit of truth, whom the world cannot receive, because it neither sees him nor knows him; you know him, for he dwells with you, and will be in you" (Jn 14:15-17).

Christian spiritual life relates to every aspect of a person's being and to every area of a person's life and work. It has to do with his or her body and behavior, as well as to his or her thoughts and feelings. It has to do with sexuality as well as spirituality, to public and political action as well as to private and personal activity. People need help in living a Christian spiritual life in its fullness and depth. People's rationally-animated bodies do not mechanically become "members of Christ" and "temples of the Holy Spirit" (1 Cor 6:15-19). And a person's corporally-enfleshed spirit does not magically possess the "mind of Christ" (1 Cor 2:16) and become "one spirit" with the Lord. (1 Cor 6:17).

Members of Christ's Church must have spiritual guidance and direction. They require pastoral attention and care. They need instruction in "fighting the good fight" by learning how to resist temptation, to reject evil thoughts, and to overcome sinful passions by partaking, through faith and grace, in Christ's victory through the Holy Spirit. Such spiritual and pastoral services must be present in an Orthodox Christian parish, if it is truly Christ's holy Church. They need not, and indeed cannot be provided by the clergy alone. It is the duty of bishops and priests, however, to see that people capable of providing these services do so, for the benefit of those willing to receive them. The Orthodox Christian parish is the proper place for this to happen. If it is not happening, then, once again, the parish community is not Christ's Church.

Mind: Education and enlightenment

Essential also to an Orthodox parish, if it is Christ's holy Church, is total mobilization of efforts to love God with all of one's mind through enlightenment and education.

Jesus' first title in the scripture is *rabbi,* which means teacher or master (Grk: *didaskolos,* Latin: *magister*). As messianic pastor and priest, Christ is also "the prophet" who brings ultimate and lasting judgment upon those who hear and reject him (cf. Jn 1:21,6:14; Acts 3:22-26). The Lord's first followers are called disciples or students. And the first thing said about those who believed in God's gospel of Christ crucified and glorified is that they "continued steadfastly in the apostles' doctrine" (Acts 2:42).

An Orthodox Christian parish, therefore, is essentially a teaching and learning community for all its members. It is a school of disciples whose master is Christ as He speaks within the company of believers, especially through the pastors and those with the charism and training for teaching and preaching.

An Orthodox parish without well-prepared evangelical and exegetical sermons at its liturgical services, and well-prepared doctrinal and catechetical sessions as part of its educational ministry, whatever else it might do, including having lots of liturgical services and loads of social events, can hardly be an Orthodox Christian church. This is especially true now in North America when Christianity generally, not to speak of Orthodoxy, is not a respected, accepted, and supported part of public life and education, but is rather warred against, scorned, and ridiculed by powerful forces in society. It is also especially true since more and more Orthodox Christians participate in parish life by choice and conviction, and not simply because of convention and custom.

Strength: Mission and philanthropy

Loving God with all one's strength, particularly according to the Hebrew text of Holy Scripture, means that we are to love God with all that we possess, primarily our money and property. Strength, in this context, does not merely mean mental, emotional, or physical might, though these, of course, are not to be excluded from our love for the Lord.

An Orthodox Christian parish, when it is Christ's holy Church, is obliged to use all of its powers for God's glory and the people's good. Christians as individual persons, as well as families, parishes and dioceses will have to give account to Christ for how they used their God-given strength. We will have to answer for our use of money and resources, property and possessions, positions and profits. We will be asked how we loved "in deed and in truth," and not merely "in word or speech," through concrete acts of charity for the hungry and thirsty, the sick and suffering, the homeless and naked, the persecuted and imprisoned (cf. 1 Jn 3:18; Mt 25:31-46).

On judgment day, the Lord will not ask us about our parish size and facilities. Nor will He be interested in our liturgical schedule or style. He will not ask us how we dressed or what we ate. He will be indifferent to how large our church temples were, where they were located, or how they were decorated and appointed. Nor will He ask us to recite the Nicene Creed or to explain the doctrine of the Holy Trinity. All of these things are essential, but their significance has only one end: the love of God with all one's heart, soul, mind and strength, expressed, as it can only be expressed in this present age, in concrete acts of love for our neighbors, first of all the members of our own families and churches, and most all for those who hate and oppose us.

Love of God with all our strength through acts of love for our neighbors and enemies is enacted primarily in acts of evangelism and philanthropy. While sacramental participation in an Orthodox parish is strictly reserved for committed Orthodox Christians who take full responsibility for the Church's faith and life, and completely identify with the Church's path through history, the philanthropic and evangelical activities of an Orthodox Christian parish, as well as its services of teaching, counseling and prayerful intercession, have no bounds or limitations of any kind. They are to be exercised freely and without discrimination for all people regardless of their religion, nationality, race, sexual orientation, or relation to Christ's Church. The first Christians, as witnessed in the New Testament writings and such saints as John Chrysostom and Olympia, Fr. John of Kronstadt, and Mother Maria Skobstova, taught and practiced this Christian truth without the slightest hesitation, equivocation or compromise.

A parish without carefully planned and implemented evangelical and philanthropic activity directed both within and outside its parochial bounds, is, once again, simply not Orthodox or Christian. This is especially the case when huge sums of money are collected in parishes through secular activities, and spent primarily, if not exclusively, for self-serving parochial purposes, like the salaries of the parish employees (including the clergy), or the acquisition of unnecessary properties and luxurious appointments.

Structure and administration

For an Orthodox parish to be mobilized to love God fully, and to prove this in concrete acts of worship, education, pastoral care, spiritual direction, evangelism, and philanthropy, requires that the parish have a proper Christian structure and administration.

The head of the parish in its total life must be the chief parish presbyter who is ordained and assigned by the diocesan bishop. This does not mean that the parish priest functions merely as the bishop's "representative" or "delegate." It means rather that he is appointed by the bishop and accepted by the parish as the community's spiritual and sacramental leader, father and pastor. He is the head of the body who images and presents God and Christ in every aspect of the Lord's messianic ministry.

The Christian parish headed by its priest shows that it is truly Christ's holy Church, and not merely a human association of like-minded people incorporated to satisfy the demands and desires of its members. When functioning properly, the properly structured parish maintains its identity and integrity as Christ's body, the household of God. It realizes itself in a sacramentally-ordered hierarchal and conciliar structure. In this way, as Fr. Alexander Schmemann used to say, a secularized hierarchy opposed to conciliarity is prevented from exercising tyranny, and a secularized community opposed to hierarchal leadership is protected from succumbing to anarchy.

The parish priest, properly understood in Christian Orthodoxy, is neither a domineering despot nor a servile hireling. He is neither an authoritarian "stand-in" for an almost always absent hierarch, nor a lackey at the beck and call of a secularized "board of trustees." He is rather a called, trained, tested and ordained teacher, pastor, and priest who guarantees the presence and action of Christ in the community. His God-given task, confirmed by the *pleroma* of the faithful, is to beget children to God through God's Word and Spirit, and to empower every parishioner to find and fulfill his or her calling as a member of Christ's body. He is the servant of God, for God's glory and the good of all people, including those outside the parish community, whoever they may be.

Unity and variety

Until God's kingdom comes with power at the end of the age, Orthodox Christian parishes around the world will be struggling to be Christ's holy Church. These parishes, certainly in the United States and Canada, will be of a great variety of sizes, shapes and styles, though each one, theologically and mystically, will be the very same Church of Christ. The parishes will be composed of different kinds of people. They will be of different cultures and traditions. They will have different emphases and possibilities in worship, education, pastoral care, and philanthropic and evangelical activity. None of them will claim that they can do everything by themselves. All of them will admit that they need each other, being constrained by truth and love, to cooperate for God's glory and the good of God's people. They will all confess that to do God's work they cannot compete with each other, but must complete each other in Christian service and ministry. They will know that the only way in which they should strive to outdo each other is in expressing godly zeal, brotherly affection, due honor and mutual respect (cf. Rom 12:9-13).

The priests in these God-guided parishes will pastor their people not by lording it over them, but by giving their life to them in godly service with diligence, patience, and love. They will not look for the kind of parishes they want, with parishioners prepared to satisfy their ideological, liturgical and pietistic passions. They will rather humbly and gratefully serve the actual parishes they are in, identifying by God's grace with the people whom God has given them. The guiding rule for such priests will be forever provided by the apostle Paul who became "all things to all people, that (he) might by all means save some" (1 Cor 9:22).

Whatever confusions and difficulties confront Orthodox Christianity in North America today, whatever their origins and causes, and whatever temptations and trials they bring to believers, there is no good reason why an Orthodox Christian parish in the United States or Canada cannot be Christ's holy Church. All that is required is that its members, beginning with its leaders, be firmly resolved to have it so. Their afflictions will be great, as Christ has promised, but their successes are assured by His victory. "In the world you have tribulation," Jesus says to his apostles, "but take courage, I have overcome the world" (Jn 16:33). "For what is impossible with men is possible with God" (Lk 18:27).

The Development of the Orthodox Parish in the United States

Thomas FitzGerald

Introduction

Orthodox Christians have been living in North America for over two hundred years. Whether in large cities or in small towns, they have gathered together in parish communities under the sign of the Holy Cross. Orthodox Christians have celebrated the Liturgy together in accordance with the Lord's command. They have proclaimed the faith together, the faith of the apostles and martyrs, the faith of the Fathers and the Mothers of the Church in other times and places. They have sought to maintain continuity with the saints, the righteous men and women in every age and in every place.

Today, there are about 1500 Orthodox parishes in the United States. Some parishes are composed of a handful of members who meet in simple surroundings. Other parishes are composed of thousands of members who gather in multi-million-dollar facilities. Some parishes bring together faithful with very specific ethnic and linguistic characteristics. Other parishes are composed of faithful who come from a variety of racial, cultural, ethnic and religious backgrounds. Some parishes bring together believers from a neighborhood or a particular part of a city. Other parishes serve the Orthodox living in a vast geographical area. Some parishes are involved in the life of the wider society and are known for their philanthropy. Other parishes are like cocoons, having little regard for the needs of the society around them. If known at all by the wider society, these parishes are often renowned only for their food festivals.

While the faith affirmations of Orthodox Christianity formally unite all of these parishes, there is a great deal of diversity among these communities of faith. In every parish, the faithful are called to bear witness to the Gospel of Christ as the Orthodox Church proclaims it. Yet, at the same time, there is a remarkable diversity to Orthodox parish life which is not always salutary. From the very moment when a parish is established, it takes on it own distinctive characteristics. After all, it is a living community of

11

faith. Yes, it is meant to be a community of faith rooted in the Gospel of Christ. Each parish, however, is also a community of faith which is truly like a family. It is a family with a history. It is a family which has its human members, who can be either faithful or faithless. It is a family which has its opportunities to serve the Lord or to serve fleeting idols.

The diverse character of the Orthodox parishes in America does not permit us to speak in absolute categories about their development as a whole. Each and every parish truly has its own story. In addition, most of these stories cannot easily be told because accurate records have rarely been kept. Indeed, some of the stories are best not told. Certainly, these stories have not been documented with a high degree of accuracy. This fact immediately confronts anyone who wishes seriously to study the development of Orthodoxy in America. Indeed, most studies of Orthodoxy in America have focused upon the development and characteristic features of the various diocesan and archdiocesan jurisdictions in this country.[1] While it is the parishes which make up the "flesh and blood" of these jurisdictions, there has been little serious effort to study these communities of faith in a manner which is realistic, honest and free from triumphalism.[2]

With these facts in mind, we will in this paper identify trends and characteristics of Orthodox parish life in America in a rather broad manner. Four major observations will be made. These observations will assist us in understanding the distinctive developmental characteristics of Orthodox parishes in the United States.

THE DIVERSITY OF PARISH ORIGINS

The first observation is that Orthodox parishes in this country have very different beginnings. There is no uniform pattern which characterizes the emergence of Orthodox parishes over the past two hundred years.

The mission parish

Some parishes are the result of a clear defined missionary endeavor. Most of us would think immediately of many of the parishes in Alaska. The majority of these parishes trace their roots back to the first missionaries of 1794, or the work of the subsequent missionaries of the early 1800's.[3] While these early missionaries confronted numerous difficult challenges, the work of Russian Orthodox missionaries in Alaska in the eighteenth and nineteenth centuries is remarkable and should never be overlooked in any study of Orthodoxy in America. From the start, the missionaries were concerned with teaching the Gospel of Christ to the native peoples which naturally led to the establishment of Orthodox parish communities. The directive given to the first missionaries by Metropolitan Gabriel of St. Petersburg says in part: "When Jesus Christ leads you to meet those who do not know the Law of God, your first concern will be to serve as an example of good works to them, so as to convert them by your personal life into obedient servants of the Lord."[4]

These words found a vivid expression in the simple witness of St. Herman of Alaska, one of the first missionaries who served from 1784 to 1837 as well as in the witness of St. Innocent John Veniaminov, who served in Alaska from 1824 to 1850. While the former was not ordained and had only rudimentary education, the latter engaged in translating the Scriptures and Liturgy into local languages and became the first resident bishop. Both are remembered for their deep devotion to the native Orthodox.

By the time Alaska was sold to the United States in 1870, it is estimated that there were over 100 Orthodox parish communities comprised of over 10,000 native Alaskan Orthodox. Regrettably, the inadequate number of trained missionaries and clergy weakened the presence of the Orthodox Church in the new American territory during the subsequent decades. Moreover, when Protestant missionaries entered the territory, they demonstrated little regard for the Orthodox Church and the customs of the Alaskan peoples. Many Orthodox believers and their parishes were the victims of a tragic onslaught of proselytism. [5]

The Alaskan Mission has been a source of inspiration for many of the subsequent missionary parishes which developed in the United States. While the intense effort of evangelization which characterized the Alaskan mission has never been repeated, there has been a concern for mission, which has taken a variety of forms over the past century especially.

Some would claim that many of the parishes established to serve the Orthodox immigrants during the late nineteenth and early twentieth century had a mission spirit to them. Devoted immigrant clergy and laity were deeply concerned about maintaining their Orthodox Christian Faith in the New World. Despite the many difficulties they faced, they were concerned with having a place of worship and fellowship.[6]

Other observers would point to those efforts in more recent decades to found "daughter" parishes from larger and more established parishes. As we shall see, these parishes often were established in suburban locations and were oriented toward newer generations of Orthodox who had moved out of the older immigrant neighborhoods.

Still others would point to the attempts to establish new parishes which have a "pan-Orthodox" character to them and are concerned with ministering to the so-called "unchurched." From the start, many of these new mission parishes have emphasized the universal character of Orthodoxy. They have not overly identified themselves with a particular ethnic group or language. They have made a commendable effort to share the Orthodox faith and worship especially with those persons who had no previous connection with Orthodoxy.

Mission is central to the life of the Orthodox Church and its parishes. Yet, apart from the unparalled effort of the Alaskan Mission, the centrality of mission has not always received the appropriate emphasis until quite recently. With the development of the parishes established by and for the immigrants in the early twentieth century especially, parish life was concerned chiefly with serving the needs of a specific group of people. In these parishes, there was generally a very close relationship between ethnicity, language and faith which led to little missionary outreach.

Prior to leaving the United States to return to Russia in 1907, Archbishop Tikhon, who world later become Patriarch of Moscow, boldly spoke of the importance of Orthodox mission in America when he said:

> Orthodox people must care for the dissemination of the Orthodox faith among the heterodox. Christ the Savior said that men lighting a lamp do not put it under a bushel but on a stand, and it gives light to all in the house. (Mt 5:15). The light of Orthodoxy also is not lit for a small circle of people. No, the Orthodox faith is catholic. It remembers the command of its founder: "Go into the whole world" (Mt 28:19.) It is our obligation to share our spiritual treasures, our truth, our light and our joy with those who do not have these gifts."[7]

The early immigrant parish

Many of the Orthodox parishes began as the direct result of immigration. Beginning in the late nineteenth century and continuing into the early twentieth century, about half a million Orthodox immigrants entered the United States. Many came from Greece, Asia Minor, Carpatho-Russia, the Ukraine, and the Middle East. Lesser numbers came from Serbia, Bulgaria, Romania, and Russia. Almost immediately, the immigrants set about to establish parishes, to construct church buildings and to find a priest. This was done often with little or no formal direction from church authorities either here or in the Old Country.

These early immigrant parishes usually served the needs of a particular ethnic or linguistic group. The church buildings not only provided a place for worship and the celebration of the Eucharist and the Sacraments but also provided a secure place for fellowship and mutual support. With these Orthodox immigrants, there was an intimate link between the family and the parish. There was also an intimate link between faith and the culture and language of the old world. Most came from places where there had been a historic, intimate relationship between faith and culture. It was natural, therefore, that the early immigrants would seek to transfer this interrelationship to the New World, a place which presented to many both opportunities and hardships.

Moreover, the large urban centers of the United States during the late nineteenth and early twentieth centuries provided the neighborhoods where the various immigrant groups could maintain their faith, culture and language somewhat insulated from the wider society. This was true not only for the various Orthodox immigrant groups. It was also true for certain Roman Catholic immigrants and certain Protestant immigrants. The early Greek and Slavic immigrants in New York, Boston, Pittsburgh or Chicago could see a certain parallel between their view of church and society, and those held by Italian Catholics and Swedish Lutherans, for example. Urban life was frequently characterized by numerous ethnic neighborhoods. In addition, these ethnic neighborhoods had their fill of ethnic parishes.

The accomplishments of these first Orthodox immigrants were truly remarkable. In 1870, there were only 3 Orthodox parishes in the United States exclusive of Alaska. Fifty years later in 1920, there were about 250 parishes comprised primarily of Orthodox immigrants.[8]

As we look back upon their experience, however, we can also recognize the limitations of these early immigrant parishes. Although they shared the same Orthodox Christian faith, there was hardly any contact among the various Orthodox immigrant groups. Episcopal oversight was not always present or even desired by some. Diocesan structures for the various parishes were not fully established, and certainly not fully accepted. Linguistic and cultural barriers were high. Different liturgical traditions sometimes served as an additional barrier. Deep animosities between various Orthodox peoples from the Old World frequently were carried into the new. The politics of the Old Country often divided parishioners of the same ethnic background.

In addition to this, the Orthodox immigrants had to formally organize their own parishes, often with little or no assistance or direction from higher church authorities. Similarly, these parishes were free from the traditional church-state affiliations which were common in many of their homelands. Usually the legal organization of the parishes placed full responsibility in the hands of the lay board of trustees. Following the practice of some Protestant congregations, lay trustees controlled Orthodox parish property and finances. The trustees hired and supervised the priest. The trustees negotiated with the bishop, when there was one available. In many cases, the lay trustees encouraged the movement of the parish from one jurisdiction to another depending upon their political allegiances. The lack of appropriate diocesan structures, limited education in Orthodoxy and the limited appreciation of Orthodox ecclesiological principals frequently led to an unhealthy spirit of "congregationalism" which continues to afflict many parishes.

While the immigration of Orthodox Christians from Eastern Europe and the Middle East has not ceased, it dramatically diminished after the 1920's. Even the recent increase in Orthodox immigrants from the Balkans and the Middle East resulting from political turmoil there has done little to change this fact. Thus, the decreasing number of Orthodox immigrants in the past fifty years has had a profound impact upon Orthodox parishes and their jurisdictions. Even with the limited information available, the picture of the situation is uneven and not always encouraging.

Some of the earliest Orthodox parishes in the United States have ceased to exist. Some have merged with more viable parishes in the same city or region. Other parishes have not had in recent years a sufficient population to support a regular parish priest. Some parishes, especially those in the urban centers, have relied upon the limited immigration to maintain a degree of viability. In order to attract the few new immigrants, and to maintain themselves, these parishes have sought to maintain a strong ethnic identity.

Other Orthodox parishes have had the ability to recognize the changing demographic realities and have been able to attract the newer generations of Orthodox Christians who are born and raised in this country. The majority of Orthodox parishes today comprise Americans of various ethnic and racial backgrounds. Many are the descendents of Orthodox immigrants. An ever-growing number of others were raised in different religious traditions and subsequently chose to enter the Orthodox Church.

Parishes coming from other traditions

A small but significant number of parishes have resulted from the community's move from a non-Orthodox Christian tradition into full communion with the Orthodox Church.

When the Carpatho-Russian immigrants came to this country in the late nineteenth century, they came as Eastern Rite Roman Catholics. Their Orthodox ancestors had united with Rome in the sixteenth century.[9] They had retained many of their Orthodox liturgical and cultural traditions. Here in this country, about 80 Carpatho-Russian parishes entered the Russian Orthodox Archdiocese (Metropolia) between 1891 and 1909 under the leadership of Fr. Alexis Toth, now recognized as a saint. These parishes radically transformed the Russian Orthodox Archdiocese, which traced its origin to the Alaskan Mission but had done little mission work outside of that region. The diocesan center was transferred from San Francisco to New York in 1905 chiefly because of the "return" of the Carpathian-Russians and their parishes.[10]

This remarkable pattern was repeated later in the 1930s. A group of former Ukrainian Catholic parishes was received into the Orthodox Church under the jurisdiction of the Patriarchate of Constantinople in 1931.[11] Another group of Eastern Catholic, Carpatho-Russian parishes numbering about 40 entered the Orthodox Church in the jurisdiction of the Patriarch of Constantinople in 1937. This group was led by Fr. Orestes Chornock, who was subsequently elected as their bishop.[12]

The story does not end there. Since at least 1958 there have been movements of entire parishes from the Episcopal or Anglican tradition into Orthodoxy. Most of these parishes did not abandon their Western liturgical traditions. Rather, they modified them and claimed that their practices reflected traditions which predated the Great Schism. At the present time, there are approximately 20 "Western Rite" Orthodox parishes which are part of the Antiochian Orthodox Archdiocese.[13]

In more recent years, about 10 parishes formerly associated with the Evangelical Orthodox Church have entered into full communion with the Orthodox Church through the Antiochian Orthodox Archdiocese. Before their reception in 1987, these former Evangelical Protestant parishes went through a process by which they gradually abandoned their Protestant worship traditions and adopted the Byzantine liturgical tradition.[14]

The examination of the Orthodox Church in the United States cannot ignore the fact that its parishes have very different origins. These diverse origins have affected the identity and development of these parishes. Many immediately think of the parishes established by Orthodox immigrants in the late nineteenth and early twentieth century. At the same time, one cannot ignore those parishes which have been established directly as missions as well as those parishes which have come into Orthodoxy with a previous history in another Christian tradition.

OLD WORLD CONTROVERSIES IN THE PARISHES

Our second observation is that many parishes, especially the immigrant parishes, have been deeply affected by ethnic, political, and religious debates centered in the so-called Old Country. These debates frequently manifest themselves in the life and organization of the new parishes in America.

In the wake of the Russian Revolution of 1917 and the subsequent Civil War, Russian Orthodox parishes in this country became deeply divided into at least four groups. This resulted from a breakdown in church leadership, the loss of financial support from the old tsarist government and Russian politics which pitted royalists against socialists.[15] After the death of Patriarch Tikhon in 1925, some parishes sought to remain attached to the beleaguered Moscow Patriarchate. Some adopted a royalist stance and eventually became part of the Russian Synod Abroad. A few parishes became associated with the "Living Church" movement. The majority of Russian Orthodox in the United States parishes chose neither to remain with Moscow nor to become aligned with the Synod Abroad. These parishes remained part of the Russian Orthodox Archdiocese (Metropolia) which declared itself "self-governing" in 1924.[16]

The difficulties which the Russian Orthodox parishes experienced also affected the Syrian (Antiochian) Orthodox parishes. Most of the early Syrian Orthodox parishes had come under the jurisdiction of the Russian Orthodox Archdiocese. As early as 1904, Bishop Raphael Hawaweeny was consecrated to lead these parishes within the Russian Orthodox Archdiocese. However, the difficulties afflicting the Russian Orthodox Archdiocese after 1917 led to a movement of some Antiochian parishes to establish a direct relationship with the Patriarchate of Antioch. This division also reflected ethnic and regional differences from the Old World. In 1936, two rival groups of Russian Orthodox bishops consecrated bishops for the two rival Antiochian groups. These two dioceses were eventually recognized by the Patriarchate of Antioch and coexisted until a full union took place in 1975.[17]

The political developments in Greece led to divisions in Greek Orthodox parishes between 1920 and 1930 especially. The clash was between the political parties known popularly known as the Venezelists and the Royalists. The politics of the Old Country found expression in the attitudes of parishioners and in the life of most of the Greek Orthodox parishes in the United States. As a result of political differences, many parishes became internally divided. New parishes were sometimes created. Parishes were often set against one another. These political differences were reflected in the "old calendar-new calendar" debate after 1923 and in jurisdictional affiliation. The parishes which sided with the Royalist cause established a rival diocese in 1923. This diocese was not in communion either with the Church of Constantinople or the Church of Greece. In the same year, these parishes and their diocese refused to accept the new calendar which was introduced by the Patriarchate of Constantinople and the Church of Greece.

These tragic divisions continued without resolution until 1930 when the Patriarchate reorganized the hierarchy and elected Archbishop Athenagoras of Kerkyra to serve as the new Archbishop. During his tenure, Archbishop

Athenagoras (1930-1948) accomplished much to overcome the political differences and to bring together most of the alienated Greek Orthodox parishes into the Archdiocese.

Archbishop Athenagoras also recognized that the lack of cooperation and, in some cases, divisions among the various Orthodox jurisdictions could continue to affect the stability of parishes. His own experiences taught him that Greek Orthodox parishes were easily disturbed by itinerant or renegade clergy who often claimed association with other jurisdictions. This led him to become an ardent champion of greater Orthodox cooperation and witness.

Reflecting upon the divisions which had afflicted the Greek Orthodox parishes and looking towards a more unified Orthodox witness, Archbishop Athenagoras wrote in 1941:

> Our Church, although she is the Orthodox Church of Christ, and although our Christian faithful have exceeded the five million mark, is still officially "the forgotten Church in America." Clergy and faithful are not sufficiently known to each other. We have made no effort to make our Orthodox Church and the immense treasures of her dogma, her moral teachings, history, tradition, and rituals known to the American government, churches of other denominations, intellectuals, and to the American public in general. We do not have the means to defend our faith against any kind of proselytism.[18]

The victory of communist governments in Eastern Europe following World War II also led to new divisions within and between many Orthodox parishes in this country. Some parishes sought to maintain jurisdictional affiliation with the "Mother Church," in spite of new political realities in the Old Country. Other parishes broke with their "Mother Church" and took up the fierce anti-Communist banner. These political and ecclesiastical divisions led to tragic consequences in many parishes. Jurisdictional divisions developed among the Bulgarian Orthodox (1947), the Albanian Orthodox (1950), the Romanian Orthodox (1951), the Ukrainian Orthodox (1950's) and the Serbian Orthodox (1963). The establishment of rival dioceses reflected the divisions primarily of a political nature which existed at the parish level.[19]

Speaking about the tragic consequences of these divisions, Fr. John Meyendorff says:

> The multiplicity of jurisdictions is the fruit of religious nationalism which was so widespread between the two World Wars. This nationalism found fertile ground in certain aspects of the American social structure. In the case of the Orthodox, the religious nationalism imported from Europe was superimposed on the American social strata. The result is that the "Russian Orthodox" is thought to belong to a different denomination from the "Greek Orthodox."[20]

The more recent political developments in the Balkan countries have also manifested themselves in the lives of Orthodox parishes, especially of the Serbian, Macedonian, Albanian and Bulgarian traditions. Many parishioners in these parishes continue to maintain deep political and emotional connections to their old homeland. At the same time, some political leaders and some church authorities in some of these countries have encouraged parishes in this country to express a partisan political and nationalistic perspective.

Many Orthodox parishes from nearly all jurisdictions have been embroiled, at one time or another, in bitter and divisive debates over the past eighty years. These debates usually were rooted in political changes in the Old Country, and the related changes in ecclesiastical jurisdictions there and in this country. The first generation of Orthodox immigrants were divided among themselves because of differences in language and customs. In subsequent decades, these divisions were compounded with additional divisions chiefly over politics. The political issues frequently were reflected in questions of canonicity, calendar and jurisdiction. Indeed, these topics frequently became 'religious' themes which masked the deeper political and nationalistic issues. As we look back upon our history, we are struck by the fact that the fundamental Orthodox Christian identity of many parishes often were distorted by partisan political agendas and ideologies.

The deep divisions which affected the Orthodox parishes of virtually every jurisdiction deeply wounded them to the core. The controversies of the Old World were manifest in the lives of parishioners and their parishes. Internal divisions within parishes frequently led to family divisions, acts of violence and to civil court cases. Some parishes never recovered from these battles. Others were profoundly affected by these battles. The mission and witness of Orthodoxy in America was severely jeopardized.[21]

The prominent historian Martin Marty says of these difficulties:

> Orthodoxy kept stating cosmopolitan Christian claims but was itself fiercely divided on national lines and subjected to local control. For such reasons, with a potent and uniting voice and movement absent, the rest of American leadership could ignore the claims and leave inhabitants of Orthodox enclaves alone, often to fight each other.[22]

AN ERA OF TRANSITION: THE BEGINNINGS OF A PARADIGM SHIFT

Our third observation is that signs of significant changes in many parishes become more pronounced in the period between 1950-1975 especially. This was especially true for parishes which were part of the Greek Orthodox Archdiocese, the Syrian (Antiochian) Orthodox Archdiocese, and the Russian Orthodox Metropolia, which in 1970 became the Orthodox Church in America.

Central to these changes was the decrease in immigration. The immigration laws of the 1920s placed greater restrictions on the flow of immigrants from Eastern Europe and the Middle East. While some Orthodox immigrants, political refugees and displaced persons continued to arrive in this country over the past eighty years, the massive immigration of the late 1800s and early 1900s would never be repeated.

This fact contributed to a dramatic change in the demographics of many parishes. From the 1950s onward, the larger Orthodox parishes were composed of a majority of parishioners born in this country. These parishioners were nurtured by this country's educational institutions and were more attuned to this country's social and political issues. They were far more comfortable with the wider American society than their parents or grandparents had been. To be sure, the majority of these parishioners were sons and daughters or the grandsons and granddaughters of the immigrants. Yet the newer generations of Orthodox were not as acquainted with the language, culture and politics of the old country. While appreciating their cultural inheritance, the newer generations of Orthodox Christians were Americans who saw themselves neither as immigrants nor as strangers in a foreign land.

Closely related to this development is the fact that the Orthodox Church has been attracting an ever-growing number of persons who come from other religious traditions and cultural backgrounds. As we have already noted, some have come as part of entire parishes which have been received into the Church. Others come into the Church as a result of their own spiritual journey. As many have noted, their journey has not always been made easy by those clergy and parishioners who place a high premium upon the old world ethnicity, language and customs.

One sure and rather prominent sign of these demographic changes has been the gradual increase in mixed marriages. The number of mixed marriages began to increase in the 1950s and 1960s. This trend became even more dramatic from the 1970s onward. Let us remember that marriage outside one's ethnic group and one's church was actively discouraged in earlier decades. Yet, especially throughout the past 25 to 30 years, mixed marriages between Orthodox and non-Orthodox Christians became the norm. Here, mixed marriage refers to a marriage blessed in the Orthodox Church in which one spouse is of another Christian church. In the Greek Orthodox Archdiocese, over 50% of marriages have been "mixed" since 1980. This percentage does not include the marriages of two Orthodox who are of different ethnic or racial backgrounds, or from different jurisdictions. Likewise, it does not count those Orthodox who are married outside

the Orthodox Church. This number, which also may be sizeable, is not
officially known.

The reality of these marriages as well as the broader change in demo-
graphics of the Church are having a profound impact upon the life of
Orthodox parishes.[23] The report to the Greek Orthodox Clergy Laity-
Congress in 1990 honestly recognized some of the challenges when it said:

> From a cultural perspective, it is a fact that we are no longer as homogeneous as
> we used to be. This, however, must be seen as a challenge that invites us to use
> the diverse experience of our people for the enriching of parish life since in
> Christ all historical, natural and physical differences are overcome. A parish
> must be prepared to deal with the many changes that take place in the church,
> the country and the local area. This does not mean that crisis in the future will
> not occur, but a community that devotes time to attending to relationships
> among its members will not be overcome easily by this crisis.[24]

Closely related to the change in parish demographics is the fact that there
has been a gradual suburbanization of parishioners and many parishes. Since
1950, the majority of new Orthodox parishes have been established in the
suburbs. In some cases, these were newly-established parishes in suburban
locations. In other cases, parishes relocated their church buildings from the
inner city to the suburbs. Most of these new suburban parishes began to
serve the needs of different types of parishioner. Some were the children
and grandchildren of immigrants. Some had come to Orthodoxy after being raised in other religious traditions. Some were the non-Orthodox spouses
of Orthodox.

These facts contributed to some important developments in parish ministries beginning in the 1950s and 1960s. During this period, the use of English
in sermons and in the liturgical services began to increase. Numerous editions, often bilingual, of the Divine Liturgy were published at both the parish
and diocesan levels. Religious education programs in English for children
and young adults became more formalized and much more emphasized.
Books and pamphlets on Orthodox beliefs and practices were written in
English and circulated. Some measure of pan-Orthodox cooperation among
parishes in many cities and regions began to increase. More retreats were
organized. Summer camps were established. Orthodox Campus Fellowships
were organized. Central to all of this was the growing expectation that clergy
be better educated and more sensitive to the spiritual needs of parishioners
who were less homogeneous, more educated and more affluent. Clearly, these
facts demonstrate that many parishes were becoming more responsive to
the deep spiritual interests of their parishioners.

There is no doubt that the changing characteristics of membership in
many Orthodox parishes have led to a tension in many parishes. This ten-

sion has often been centered upon the question of the degree of adaptation that Orthodoxy has had to undergo in order to serve the spiritual needs of new generations of parishioners, to be missionary-minded, and to be a witness to the Gospel in this society.

On the one hand, there have been those who advocate little, if any, adaptation in parish life. They feel that the ancient liturgical language and the myriad of ethnic customs are essential to the Orthodox faith. For them, ethnicity and religion are intimately related. The distinctiveness of Orthodoxy is to be found in certain external characteristics carried from the Old Country. The advocates of this viewpoint do not easily make a distinction between the unchanging truths of the Orthodox faith and those changing characteristics of the church through the ages.

Others have had a different perspective on parish life. They believe that the Orthodox Church in this country is neither living in exile nor in a diaspora. It has been planted here by missionary and pious immigrants to be the Church of God in this place. These persons recognize that in the past Orthodoxy has penetrated a wide variety of cultures and evangelized a wide variety of peoples precisely because of its ability to engage a new culture and to preach the faith in a meaningful way. While not altering the Apostolic Faith, the Church throughout the ages has lived in a wide variety of cultures and used many languages in order to honor God in worship and to nurture God's people in the faith.

Archbishop Iakovos, one of the foremost protagonists for the development of Orthodoxy in America, boldly opposed the extremists and exhorted the faithful of the Greek Orthodox Archdiocese to look to the future when he said:

> I believe that our Church, without ceasing to be racially rooted in Greece and religiously in the Phanar (the Ecumenical Patriarchate), must accept the fact that America is the place to which God has intended it to grow and bring many more into its fold; and that it has an obligation, without compromising in matters of faith, to adapt itself to the existing conditions and needs, changing in the final analysis even the language, but never its spirit or ethos.[25]

Given the various parish demographics and history, there was no easy formula that could be followed by all parishes. The tension within parishes often found expression over the practical questions of the religious formation of young people, the use of English in the Liturgy, perspectives on moral issues, or the educational background of the priest. Some larger parishes consciously attempted to serve at least two general groups of parishioners. Smaller parishes had fewer options available.[26]

After reviewing many of the challenges facing the Church, Fr. Nikon

Patrinakos had the courage to raise the question of the survival and to offer some bold perspectives. He said:

> If the Orthodox Church is to survive in this country and finally to assume her proper place in the hearts of her own people, let alone in the society at large, she will not survive as a religious ghetto, and a kind of "privileged" by definition religious community. We expect our church to survive but in the open and only after a struggle to substantiate her claim of being truly Orthodox, that is, of correctly believing and correctly practicing. This, not by keeping the Orthodox people in spiritual and ecclesiastical seclusion from the fear of becoming polluted, but by allowing us to offer our minds and our hearts, our wisdom and our theology, our ritual and religious art.[27]

THE ORTHODOX PARISH AS A VOLUNTARY COMMUNITY OF FAITH

This leads us to our final observation on the development of the Orthodox parish. The Orthodox parish in America today is very much a "voluntary community of faith." Or, to state it differently, our parishes are composed of persons who have freely and consciously chosen to become associated with a particular parish. This does not deny the preeminent sense of a calling by the Christ to be a follower and to be a member of His Church. This is always primary. Rather, it does recognize that each person must freely and consciously respond to that call. Far from being a once in a lifetime response, it is a continuous response of faith to the One who calls each of us to His fellowship and service. It is for this reason that the prayer of the Church calls upon us regularly to "commit ourselves, one another and our whole life to Christ our God."

Freedom of choice is not something new. After all, the freedom to choose is a gift of God and a characteristic of the human person. The Fathers of the Church frequently emphasize that our free will is an essential aspect of human nature. Let us also remember that "freedom" and the "freedom to choose" are very much characteristics of American life. Our society emphasizes the fact that we are free to choose. Indeed, when it comes to religion, we are also free to choose whether or not to believe in the Christian Faith. We are free to choose whether or not to belong to a particular church. And, we are free to choose whether or not we will participate in the life of a parish community.

Given their times and circumstances, our parents and grandparents were not in a position to exercise much choice when it came to religion. This does not mean that they lacked free will. It simply means that they more easily conformed to the expectations of their elders. They simply followed the example of their parents and the mores of their society. They generally accepted the religion of their parents, and they normally belonged to the parish of their parents, if they were in this country. Not to do so was viewed as an abandonment of family values and cultural tradition.

Today, some Orthodox continue to follow this pattern with little question. Often, they follow the religion of their parents and choose to be a member of the same parish as their parents. This is certainly true in locations where there is only one Orthodox parish immediately available and where families have not been uprooted.

Yet, there is an unease among many Orthodox parishioners. Many are disappointed with the quality of their parish life, with the lack of spiritual emphasis, with petty squabbles, and with misplaced priorities. The report to the Greek Orthodox Clergy-Laity Congress in 1990 honestly recognized some of the difficulties when it said:

> The reality is that there are many parishioners who do not find their parishes helpful or meaningful in their lives. They are unhappy with the liturgical life of their parish, they are dissatisfied with the quality of preaching, they do not find much assistance in addressing personal issues, they often find the administrative life of the Church authoritarian or closed, and parish life frequently limited in activities.[28]

At the same time, it appears that an increasing number of Orthodox, especially those who have a deeper concern for spiritual life, are placing greater expectations upon parish life. They want the parish to truly be *the Church*. They are seeking a community of worship, of Christian fellowship and nurture. As a result of this, they are conscious of the freedom of choice which they have. They are ready and willing to support fully a parish in which the emphasis is clearly upon Christ and His Gospel as expressed through the Orthodox faith. Likewise, when necessary, they are ready and willing to find a "new" parish which will support their growth in Christ, their growth in life, holiness and spiritual maturity. As the Greek Orthodox Report says:

> As our people become more educated and more cosmopolitan, they are looking for more persuasive preaching and more prayerful liturgy than they once needed. It is an interesting phenomenon that just when presbyters have become more sophisticated and sensitive in their pastoral ministry, the laity have raised their level of expectations.[29]

Today, many Orthodox are asking serious questions about the quality of parish life. Many are selecting a parish, first of all, because it is a community where the centrality of Christ and His Gospel are proclaimed and expressed through the Orthodox faith, and are made relevant to their lives. It is a community which truly nurtures their faith, through the Liturgy, through instruction, through fellowship.

Many Orthodox parents are selecting a parish because their children can be nurtured in the faith and strengthened in Christian values. They expect that their daughters as well as their sons will be treated in a loving and respectful manner.

Many newcomers to Orthodoxy are selecting a parish because they feel accepted and wanted, and are not characterized as being "outsiders" or "second class."[30]

Many Orthodox women are selecting a parish because they are treated with respect, and they have their talents and concerns valued.

Many Orthodox in mixed marriages are selecting a parish because they feel that their non-Orthodox partner is not ignored, but welcomed warmly.

Let us also remember three important facts about American society today. First, the decision to be a believer and to choose a parish takes place in the context of a society which is increasingly secularized. Society today does not offer the same degree of support to religious faith and conviction that it did only a few decades ago. Our grandparents and many of our parents lived at a time when society and family worked hand in hand to support religious belief and morals. This cannot be easily said today. It is true that there are some signs of a renewed appreciation of the importance of spirituality within the larger society. Yet, religious faith and values are often treated with little positive regard by the major institutions of our society and in the popular media. American society has generally desacralized Sunday. It is no longer regarded chiefly as a day set aside for worship and family. Sunday morning presents many options in addition to the opportunity for worship and Christian fellowship.

Second, this is a society which presents all with many religious options. For those who are interested in spiritual concerns and moral issues, there is a whole "supermarket" of churches of various traditions. In addition, there are meetings places which bring together followers of other world religions. There are religious associations and ethical groups. There are also numerous "recovery groups" which offer spiritual perspectives and fellowship. Many of these assist their participants to engage deeply spiritual questions and concerns.

And third, there is a great deal of mobility in American society. Americans are not as oriented to their neighborhood or city as were our grandparents. Because of employment, education and recreation Americans have become accustomed to movement. While this can create a sense of "uprootedness," it can also contribute to a desire to find a parish which provides thoughtful guidance in the faith and a nurturing Christian community.

Yes, there is a very interesting paradox here. While the society exhibits some significant secularistic tendencies, there is at the same time a profound interest in issues of spirituality broadly defined. Indeed, many

Americans, and this includes many Orthodox, who reject the precepts of traditional religions are at the same time concerned with profoundly spiritual questions. They often feel that their spiritual concerns are not addressed by their parish!

With this in mind, there is a need to recognize the reality of our situation today. The choice to be an Orthodox Christian and to be a member of a parish is a major decision in the lives of many today. We can no longer take for granted that our relatives and friends, that our sons and daughters will choose Christ and the Orthodox Church. We can no longer expect that they will passively "attend" church services they do not understand. We can no longer expect that they will tolerate our foibles and our divisions, our pettiness and our triumphalism. If we have eyes to see, we must recognize that some have left the church because they have not found Christ and His Church.

Writing two decades ago, Fr. Leonidas Contos said:

> Once again, at the risk of dealing with truisms as if they were revelations, the process of change in the composition and orientation of the local church is deep and irreversible. It carries implications for us – our self-perception, our ministry, our mission, our worship, our very future – which we will continue to ignore, or gloss, to our peril.[31]

THE CHALLENGES BEFORE THE PARISH

There is no doubt that the development of Orthodox Christianity in this country is a remarkable phenomenon which bears witness to the reality of Christ and His Gospel. Yet, at the same time, it must be said that the development of Orthodox parishes in the United States has more often than not been rather haphazard. The development has been deeply wounded by jurisdictional divisions as well as by ideological and political debates. Until quite recently, there has been precious little reflection about the direction of parish life either at the local level or at the jurisdictional level. Both parishes and jurisdictions have generally responded to events and crisis. There has been little analysis of trends in parish life or the complexity of the American social reality especially its religious dimension.

With this in mind, we must recognize that there are important challenges which face the Orthodox Church and its parishes in America today. These challenges demand attention by clergy and lay leaders both at the parish level and at the levels of dioceses and jurisdictions. Indeed, they are challenges which face most parishes regardless of their size, their history or their jurisdiction. As such, they are challenges which deserve to be discussed and attended to in a fully pan-Orthodox manner.

The Challenge of the centrality of Christ and His Gospel. The Orthodox parish is meant to be first and foremost a community of believers centered upon the reality of Christ and his teachings as expressed by the Orthodox Church. Nothing in the life of the parish can be more important than Christ and his Gospel. Every activity of the parish must relate to the Gospel and bear witness to the Lordship of Christ. Parish priorities must reflect the prayer of the Church to "commend ourselves, one another and our whole life to Christ Our God."

The challenge of the parish liturgy. Worship is central to the life of the Orthodox parish and the life of each parishioner. The celebration of the Liturgy and the other services of worship provide the parishioners with the opportunity not only to praise and thank God but also to be formed in the Orthodox faith, and thereby transformed ever more deeply into sons and daughters of God. This requires, however, that the worship of the Church be understandable and accessible. With the leadership of the priest, the worship of the parish must be truly the "action of the people" and not a performance by their "representatives." The recovery and development of an order (typicon) of liturgical life for the parish is a critical necessity. Such an order must be rooted in the rich tradition of Orthodoxy while at the same time remaining sensitive to the realities of the parish community and the society. Is the parish a community of faith where the liturgical life is both central to its life and to the formation of the whole People of God?

The challenge of a healthy and mutually supportive relationship between clergy and laity. According to Orthodox theology, the parish priest is the father of the parish. He is called to lead the community's prayer, to teach, and to guide the People of God as they grow in holiness, develop their spiritual gifts, and give service in Christ's name. There are many parishes where this relationship is in place and leads to spiritual benefits for both the priest and the parishioners. In some parishes, however, the priest continues to be seen as an "employee" who serves at the whim of the parish council. Such a view of the relationship profoundly hinders the ministry of the priest and the identity of the parish. This is further compounded in those places where the parish cannot provide the priest with sufficient financial support. Is the parish a community of faith where priest and people work together for the ultimate glory of God and the salvation of the world?

The challenge of pastoral care. Our people look for support and assistance as they seek to live their lives as faithful Orthodox Christians. The parish is meant to be a community of faith through which believers can deepen their relationship with God, one another, and with the creation in the midst of their responsibilities and life challenges. The life of the parish and the activity of the parish priest must always sensitive to the challenge of providing pastoral care, mutual support, and spiritual guidance to the members of the parish. Clearly, the fact that the composition of parishes is changing means that the concerns and needs of parishioners are not entirely the same as those of earlier periods. Is the parish a community of faith where believers find the truth of the Orthodox faith expressed not only in worship but also in pastoral care, spiritual direction, and in mutual support?

The Challenge of Formation. The Orthodox have a distinctive vision of God, ourselves and the world which is rooted in the Gospel of Christ and passed on by the Church through the ages. This vision is expressed through the Eucharist and the Scriptures as well as through the sacraments, prayers and icons. Yet, this vision is made immediate and relevant to particular concerns through preaching, through teaching, and the events of the parish community's life. Nurture and formation take place in a variety of ways. The opportunities for religious education and nurture, which are provided by the parish, must be seen as complementary, and not in opposition, to the liturgical life of the believing community. Is the parish a community of faith through which all the believers are nurtured in their identity as followers of Christ?

The challenge of children and young people. Our children are maturing in a social and educational environment where there are a wide variety of religious and ethical viewpoints. If we wish to assist parents in nurturing their children in the Orthodox faith and values, the parish must take very seriously its responsibility to young people. This begins when priests and lay leaders treat children and young people as honored and welcomed members of the parish. The parish must consciously make an effort to involve children and young people fully in the life of the believing community. This begins with the liturgical life but it certainly does not end there. Is the parish a community of faith in which our children feel "at home" in the worship as well as in the Christian formation programs?

The challenge of financial responsibility. With few exceptions, each parish is responsible for raising sufficient funds to support its ministries, programs and facilities. In some parishes, the concept of "stewardship" has led to a very positive understanding of the responsibilities of the parishioners to their parish and its ministries. However, the old system of "membership dues" is still quite common in many parishes. This concept tends to equate parish membership with financial obligations. This leads to a practical diminution of the centrality of Baptism, the importance of regular participation in the Liturgy, and the responsibilities of Christian life. This becomes even more problematical in those parishes where the impression is given that one is obliged to pay a fee for the celebration of sacraments. The reliance of some parishes upon revenues from "games of chance" only compounds the problem. The manner in which a parish raises its funds and disperses them may indeed be very telling indicators of its identity, values and stability. Is the parish a community of faith in which the raising and disbursement of funds are done in a transparent and honest manner which is faithful to its true identity and mission?

The challenge of pan-Orthodox cooperation. While some parishes continue to reflect the isolationist mentality of their past, many of our parishes have come to recognized the importance and value of cooperation with other Orthodox parishes in the same neighborhood or city. In the first instance, this normally takes place with parishes of the same jurisdiction and then reaches out to parishes of other jurisdictions. This is often manifested in joint liturgical services, in retreats, in campus ministry and in special religious education programs. In some places, there are outstanding examples of a unified Orthodox witness in the area of social services and in the pastoral care for the elderly, the hospitalized and new immigrants. Is the parish a community of faith which seeks to build relationships with other Orthodox parishes for the sake of common witness and service?

The challenge of ecumenical relations. The local parish cannot easily ignore questions related to the unity and disunity of Christians and their churches. As already noted, the prevalence of "mixed marriages" blessed by the Orthodox Church means that many families in our parishes must face the practical and theological consequences of the disunity of the historic churches. Likewise, while being faithful to Orthodox teaching, our priests and parishes are frequently involved in ecumenical activities with neighboring Roman Catholic and Protestant parishes. This may involve participation in special services of prayer for Christian unity, study groups, and common service in the society. Is the parish a community of faith which recognizes the tragic consequences of Christian disunity and seeks to contribute to the process of reconciliation in accordance with Orthodox teachings?

The challenge of witness in the society. The Liturgy is offered "for the entire world," as the anaphora of St. John Chrysostom tells us. Just as our Lord came "for the life of the world," the Church exists in the world for the sake of the world. Thus, our eucharistic action must also be made manifest in our concern for the good of the society and the salvation of all. When a parish demonstrates its concern for the society and the well-being of all, especially through acts of philanthropy and generosity to those in need, it is giving a very important witness to the ultimate value of the Gospel. Is the parish a community of faith which is known in the neighborhood and the city to be a sign of the Gospel and a channel of God's philanthropy in the world today?

The challenges before the contemporary Orthodox parish in the United States today are immense. Moreover, the challenges which we have noted are intimately related to other challenges facing the Church as a whole. These include a number of issues related to leadership, especially the quality of priestly preparation and the quality of episcopal oversight. These include issues related to the accurate analysis of the characteristics and spiritual issues of American society. These also include the issues related to the overcoming of jurisdictional divisions and the establishment of a more administratively united Church in the United States. At the heart of all these is the ultimate challenge to the Church to truly be the Church of God today in this society. As Fr. Georges Florovsky said:

> Orthodoxy cannot be maintained simply by inertia. No tradition can survive unless it is continued through creative effort. The message of Christ is eternal and always the same, but it must be reinterpreted again and again so as to become a challenge to every new generation. We have not simply to keep the legacy of the past, but must first realize what we have inherited and do everything we can to present it to others as a living thing.[32]

NOTES

[1] For a comprehensive introduction to the development of Orthodox Christianity in America, see Thomas FitzGerald, *The Orthodox Church* (Westport, CT: Greenwood Press, 1998).

[2] The Hartford Study on Religious Congregations, which has included the Orthodox, should prove to be a very valuable resource.

[3] For an introduction to the mission, see Michael Oleska, *Orthodox Alaska* (Crestwood: St. Vladimir's Seminary Press, 1992).

[4] Cited in Bishop Gregory Afonsky, *A History of the Orthodox Church in Alaska* (Kodiak: St. Herman's Theological Seminary, 1977), p. 23.

[5] Afonsky, *A History of the Orthodox Church in Alaska*, pp. 78-81. See also Robert Berkhofer, *Salvation and the Savage: An Analysis of Protestant Missions and the American Indian Response, 1787-1862*.

[6] Alexander Doumouras, "Greek Orthodox Communities in America Before World War I," *St. Vladimir's Theological Quarterly* 11:4 (1967), pp. 44-52.

[7] A portion of this text is found in Constance Tarasar and John Erickson, eds., *Orthodox America, 1794-1976* (Syosset, NY: Orthodox Church in America, 1975), pp. 100-101.

[8] FitzGerald, *The Orthodox*, p. 23.

[9] Lawrence Barriger, *Glory to Jesus Christ: A History of the Carpatho-Russian Orthodox Diocese* (Brookline, MA: Holy Cross Orthodox Press, 2000), pp. 10-22. This is a very valuable study on the background and development of the Carpatho-Russian Orthodox Diocese.

[10] Ibid., pp. 23-35; FitzGerald, *The Orthodox Church*, pp. 27-30.

[11] FitzGerald, *The Orthodox Church*, p. 49.

[12] Barriger, *Glory to Jesus Christ*, pp. 76-92.

[13] On the early development, see William Paul Schneirla, "The Western Rite in the Orthodox Church," *St. Vladimir's Theological Quarterly* 2:2 (1958), pp. 20-46.

[14] See Peter Gillquist, *Coming Home* (Brentwood, Tenn.:Wolgemuth and Hyatt, 1989).

[15] FitzGerald, *The Orthodox*, pp. 41-45.

[16] Ibid., p. 46.

[17] FitzGerald, *The Orthodox*, p. 47.

[18] Letter from Archbishop Athenagoras to Metropolitan Theophilos, cited in George Papaioannou, *From Mars Hill to Manhattan*, (Minneapolis: Light and Life, 1976), p. 173.

[19] See Alexander Schmemann, "Problems of Orthodoxy in America: The Canonical Problem," *St. Vladimir's Theological Quarterly* 8:2 (1964), pp. 164-185.

[20] John Meyendorff, "Orthodoxy in the U.S.A.," in *Orthodoxy: A Sign From God* (Athens: Zoe, 1964), p. 355.

[21] For a rather biting review of these developments from a prominent Protestant author, see Martin Marty, *Modern American Religion: The Irony of it All*, (Chicago: The University of Chicago Press, 1986), pp. 125-130.

[22] Ibid., p. 130.

[23] The 2001 Year Book of the Greek Orthodox Archdiocese provides statistics on mixed marriages celebrated in the Archdiocese for the past twenty years.

[24] *Report to His Eminence Archbishop Iakovos Concerning the Future Theological Agenda of the Greek Orthodox Archdiocese* (Brookline: Holy Cross Orthodox Press, 1990), p. 8.

[25] Archbishop Iakovos, *Toward the Decade 1970-1980* (New York: Greek Orthodox Archdiocese, 1970), p. 22.

[26] For a brief but valuable study of the developments among some of the Orthodox parishes in Connecticut, see Robert John Klancko, "The Russian Orthodox Parishes of Connecticut," *Eastern Churches Journal*, 4:2 (1977), pp. 73-78.

[27] Nikon Patrinakos, *The Individual and His Orthodox Church* (New York: The Orthodox Observer Press, 1970), p. 82.

[28] *Report to His Eminence*, p. 8.

[29] Ibid., p. 8.

[30] The false distinction between "native" Orthodox and converts is one which is not consistent with the theology of the Church and one which is very divisive. The false distinction is avoided in this paper. For some further observation on this, see Theodore Bobosh, ed., *Come and See: Encountering the Orthodox Church* (Syosset, New York: Orthodox Church in America, 1983).

[31] Leonidas C. Contos, *2001: The Church in Crisis* (Brookline: Holy Cross Press, 1981), p. 49.

[32] Georges Florovsky, "To the Orthodox People: The Responsibility of Orthodox Believers in America," *Russian Orthodox Journal*, 23:6 (1949), p. 18.

Orthodoxy and the Pluralistic Challenge

Peter L. Berger

First let me say that I'm greatly honored by the invitation to address this gathering. As some of you know, I'm not Orthodox (I'm an unrepentant and unapologetic Lutheran), but I have had many ties with American Orthodoxy and have long had a sympathetic interest in its affairs. Consequently, I speak to you as an outsider, but also as a concerned friend. Secondly, let me explain that I'm deviating from the title given to my address by the organizers of this conference. I will speak about the challenge of contemporary pluralism to American Christianity in general and to Orthodoxy in particular, but I have little use for the term "postmodern" of the assigned title. But my rejection of this term actually serves as a good introduction to what I have to say.

The term "postmodern" has come to mean quite different things (which is, precisely, why I don't like it), but in the context of thinking about contemporary religion it has been closely associated with the notion of secularity: Supposedly we not only live in a "postmodern" age, but also in a post-Christian or post-religious one. Thus the challenge to the Christian churches is supposed to be the alleged situation in which secularity dominates: How is one to present the Gospel, or even more generally to speak about God, to people for whom religion has become largely irrelevant? I would put it to you that this view of our situation is misleading. If one looks empirically at the contemporary world, one finds it almost everywhere in the grip of powerful religious upsurges. There is indeed one geographical area where one can plausibly speak about a secularized situation, and that is western and central Europe – a "Euro-secularity," which originated in northern Europe and has, since the 1950s, been spreading south and east (incidentally, including Greece). Why this should be the case is not something I can go into here. But an important thing to understand is that the United States is a very different case: It is quite clearly *not* a secularized society (although it has a secularized cultural elite, which is yet another story), but what it shares with Europe and indeed most of the world is a different challenge – namely, that of pluralism. If we were meeting in Athens, we would want to consider the challenges of secularity *and* of pluralism to the Christian community;

since we find ourselves in Boston, I will limit myself to the latter challenge.

The meaning of "pluralism" is quite straightforward: it means the co-existence, under conditions of civic peace, of people of different ethnic and religious backgrounds. For well-known historical reasons, the United States has been an increasingly successful experiment with pluralism for a long time, with far-reaching social and political consequences. As far as religious institutions are concerned, this has meant an ever-expanding market of religious options, beginning with the historic Protestant churches, then coming to include the newer Protestant denominations, the Roman Catholics, and the Jews, and today including just about any religious community that does not encourage its members to break the laws. As was already noted by Alexis de Tocqueville, this freedom of religion has been an important factor in the vitality and public influence of the churches in America. But it has also confronted the churches with the problem of having to compete in retaining or gaining the adherence of an uncoerced population. This has been especially difficult for churches with a claim to exclusive authority and a history of relying on the state to enforce a religious monopoly. The drama of Roman Catholicism in America, from its beginnings as a defensive subculture to the self-confidence expressed in the declaration on religious liberty of Vatican II, is very largely the drama of coming to terms with pluralism.

However, while pluralism presents a challenge to religious *institutions*, it brings about an even deeper challenge on the level of religious *consciousness* – that is, on the place of religion in the minds of individuals. This challenge too can be described rather simply: it is a shift from religion as a taken-for-granted reality to religion as a matter of deliberate choices. Put differently: certainty in the matter of religion becomes harder to get. The social-psychological reasons for this are not mysterious: human beings are social beings, and they take anything for granted about which there is consensus in their social environment. For example, if one lived in a remote community in rural Greece – say, one hundred years ago – a community in which every significant person one dealt with was Orthodox and into which non-Orthodox individuals or communications rarely if ever penetrated, then being Orthodox would have been taken for granted as much as being a man or a woman, being Greek, having dark hair or being allergic to this or that food. It is precisely this taken-for-grantedness that is undermined by pluralism – because now there is no longer the traditional consensus as the individual is ongoingly confronted by a plurality of beliefs, values and ways of life, and is therefore compelled to make choices between them. This is a challenge that may or may not be linked with secularity, but that in either case is quite different from the challenge of secularity. One could put it this way: secularity challenges religion by creating an environment in which there is too little religion; the challenge of pluralism, on the other hand, comes from an environment in which there is *too much* religion – or, more precisely, in which there is a multiplicity of religious possibilities to choose from. It is this situation, I would argue, that is characteristic of contemporary America.

Needless to say, what happens on the level of individual consciousness has implications on the institutional level. The churches have to face the fact that they can no longer count on the taken-for-granted allegiance of their traditional clienteles. What is more, even those who retain an institutional allegiance are prone to pick and choose from the tradition, constructing their own version of it rather than accepting it as an undivided whole. This, of course, is very irritating to the official guardians of the tradition. Robert Wuthnow, one of the best sociological analysts of contemporary American religion, has coined the phrase "patchwork religion" to describe this phenomenon: reminiscent of children putting together building blocks, individuals now put together their own, often quite idiosyncratic version of what it means to be a Roman Catholic, Jew, or what-have-you. Another way of putting this is to say that more and more individuals become "heretics": I don't have to remind this audience that the Greek word *hairesis* means "choice." It is important to point out that even if an individual identifies himself as being in total conformity with this or that religious tradition – that is, he declares himself to be an orthodox (with a small "o") or neo-orthodox Catholic, Jew or what-have-you, *that too is the result of choice* – and, what is more, a choice that is not irrevocable.

The American language reflects this state of affairs. It speaks of people having a "religious preference" – a term that comes from the world of consumption, of choices made in a market economy. People also say that, for example, they "happen to be Catholic," which phrase is often followed by an explanation of where they "happen to" disagree with the Pope. Using a more Californian discourse, people may say that they are now "into meditation" – a phrase that adumbrates the possibility that, at some future time, they may again be "out of" it.

America today does not suffer from a deficiency of religion; if anything, it suffers from a surplus. Let me suggest a small field exercise in the sociology of religion: Go to Washington to the corner of Lafayette Park and 16th Street, turn your back on the White House, and go north on 16th Street. From that starting point all the way to Walter Reed Hospital you can experience a veritable orgy of religious pluralism. There are Catholic churches and churches of every conceivable Protestant denomination, at least one

Orthodox church, several synagogues, a mosque, one or more Buddhist temples, a Baha'i meeting place, the temple of a Vietnamese syncretistic cult, and some others that I cannot recall at the moment. Incidentally, I have not been able to find out *why* this particular street has become such an emporium of religious possibilities (it may have something to do with zoning regulations). But, whatever the reason, 16th Street Northwest provides a vivid metaphor of the condition of religion in contemporary America, a physical embodiment of the challenge of pluralism. (By the way, if you want to do your sociology of religion in a more tropical setting, you can have an even more exuberant experience of pluralism by going to Hawaii and following the Pali Highway, which goes from Honolulu north across the island of Oahu. And if you do this, you can reflect on the possible fact that Hawaii is one state of the Union in which Christians may now be a minority, and on the probability that much of mainland America, beginning with California, may look more and more like Hawaii, ethnically and religiously, in the twenty-first century.)

Let me, for a moment, jump out of the role of sociologist and say something as a Christian believer: I don't deplore this situation. I cannot understand why one would theologically prefer a situation in which religion is taken for granted to a situation in which one must make religious decisions. Rather, it seems to me that only in the latter case can one meaningfully speak of *faith*. What is more, there is a remarkable similarity between our contemporary pluralism and the pluralism of the Greco-Roman world with which the early Christians had to contend. At least until the Constantinian establishment of Christianity, and probably for some time after that, the early church found itself in a pluralistic market of religious possibilities probably as diversified as the one we encounter today. And, again, I need not remind this audience that I'm speaking of the age in which the great works of Patristic theology were written. Let me put it this way: Should we deplore the fact that, sociologically speaking, our situation today is more similar to the Cappadocian Fathers as against, say, the situation in which Orthodoxy existed as a closed-in (and, I think, a taken-for-granted) subculture under the Ottoman *millet* system? You must reach your own conclusion, but I, for one, find this similarity inspiring rather than depressing.

To return to America, while there was a separation of church and state from early on, there was also what has been called "social establishment" of religion, covering an ever-expanding group of religious institutions. A benchmark could be an influential book published in 1955 by Will Herberg under the title *Protestant-Catholic-Jew*. Herberg, writing in the so-called "religious revival" during the Eisenhower administration, argues that there were now three respectable religious identities in America, the three mentioned in his title. One may recall that this was also the period in which it became conventional to say that American democracy was based on so-called "Judeo-Christian values." I think that, for his moment in history, Herberg's analysis was quite accurate. But think of all that has happened since then! When Herberg spoke of Protestantism, he had in mind the mainline denominations – Evangelical Protestantism was off his map, and he did not (I suppose, could not) foresee the powerful upsurge of this version of Protestantism that began in the 1970s. Since Herberg's book, the Roman Catholic church went through the earthquake of Vatican II, there occurred the powerful upsurge of orthodox Judaism, with feminism cutting across all three communities. Also, there has been an increasingly noticeable presence of Islam and the major traditions of eastern and southern Asia, as well as the important phenomenon of New Age religiosity. I need hardly add that Herberg had nothing interesting to say about Eastern Orthodox Christianity; it too was pretty much off his map. What is more important, Orthodoxy today still occupies a place somewhat removed from the turbulence of American religious pluralism, although it is clear to me that it is increasingly affected by it. I have thus reached the point where I should speak directly about Orthodoxy.

The comparison with American Judaism is thought-provoking. There are roughly as many Eastern Orthodox Christians in America as there are Jews. In the course of the past century, the Jewish community, including its religious sensibilities, has had a considerable impact on American culture (including the American language and the American sense of humor); there is no comparable impact by the Orthodox (although, of course, Orthodox individuals have been prominent in various areas of American life). You are better qualified than I to explain this difference. I suppose that at least one explanation comes from the fact that Orthodoxy in America (with the notable exception of the Orthodox Church in America) continues to be a diaspora phenomenon, not only organized along ethnic lines but thinking of itself in ethnic terms. But I also think that, beyond this, Orthodoxy has not as yet perceived its situation as, willy-nilly, that of a player in the great game of American pluralism. Perhaps this is not surprising, for unlike the two major branches of western Christianity, Orthodoxy's experience with pluralism is very new.

Since the Patristic age, I think it is fair to say, Orthodoxy has essentially experienced four social contexts. First, it experienced itself in the position of a privileged state church – first in the Byzantine Empire, then in Russia, then in the newly independent Orthodox nations of southeastern Europe. This is the phenomenon that Max Weber called "caesaropapism." It is my impression that this relationship with society has become paradigmatic in the Orthodox mind, and it keeps resurfacing. It has resurfaced dramatically in Russia, where an outside observer gets the impression that, notwithstanding seven decades of Communist persecution and marginalization, important elements in the Russian church understand its role in pre-1917 terms, as if the Bolshevik revolution had never occurred and as if nothing much is to be learned from the fate of the church during the Soviet period. It hardly needs emphasizing that the "caesaropapistic" paradigm does not work in America. Secondly, Orthodoxy experienced itself as a persecuted community, intermittently under Muslim rule and then, catastrophically, under Communism. This experience, too, is not applicable to America (thank God, one should add). Thirdly, Orthodoxy served as one of the organizing principles of the Ottoman *millet* system, a relatively tolerant arrangement much of the time, but one that encapsulated Orthodoxy in a sort of religious caste system that precluded its influence on the larger society (although Orthodox individuals attained positions of power and privilege in Ottoman society). Although this system was organized under religious rather than ethnic categories, it led to a powerful merging of ethnic and religious identities: To be Greek, or Serbian, or Bulgarian, etc., meant *ipso facto* to be Orthodox, and to identify oneself as, say, Greek, but *not* Orthodox was not only morally repugnant but cognitively incoherent. While the *millet* system as such disappeared with the Ottoman empire, I think one can say that some of its mindset survived in the nation-states that succeeded that empire and carried over into the Orthodox diaspora. Fourthly and finally, Orthodoxy existed in diaspora communities, defined in ethnic terms, both in Western Europe and in America. This has indeed been a paradigm that could be maintained with a good deal of empirical plausibility – *as long as the relevant ethnic identities could be taken for granted.* My argument concerning pluralism is, precisely, that this taken-for-grantedness is progressively under pressure in contemporary America (I really don't know how this plays out in Western Europe, where in any case the Orthodox community is much smaller).

In Vienna, my home town, there is a street called Greek Alley. It still contains a very beautiful Byzantine – style church, Greek ecclesiastical offices, and some commercial establishments owned by individuals of Greek origin. I don't know anything about the Greek Orthodox community in Vienna today, but in my own mind this little urban scene is a perfect image of diaspora existence. I can easily imagine that until recent times, and under the Habsburg regime that had established religious tolerance already in the eighteenth century, an individual growing up in the Greek community in Vienna would be both Greek and Orthodox in a taken-for-granted way (though probably there were a few defectors, mostly in the direction of Roman Catholicism). Diaspora communities of this sort can be close-knit and closed-in over long periods of time, and they were just that for some time in America. For all I know, there are still analogues of Vienna's Greek Alley in various American locations. But, increasingly, they are hard to maintain amid the exuberant diversity of contemporary American culture. And I would propose that Orthodoxy has yet to come to terms with this novel experience.

This fact is reflected in the way that other Christians perceive Orthodoxy in America. They are not hostile to it, but neither do they see themselves as being in competition with it (as Protestant and Catholics see one another, even if – and perhaps especially if – they are mutually tolerant). As Alexander Schmemann often pointed out, Orthodoxy is perceived as being "colorful," "exotic" and by the same token as not to be taken seriously as a theological interlocutor, except among very small coteries of ecumenists who mainly speak with one another. Thus, even where Orthodoxy has participated in ecumenical bodies such as the National Council of Churches and the World Council of Churches, its role has been largely defensive. Given some of the inanities that these two bodies have put forth in recent decades, I am grateful for the role of the Orthodox as nay-sayers, but that is a different thing from direct and positive influence. Put differently, the Orthodox witness has been largely negative. It has been useful in reminding Protestants that there is a Christian world different both from theirs and that of Rome, but I don't think that it has changed many minds in an ecumenical movement that, when all is said and done, has remained a rather provincial Protestant enterprise. I am not familiar with sociological studies of American Orthodoxy, but I find it interesting that there are two, seemingly contradictory trends to be observed. One trend is the increasing rate of intermarriage – that is, of Orthodox individuals marrying non-Orthodox spouses – apparently with the result that the offspring of these marriages tend to be non-Orthodox. I understand that this "demographic hemorrhage" is considerable. The other trend is a still numerically small but significant movement *into* the Orthodox community by individual converts. Again the comparison with the Jewish community is instructive. The movement *out* as a result of intermarriage is very comparable (and, of course, it has been a matter of great concern to Jewish leaders). The movement *in*, however, is different. As far as I know, there are few conversions to Judaism that are not motivated by non-Jewish individuals deciding to share the religion of their Jewish spouses. This does not seem to be the case with most conversions to Orthodoxy, where the motive is religious rather than familial. What may be learned from this?

An increasing number of observers of the American Jewish scene have concluded that Jewish identity can no longer be taken for granted on the grounds of ethnic loyalty, that neither Israel nor the Holocaust can serve as anchors of Jewish identity for young American Jews, and, therefore, that the only reliable anchor for such an identity is a rediscovery of the religious genius of Judaism. The resurgence of traditional Judaism among American Jews supports this conclusion. So does the fact that, apparently, the movement *out* through intermarriage is minimal where Jewish identity has been grounded in religious rather than ethnic motivations. Christian Orthodoxy, of course, has no analogue to either the geographical signifier of the state of Israel or the historical signifier of the Holocaust, but the analogy is strong when it comes to the fragility of ethnic loyalty: when such loyalty can no longer be taken for granted, it must be re-established on different grounds – and these can only be religious. There is a curious implication here (it applies to both Jews and Orthodox Christians): it is no longer plausible to use different languages when speaking to insiders and outsiders. Put differently: if you want to keep your own children within your community, you must use with them the same language with which you would entice an outsider to join your community, and vice versa. (This is more difficult for Jews, whose religion has not been missionizing among outsiders for many centuries; it should be easier for Orthodox Christians). Let me concretize this: if you are a third-generation Greek-American and you want your children to go to church with you, it is going to be more and more difficult to motivate them simply by referring to their putative Greekness. Rather, you will have to tell them about the *religious* riches that await them if they participate in Orthodox worship. But that is exactly what you would say to a Protestant or agnostic acquaintance who has asked you about Orthodoxy!

Some years ago I met a Sufi poet. In one of his poems he referred to the boundary which, in traditional Muslim thought, divides the lands of Islam from the lands of the unbelievers. And he wrote: "Today this boundary runs across the soul of every Muslim." Something like this can be said about all of us who are caught in the dynamic of modern pluralism. The boundary between belief and unbelief, between insiders and outsiders, has become porous and fragile. For the believer this means that he must constantly speak *across* this boundary, even when he speaks to those who are supposed to be inside his community. In a way, though, this means taking on the role of the missionary, even when one is, so to speak, "at home."

What about Orthodoxy in America, then? Over and beyond the question of its ecclesiastical organization, it seems to me that it ought to move from its traditional defensive posture to one of aggressive self-assertion – not, of course, in a spirit of arrogance or intolerance, but with an awareness of what it has to offer to both insiders and outsiders. Put simply, it ought to *engage* American pluralism rather than just trying to hold it off. There is no guarantee of success here, but it seems to me that such engagement would mean taking advantage of a great opportunity – with a strange similarity, let me say again, to the opportunity facing the early church in the great cities of the late Roman empire.

As I conclude, I should probably respond to a question that must me in your minds: why should this Lutheran be interested in American Orthodoxy becoming more assertive? Well, let me assure (or perhaps disappoint) you by saying that I do not see myself as a potential convert. But I believe that all of us, who are Christians in contemporary America, need the Orthodox witness. There is, of course, a wealth of theological and liturgical resources of which the non-Orthodox communities are largely ignorant and from which they can learn a lot. But there is something more fundamental: one of the most destructive tendencies in western Christianity over the last century or so (very strongly in Protestantism, somewhat less in Roman Catholicism) has been *a loss of transcendence*. Christianity has been understood in moral, political, or psychotherapeutic terms – rather than in terms that the New Testament presents the Gospel – as the breaking-in of a cosmic power of redemption into the world of empirical reality. I don't suppose that Orthodoxy is immune to these aberrations, but so far at least it has been much less susceptible to them. It is impossible to attend the Divine Liturgy in any Orthodox church without realizing at once that what is being celebrated here is not a moral code, a political program, or a therapeutic method, but the drama of redemption initiated by the God who transcends all the realities of this world. It is this realization that supposedly overcame the emissaries of the Russian tsar when they attended the liturgy in Hagia Sophia in Constantinople, making them report that they had experienced "heaven on earth." This, in my view, is why the Orthodox witness is needed in America.

Ecclesial and Ethnic Identities Within the American Religious Scene

Stanley Samuel Harakas

Introduction

In the conference program, this presentation is listed under the heading of "Pastoral Perspectives." Yet to arrive at a functional set of pastoral guidelines, it is important first to examine the central terms of the assigned topic. We first need to examine carefully, as space allows, the meaning of "identity" in the current discussion. To this rather fluid reality, secondly, we also need to describe honestly the tensions and paradoxes that flow from our Orthodox theological affirmations as they have impact on our multiple ethnic and religious existence. Next, we need to pay some attention to what we mean when we speak of American identity and how some American religious experiences in the past and present can illumine our own Orthodox journey in this country. Finally, this presentation will make an effort at drawing from these observations some pastoral guidelines for addressing the ongoing tensions expressed in Orthodox "Ecclesial and Ethnic Identities within the American Religious Scene."

Identity dilemmas: Matryoshka dolls, multicolored umbrellas, and changing hats

We Orthodox in America, with our ethnic-based roots in the Old World, tend to feel that we fully grasp the interconnectedness of ethnic and religious identity. Out of our cultural and religious experience we conceive of the identity question as a tri-polar reality: Orthodox religion, our particular national heritage, and the realities of American existence.

Contemporary scholarship, however, draws a much broader, complex and ambivalent picture. Identities are multifaceted and interrelated and in an ongoing flux. Take, take for example, a sample of ten titles of books on this topic published after 1990. These are: *Religion, Ethnicity, and Self-Identity: Nations in Turmoil*[1]; *One America Indivisible: A National Conversation on American Pluralism and Identity*[2]; *Diversity in America*[3]; *People, Nation &*

State: The Meaning of Ethnicity and Nationalism[4]; *The Dynamics of American Ethnic, Religious and Racial Group Life: An Interdisciplinary Overview*;[5] *The Divine Call: Religious Identity in the North American Cultural Mosaic*[6]; *Citizenship and National Identity: From Colonialism to Globalism*[7]; *The American Nation, National Identity, Nationalism*[8]; *The Next Religious Establishment: National Identity and Political Theology in Post-Protestant America*[9] and *The Tribal Basis of American Life: Racial, Religious, and Ethnic Groups in Conflict.*[10]

The one commonality to all of these books is the sense of complexity, overlap, interpenetration and unclearness of the meaning of the terms religious and ethnic identity, especially when coupled with realities such as territoriality, nation, state, organized religion, personal religion, gender, racism and civil religion. For example, there are two major theories on how ethnicity comes into being, one is called "Primordialism" and the other "Constructivism." A primordial view of ethnicity places important weight on the congruities of blood, kinship and belief; the view that ethnicity is constructed holds that ethnicity is historically invented and imagined. Both views are able to provide historical examples. Constructivism argues that ethnic identity is a cultural construct that is malleable and can be constructed at will. Of course, there is a third alternative that ethnicity is both a primordial given and malleable concurrently. The fourth logical alternative is that it is neither.[11]

One way of understanding the complexity of ethnic and religious identities is to use illustrations that serve to aid us in conceptualizing the problems. One of the works not mentioned above provides such an illustrative image. The book I have in mind is titled *Nested Identities: Nationalism, Territory and Scale.*[12] The editors begin their work with this observation: "Identities are not fixed or immutable but are accumulated over the course of a lifetime; they are part of the process of creating psychological stability."[13] Obviously, they are among those who see identity in some fashion as an ongoing construction project. Their book focuses primarily on the sense of identity imparted by territories, nations and localities on various geographic scales. The book covers the identity provided by vast territorial areas, dealing with Europe, the Caribbean and Russia. It also deals with middle-sized areas such as Finland, Estonia, Nigeria, Sri Lanka, and regional or micro-scale areas such as those represented in Spanish Basque nationalism, Palestinian Arabs in Israel, Hungarian and Romanian Transylvania, and Welsh identity in England. But eventually the focus comes down to personal identity. The volume on "nested identities" ends with a summary chapter which begins:

The term *nested identities* nicely captures an essential attribute or "identity," inasmuch each person gains an understanding of who she/he is by considering "self" in relation to others in a variety of different ways that can and generally do include differing scales of levels of abstraction."[14]

I am suggesting that "nested identities" are even more complex, nicely illustrated by the colorful Slavic tradition of matryoshka dolls in which the same figures, in increasingly smaller and tighter sizes are nested inside each other. Our identities are multilevel and included in one another. The most outward doll is not necessarily the most significant doll. Perhaps the most hidden and most difficult to access is the most important to us. The external appearance may be just that, a public face which does not disclose the defining inner identities. Thus, religious and ethnic identities may be more important to a person than the external mask that only serves to hide what truly matters.

When we move away from a set of personal identities to our social and organized life, another image aids us in understanding what is at work. In Vincent N. Parrilo's book *Diversity in America*, there is a discussion of the American mosaic of religions, ethnic traditions, race and gender issues, which has come to be described as "multiculturalism." He points out that the very term is subject to multiple interpretations and understandings, so that *inclusionists* argue that a society such as ours must emphasize the presence and contributions of non-Europeans; *separatists* call for "minority nationalism" and "separate pluralism" in America, and the *integrative pluralists* call for a mutual sharing of diverse subcultures. The authors seem to opt for the latter, but not uncritically, identifying both good and bad in the mix and relationships of the immigrant, religious, ethnic, racial, language and cultural dimensions.

The image Parillo uses is the umbrella. As groups, we stand under the identity of umbrellas that are not of one color only. Our group identities vary from one another perhaps in only small ways. Assuming a color for a commonly held religious identity, this color may appear on several umbrellas under which certain groups stand. Irish, Italian, Slovenian, Mexican and French-Americans may have the color of Roman Catholicism on their umbrella, but also they may each have a different color peculiar to their national origins. The case is similar with Protestants of various stripes. Presbyterians may be one denominational family in religious identification, but reflect various ethnic identities. A recent newspaper article described how Scottish dancing companies are cultivated in the United States. The dancers appear frequently at widely attended Scots Highlander gatherings throughout the nation.[15] Scottish identity and not Presbyterianism is the dominant color of the umbrella there. In fact, the color of Presbyterian identity is so subdued that though it may be present, it is not identified publicly.

Ethnic and religious groups protect their identities by holding multicolored umbrellas over their heads. But there is one more illustrative image that may complete the picture for us.

Our late fellow faculty member here at Holy Cross, Fr. Nomikos M. Vaporis, frequently described to us his feeling of changing hats, depending on the environment in which he found himself. When in an ethnic Greek environment, language, thought patterns, the senses of fitness and appropriateness took on a particular configuration. When at an academic meeting, the mix and tone of these changed. When functioning as a priest in a parish situation the blend of identities and roles was strongly influenced by the ecclesial environment. Applied to the matryoshka doll image, it means that sometimes what is core to us might remain mostly hidden as a committed Russian Orthodox person might be when she is functioning as a bank teller. In terms of the umbrella image, it may mean that group identities can expand to include co-religionists even though they are not of our own ethnicity, as many non-Serbian Orthodox Christians felt at the NATO bombing of Kosovo.

Orthodox theological and ecclesial identity tensions: True faith, incarnation and contrasting/complementary typologies

When we seek to bring to bear Orthodox theological and ecclesial teachings on the question at hand, a series of affirmations readily comes to the fore, but the Orthodox theological matrix does not necessarily reduce the tensions that accompany the issue of ethnic and religious identities within the American scene.

While there are many theological and ecclesial teachings that can be raised in such a discussion, two provide alternate if not contrasting foci for the discussion. The first is the identity that Eastern Orthodoxy claims to be the fullness of the true Christian Faith. It is not the place in this paper to enter into a defense or exposition of this claim. Whether understood as "True Faith" or "True Worship," the exposition, proclamation, defense and affirmation of Orthodox Christianity before all is an essential mark of its identity. The foundations of Holy Tradition, Holy Scripture, the patristic mind, liturgical practice, monastic and spiritual life, architecture and art make statements that affirm a unique and unwavering consciousness of the identity of Orthodox Christianity with the One, Holy, Catholic and Apostolic Church. As Orthodox Christians we hold this perspective as a precious treasure, a *parakatatheke*, which may not be compromised, abandoned or distorted.

On the other hand, Orthodox Christianity has taken seriously throughout the centuries the view that God's creation of the world, and the Incarnation of the Son of God in the person of the *Theanthropos* Jesus Christ gives special meaning to human life and culture and even ethnic identities. As St. Paul said to the Athenians on Mars Hill, God "made from one every nation of men to live on all the face of the earth, having determined allotted periods and the boundaries of their habitations" (Acts 17:26). One of the striking things about the description of Pentecost in the book of Acts was that people of many different ethnic backgrounds experienced the giving of the Holy Spirit. The rise of traditionally Orthodox *ethnoi* in history, and the recent nineteenth century creation of nation-states with Orthodox religious and cultural identity are brought into sometimes harmonious, sometimes conflicting, sometimes supplementing relationships. Orthodoxy, however, as it is incarnated in multiple ethnic and cultural traditions, faces a new kind of challenge in the cauldron of American multiculturalism.

An example of the complexity of this challenge is to be found in Fr. George P. Liacopulos' book *Lights of the Modern World: Orthodox Christian Mission and Evangelism in the United States.*[16] While the focus of the work is the development of a missionary mentality and outreach, the volume is instructive for the discussion regarding the relationship of religious and ethnic identities of the Orthodox Church here in the United States. Fr. George develops a three-sided typology, describing the perspectives of the Old Calendarist Movement in America, contrasted secondly with the Greek Orthodox Archdiocese of America, and thirdly with the Evangelical Orthodox Mission of the Antiochian Archdiocese in America. The work is valuable and insightful on several levels, but at the level of ethnic and religious identity, these three Orthodox bodies in the United States exemplify different responses to the identity question.

The sectarian tendencies of the Old Calendarists seem to indicate a sharp line of distinction from whatever is perceived as American culture. Rather, bodies like the Russian Orthodox Church Outside Russia seem to identify with a nineteenth-century Russia which is no more. The Greek Orthodox Archdiocese of America is presented as most conflicted in its struggle to determine the mix of religious and ethnic identities. Among the tensions described are what the author calls "The Ethnocentric/Traditionalist Approach," the Americanizing "Orthodox Christian Laity Movement," and paradoxically, the development of "The Archdiocesan Mission Center as an Instrument of Evangelistic Renewal in the Church." To this perplexing mix, Fr. Liacopulos provides one of the first analyses from outside, of the Evangelical Orthodox Christian Movement (AEOM). In two short sections he describes a range of positions regarding the American religious and ethnic scene.[17] In the AEOM perspective, America is a place that has no place for exclusivistic religious positions, with which Orthodoxy is identified. Civil religion displaces authentic faith. Thus, the watered down religious life of America provides an arena for Orthodox missionary activity. These alternative AEOM affirmations of the American religious scene evaluate American ethnic identity in almost totally negative terms.

Fr. Liacopulos also points to alternative views that have been considered by the AEOM that are more open to the potentiality of American ethnicity for the Orthodox Church and which express a more centrist approach.[18]

If anything, Fr. Liacopulos' study shows a significant difference among Orthodox thinkers in America regarding the relationship between and among ethnic, religious and American identities. I would suggest that some of the tensions would find a more hospitable venue, if we accept the view presented in the previous section that keeps in the forefront of consideration the insights of matryoshka dolls, multicolored umbrellas, or different hats in different situations, coupled with an uncompromising commitment to the True Faith of Orthodoxy.

The American religious scene: American identity, resolutions, future expectations

Scholars of American identity are as perplexed about it as any Orthodox theologian or serious Orthodox person reflecting on what it means to be an Orthodox Christian in America. However a modest consensus exists. While other nations and ethnic groups may readily appeal to identities based on real or imagined shared "blood, kinship, language and belief," the United States of America cannot. Though an exaggeration in the light of other multicultural political and ecclesial bodies such as Byzantium,[19] there is a recognizable truth in what one scholar has said about the United States of America, that it is the "first universal nation."[20]

What makes America "America" is not the content of its culture in terms of language, religion, ethnicity, racial composition or even some of its philosophical traditions or its manifestations of its popular culture. All these form a constantly changing kaleidoscope of expressions. As one commentator has put it: "By far the most powerful popular conception of America is that it is an idea and not just a place or an ethnic group. It is the idea of democracy."[21] He adds, honestly, that many problems, inconsistencies, frustrating contradictions of American democracy are provoked by "the problem that is inherent in our democracy itself, the problem that flows from the fact that we committed ourselves in the beginning to both liberty *and* equality." He asks plaintively, "How can we honor both of these transcendent ideals at the same time?"[22]

Critical to responding out of an Orthodox theological and ecclesial perspective to the question of ecclesial and ethnic identities in the American religious scene is the truth that the democratic framework with its dual paradoxical appeal to liberty *and* equality is *the only essential element of what America means.* All else that is presented as American is part of constantly changing and modulating cultural pluralism.

That is extremely important for the self-identity of Orthodox Christianity in this country. We need not absolutize any aspect of past or current dimensions of the content of the American experiment. We cannot ignore it, we must engage with it, but we ought not allow ourselves to be determined by it.

What we do with our own cultural diversities in which Orthodox Christian truth was incarnated in multiple cultures requires that we respect the identities of our own members as they develop on different trajectories and at varying paces, not simply as ecclesial organizations, but as persons in parishes. Matryoshka dolls illustrate the truth that growth in Orthodoxy will express itself differently; the various Orthodox umbrellas will continue to carry multiple ethnic, language and cultural identities; and we will find ways to engage mutually with our different identity hats as we make our way as a Church toward a greater embodiment of our shared Orthodox True Faith.

Let liturgical language illustrate what I mean. Presbytera Emily and I are members of five parishes in the part of Florida where we live. One is a large parish which is located in a town that has a longstanding powerful ethnically Greek and Orthodox presence.[23] This parish has addressed the language-cultural aspect of its people by conducting two Divine Liturgies each Sunday. The first service is celebrated ninety percent in Greek and ten percent in English and is attended each Sunday by about 500 people. The second Liturgy is ninety percent in English and ten percent in Greek. About 100 people attend this service. Approximately ten miles north is the second parish.[24] Here the priest scrupulously seeks to maintain a balance between Greek and English in order to meet the needs of both the many Greek and Cypriot-born members, on the one hand, and the increasing number of third-generation Hellenes, and non-Greek convert-members of the parish, on the other hand. Some fifteen miles north is the third Greek Orthodox Church,[25] which is very small, in which not only is the Divine Liturgy conducted ninety-eight percent in English, but the congregation, led by the presbytera, sings all of the responses. Another fifteen miles to the north is the fourth parish,[26] where the congregation calls for mixed use of both languages in the proportion of about seventy percent in Greek and thirty percent in English. The fifth parish we attend right in my hometown, is a parish of Slavic background that advertises itself as "American."[27] Ninety-five percent of the Liturgy is, indeed, in English. But not only is five percent in Slavonic, it is sung neither in Byzantine melodies, nor in Russian Znameny chant, but in the plainsong of the Carpathian Mountains.

From the perspective of this presentation, all of these varied practices are valid expressions of ethnic and Orthodox religious identity in the American religious scene. As the matryoshka doll identities evolve and change, so will the language use and the face of these parishes move back and forth from the forefront. The umbrella colors will change and adapt in response to the cultural identities of the people who compose them. Cultural identities will require caps and hats of different styles and forms. The critical issue for the Orthodox Church here in the United States is that it remain committed to the True Faith, the core Orthodox identity, without which there can be no future for Orthodox Christianity in America.

Pastoral guidelines: Ecclesial unity; cultural diversity; for the life of the world

It is for this reason that we Orthodox are called in America to concurrently recognize and serve the diverse cultural and ethnic and linguistic constituencies where we find them. We do no un-Orthodox, nor un-American thing in fostering or responding pastorally to this cultural diversity. But we must acknowledge concurrently that history teaches us that we must prepare our people, so that they are deeply grounded in the True Faith, a grounding that transcends the heritages of each of us, precious as they are. Demographics point to forces at work in America that have affected other religious groups. These can be shown empirically to point to either a consolidation of Orthodox Christianity in this country, or its eventual dissolution.

An example is found in the story of one of the major Protestant denominations in the United States, whose members first came to the United States in the early 1800s. These local churches were organized into various synods based on the lands of their ethnic origins, mostly Germany, Holland, Norway, Sweden, Denmark, Finland and even Iceland. By the third generation, while ethnic identities continued to be cultivated, English began to replace some of the national languages in worship. A century later, in 1917 and 1918, a merger between two ethnically diverse synods of this same denominational family began to take place, forming larger ethnically-based jurisdictions.[28] Cooperative work between the two during World War I was fostered by a joint agency for social work. After the war the laypeople of the denomination formed an inter-synodal lay organization. By 1945 several of the ethnically-based synods unified to form more inclusive ethnic church bodies. By 1960 some German, Danish and Norwegian bodies united, and two years later a parallel organization composed primarily of German, Slovak and Icelandic synods merged with Finnish and Danish bodies into a body which included the word "American" in its title.[29] In 1977 three of the four major bodies of this denomination called for planning to proceed toward creating a single church body. This resulted in a two-year study process begun in 1980. After six years of intensive studies and meetings, the three bodies voted to unite, holding their "constituting convention" in 1987.[30]

There are, of course, many fundamental theological and canonical differences between this body and the Orthodox Christian Church, which cannot be discounted. But we Orthodox also struggle to define ourselves, not always in the same way. Nevertheless, I have deliberately highlighted the plural ethnic diversity of this denomination, to emphasize that our own Orthodox experience in the United States has significant historical parallels. We are not unique in this aspect of our existence in the United States. Further, I have outlined this historical convergence so as to underscore the fact that the process took almost two centuries to accomplish even partially, because the fourth of the major bodies of this denomination has refused to join in the uniting effort.[31]

What do all these things mean in terms of pastoral guidelines for the issue of ecclesial and ethnic identities within the American scene for the Orthodox Churches in the United States?

Numerous other Orthodox writers such as Nicholas Apostola,[32] Demetrios Constantelos,[33] Thomas Hopko,[34] Ihor Kutash,[35] D. Mihas,[36] Maria-Fotini Polidoulis,[37] Samuel Rubenson,[38] Mikhail Sergeev,[39] Constance Tarasar[40] and others have sought to sort out the questions of Orthodox identity. Based on what has been presented in this paper, I summarize what some pastoral guidelines might well be, as a contribution to the ongoing discussion.

A. In our jurisdictional and parish existence, ethnic identities coupled with our Orthodox identities are real, but they are also multidimensional, and in process of taking on changing identities, with new expressions and colors and hues.

B. A pastoral approach within parishes, specific jurisdictions and between Orthodox ecclesial bodies will, on the basis of authentic Orthodox theological affirmations, acknowledge and affirm the identities of our varied concrete ethnic and cultural expressions, recognizing that an incarnational approach has characterized Orthodox Christianity throughout the ages. Within this, however, American identity is defined and understood, Orthodoxy must also work to affirm the American identity, into which we must seek to incarnate the True Faith.

C. In the long perspective, responding to the American social and cultural matrix, there is need for theologically-informed insight and critical judgment. Orthodox evaluations must be cooperatively made among us regarding what is contrary to the True Faith, what can be affirmed and endorsed, what can be transformed and incarnated with the Spirit of Orthodoxy and what must be vigorously rejected and condemned.

D. At the same time, the Orthodox bodies in the United States on every level of ecclesial existence need to foster mutual understanding and appreciation for the varied ethnic and ecclesial Orthodox traditions among us. Included in this is the strengthening of intra-Orthodox cooperation, common Orthodox study efforts and unified position-formulation regarding contemporary public issues. We must pursue also shared men's, women's and youth programs, church rubrics and music, and social service programs. We need to become much clearer in regard to what we are for in American life, as well as what we are against.

E. Special attention and encouragement must also be given to the efforts of good-willed, reverent and well-informed lay leaders in the efforts they are making to contribute to the growth and development of Orthodoxy in America.

F. Finally, our hierarchical leaders, here in this country, those that are abroad, and most importantly the Ecumenical Patriarchate, are under a divine mandate from the Lord Jesus Christ who said "feed my sheep." Surely this implies a call by our Orthodox leaders to protect, enhance and unify the flock of Christ here in the United States of America, regardless of how lengthy and difficult a process it will be.

Conclusion

The response to the issue of ethnic and religious identity in America outlined in this paper is simultaneously a call to respect and honor our varied ethnic identities, while making efforts to discern the meaning of our common American identity. Further, this presentation has sought to locate in a central place our shared identity in the True Faith, the True Orthodox identity as jurisdictions, as parishes and as individual Orthodox persons in communion with each other in the One, Holy, Catholic and Apostolic Church of Christ.

NOTES

[1] Martin E. Marty and R. Scott Appleby, Eds. *Religion, Ethnicity, and Self-Iden-*

tity: Nations in Turmoil (Hanover, NH: University Press of New England, 1997).

[2] Sheldon Hackney, *One America Indivisible: A National Conversation on American Pluralism and Identity.* (Washington, DC, 1998).

[3] Vincent N. Parrilo, *Diversity in America* (Thousand Oaks, CA: Pine Forge Press, 1996).

[4] Edward Mortimer, *People, Nation & State: The Meaning of Ethnicity and Nationalism* (New York: I.B. Tauris Publishers, 1999).

[5] Philip Permutter, *The Dynamics of American Ethnic, Religious and Racial Group Life: An Interdisciplinary Overview.* (Westport, CT: Praeger, 1996).

[6] John H. Berthrong, *The Divine Call: Religious Identity in the North American Cultural Mosaic* (Maryknoll, NY: Orbis Books, 1999).

[7] T. K. Oommen, *Citizenship and National Identity: From Colonialism to Globalism* (Thousand Oaks, CA: Sage Publications, 1997).

[8] Knud Krakau, *The American Nation, National Identity, Nationalism* (Munster: LIT, 1997).

[9] Eldon J. Eisenach, *The Next Religious Establishment: National Identity and Political Theology in Post-Protestant America* (Lanham: Rowan & Littlefield, 2000).

[10] Murray Friedman and Nancy Isserman, *The Tribal Basis of American Life: Racial, Religious, and Ethnic Groups In Conflict* (Westport, CT: Praeger, 1998).

[11] See, for example, Edward Mortimer, *People, Nation and State*, chs. 1 and 2.

[12] Guntram H. Herb and David H. Kaplan, *Nested Identities: Nationalism, Territory and Scale* (New York: Roman & Littlefield Publishers, 1999).

[13] Herb and Kaplan, p. 1.

[14] David B. Knight, "Afterword: Nested Identities – Nationalism, Territory, and Scale," in Herb and Kaplan, p. 317.

[15] "Reminders of Scotland in the Dance," *Hernando Today*, Sunday, September 17, 2000, section B, pp. 1-2. "A way we have come together as Americans and appreciate each other is to learn about our cultures. By keeping the traditions of our homelands, passing them on to our children and sharing them in our community, we can celebrate and value our differences in unique and interesting ways," says Amy Brijbag, the author of the article. The article, of course, reflects the view that cultures and religions can share the American space while maintaining an ethnic identity.

[16] Fr. George P. Liacopulos, *Lights of the Modern World: Orthodox Christian Mission and Evangelism in the United States* (Minneapolis: Light & Life Publishing Co., 2000).

[17] Liacopulos, "An AEOM Assessment of Modern American Society," pp. 148-149, where the views of Frank Schaeffer, Ron Roberson, Gordon Walker, and Peter Gillquist are discussed.

[18] Liacopulos, "The Relationship Between Orthodoxy and American Culture," pp. 149-155, in which the views of three OCA thinkers were published in the AEOM periodical *Again*. They are Frs. Leonid Kishkovsky, Joseph Fester, and Michael Oleksa.

[19] Fr. John Meyendorff pointed to the cultural pluralism of the Byzantine Empire and the Orthodox Church in many places. One of his statements follows. "The issues of cultural pluralism within the Church took a quite different shape in

the East. Here a diversity of venerable Christian traditions had existed since the very origins of Christianity, and will constitute a significant factor in the missionary expansion (of the Eastern Church). If, as already in New Testament times, the Greek language served as a major tool of intercultural and international communication, Syria and Egypt preserved not only their cultural identity, but also their respective languages, and gave birth to daughter-churches and daughter-civilizations in Armenia, Georgia, Mesopotamia, Persia, India, Arabia, Ethiopia and Nubia. In all these cases, the model given at Pentecost (Acts 2) of each nation accepting the Word of God in its own language was applied; and Greek – in spite of its being the principal tool of theological creativity and doctrinal debates – was never seen (as Latin was in the West) to be the only available vehicle of civilization." *Imperial Unity and Christian Divisions: The Church 450-680 A.D.* (Crestwood, NY: St. Vladimir's Seminary Press, 1989), p. 24.

[20] Ben Wattenberg, *The Birth Dearth,* 2nd Ed (New York: Pharos Press, 1989). Quoted in Parrillo, *Diversity in America,* p. 190.

[21] Sheldon Hackney, *One America, Indivisible,* p. 55.

[22] Hackney, p. 56.

[23] St. Nicholas Greek Orthodox Cathedral, Tarpon Springs, FL.

[24] St. George Greek Orthodox Church, New Port Richey, FL.

[25] St. Nicholas Greek Orthodox Chapel, Brooksville, FL.

[26] St. Michael the Archangel, Lecanto, FL

[27] Holy Trinity Carpatho-Russian Church, Spring Hill, FL.

[28] This account refers to the developing organization of the various Lutheran jurisdictions in the United States, and in particular, this stage of the uniting of various ethnically-based synods among Lutherans from Norway (Norwegian Lutheran Church of America) and the union of three German-based synods into the United Lutheran Church in America. "Roots of the Evangelical Lutheran Church in America." www.elca.org/co/roots.html, pp. 1-2.

[29] "In 1960 the American Lutheran Church (German), United Evangelical Lutheran Church (Danish) and the Evangelical Lutheran Church (Norwegian) merged to form the American Lutheran Church (ALC). The Lutheran Free Church (Norwegian), which had dropped out of merger negotiations, came into the ALC in 1963. Ibid. p. 2.

[30] There is some value in quoting more extensively from the account of the process leading toward merger of these ethnically disparate Lutheran bodies. "The 1978 ALC and LCA conventions adopted resolutions aimed at the creation of a single church body. The AELC joined them, and the ALC-LCA Committee on Church Cooperation became the Committee on Lutheran Unity (CLU) in January of 1979. Presiding Bishop David Preus (ALC), Bishop James Crumley (LCA) and President and later Bishop William Kohn (AELC) met with the CLU over the next sixteen months, and the 1980 conventions of all three church bodies adopted a two-year study process. Documents were in the hands of congregational leaders by November of that year, and by 1982 all the pieces were in place for the three churches to have simultaneous conventions so that, on September 8, 1982, with

telephone hookups so each could hear the others' votes, all three church bodies voted to proceed on the path toward a new Lutheran church.

The ELCA takes shape

The CLU proposals included the structure and operating procedures for a new group, the Commission for a New Lutheran Church (CNLC), and a timetable for the churches: The 1984 conventions to discuss, review and respond to a statement of theological understandings and ecclesial principles, and a narrative description of the new church; The 1986 conventions to discuss, review and respond to the articles of incorporation of the new church, the constitution and bylaws of the new church, and be able to take action to cease functioning by Dec. 31, 1987. The 70-member CNLC, its members deliberately chosen to be widely representative of the membership of all the merging bodies, met ten times over the next five years, making full reports which were widely disseminated to church members. By August 1986 the CNLC had completed its work and again the three church bodies met in simultaneous conventions, again with telephone hookups, and voted overwhelmingly to accept the constitution and bylaws of the new church as well as the proposed agreement and plan of merger, thus creating the fourth largest Protestant body in the United States. The ten-member Transition Team met fifteen times in the process, hiring a coordinator and settling issues such as specific location, staffing and budget for the new church. The Evangelical Lutheran Church in America was finally born at its constituting convention in Columbus, Ohio, April 30-May 3, 1987. The three churches had "closing conventions" the day before, taking care of constitutional matters and saying goodbye. In the four days of the first convention of the new church delegates finalized legal details and elected the ELCA's first bishop, Herbert Chilstrom, other officers and 228 other people to various boards, councils and committees. At 12:01 a.m., Central Standard Time, January 1, 1988, the ELCA became the legal successor to its predecessors, a mosaic reflecting not only the ethnic heritages of traditional Lutherans through its original churches, but also the full spectrum of American culture in which it serves, proclaiming the Gospel of Jesus Christ to the world." Ibid. p. 4. Of interest for the purposes of this paper in which "identity" has a central role, is the only link on this ELCA page, named, significantly, "Who We Are."

[31] The Lutheran Church – Missouri Synod (LCMS).

[32] Nicholas K. Apostola, "Moving Towards an Administratively United Church." *St. Vladimir's Theological Quarterly*, 40:1-2 (1996), pp. 95-114.

[33] Demetrios J. Constantelos, "Ethnic Particularities and the Universality of Orthodox Christianity Today." *Journal of Modern Hellenism*. 7 (1990), pp. 89-105.

[34] Thomas Hopko, "The Narrow Way of Orthodoxy."
St. Vladimir's Theological Quarterly, 40:1-2 (1996), pp. 3-15.

[35] Ihor G. Kutash, "The Nationalism of the Ukrainian Autocephalous Orthodox Church: A Stage in Global Consciousness." *ARC: Journal of Faculty of Religious Studies, McGill University*. 19 (1991), pp. 109-121.

[36] D. E. M. Mihas, "Religion in Albania." *Modern Believing*, 38:1 (1997), pp. 33-40.

[37] Maria-Fotini Polidoulis, "The Christian Call to Love: The Influence of the Greek Orthodox Ladies Philoptochos Society on the Social Ethos in America." *Greek Orthodox Theological Review*, 39:3-4 (1994), pp. 356-375.

[38] Samuel Rubenson, "Kyrka eller folk – den syrisk-ortodoxa kyrkan och det svenska samhallet" (Church or People – the Syrian-Orthodox Church and Swedish Society). *Svensk Teologisk Kvartalskrift*, 68:2 (1992), pp. 71-79.

[39] Mikhail Sergeev, "Russian Orthodoxy: Renewal or Revival?" *Journal of Ecumenical Studies*. 33:1 (1996), pp. 36-43.

[40] Constance Tarasar, "Sophie Shidlovsky Koulomzin: Architect of Cooperative Orthodox Education." *Religious Education*, 73:5 (1978), pp. 91-99.

A Response to Fr. Stanley S. Harakas' "Ecclesial and Ethnic Identities within the American Religious Scene"

Robert M. Haddad

Because my disagreement with Fr. Harakas relates more to emphasis than to substance, I shall pursue "response" less as antithesis than as commentary but not without intruding, particularly in my concluding remarks, some of my own thoughts on ecclesial and ethnic identities.

In the space allotted I cannot hope to do justice to the richness of Fr. Harakas' effort to relate shifting ethnic and linguistic identities to an Orthodox identity that vastly transcends both sets of distinctions. His exposition, although a model of clarity, displays a tolerance of ethnic and linguistic, not to mention jurisdictional, diversity that far exceeds mine.

Fr. Harakas begins by clarifying two major theories of the genesis of ethnicity: primordialism, which holds ethnicity to be a given; and constructivism, which sees ethnicity as "a culture construct that is malleable and which can be constructed at will." Malleable certainly but "constructed at will" improbably. In considering, for example, the well-known phenomenon of "going native," one might well question the degree to which such a metamorphosis is ever completely successful. The new identity sought – hedged about as it is by linguistic, social, economic, as well as ethnic barriers – is rarely attainable in its fullness. Fr. Harakas would agree that the experience of millions of immigrants in America would testify to the difficulties in constructing a new self, even when one is inclined to do so.

Fr. Harakas judiciously favors the view that ethnicity is generally both a primordial given and a culture construct, although he does cite favorably the observation of Martin Marty and R. Scott Appleby that "identities are not fixed or immutable but are accumulated over the course of a lifetime." One might note, however, that this apparently constructivist perspective reduces ethnicity to only one component of "identity." In this regard, one might usher forth the example of the late lamented Fr. Nomikos Michael Vaporis who described to Fr. Harakas his "feeling of changing hats," depending on whether he found himself in an ethnic Greek, in an Orthodox ecclesial, or in a secular academic environment. Any Orthodox pursuing a career in the secular academy recognizes immediately Fr. Vaporis' inescapable though not always discomfiting or unwelcome "feeling of changing hats." And this is not always a function of ethnicity. For Fr. Harakas, the matryoshka dolls of Slavic tradition, the same figure in differing sizes fitting into smaller or larger replicas, also illustrate the complexity of identity. To employ a different metaphor to comparable effect: we all tend to live within our concentric circles: linguistic, ethnic, territorial, sexual, social, economic, professional and, for some, religious.

Moving from the issue of personal identity, Fr. Harakas discusses briefly the communal – more specifically, the American mosaic which lately has come to be described by many as "multiculturalism." In paraphrase of Vincent N. Parrilo, Fr. Harakas notes three different interpretations of that truly slippery concept: those of the "separatists," the "inclusionists," and the "integrative pluralists." Although Fr. Harakas does not choose sides in this debate, I feel compelled to do so. I have scant patience with the "separatists" and their advocacy of "minority nationalism" and "separate pluralism" – prescriptions, it seems to me, for a politically divided United States. I am only slightly less intolerant of the "inclusionists" and their call to "emphasize the presence and contributions of non-Europeans." Where it matters most in the public sphere, and that pertains to American language, law and political institutions, the fundamental contributions have come from White Anglo-Saxon Protestants, and this much-maligned group has served well the nation (always excepting the aboriginal population and, until recently, Asians and Afro-Americans). Their formulations have provided Americans of European and non-European derivation alike ample scope for realization of their mundane and even their religious aspirations, despite the heavy hand of American secularism. The same considerations lend an aura of unreality to the "integrative pluralists," and their program "for a mutual sharing of diverse sub-cultures." I wish neither to deny the existence of these sub-cultures nor to will their dissolution. Singly or collectively, however, they remain subordinate to the dominant culture spawned, to be sure, by White Anglo-Saxon Protestants but now universalized to encompass, in greater or lesser degree, all Americans and, indeed, much of the world. The Orthodox task to transform that culture presupposes immersion in it.

Nor are my remarks intended to invalidate entirely the "umbrella" image next employed by Fr. Harakas as he draws closer to the subject of ethnic diversity within the American Orthodox community. Roman Catholics of Irish, Italian, French and other ethnic derivations do indeed sport a distinctive jurisdictional umbrella over their ethnic particularisms. The same is somewhat less true of most Protestants who, collectively and denominationally, lack the sturdy hierarchical arrangements of the Roman Catholics. Obviously and alas, however, the Orthodox umbrella hovering over ethnic particularisms lacks the jurisdictional unity emblazoned on the Roman Catholic umbrella, while the variegated Protestant pattern, characterized by a wholly alien ecclesiology, is largely irrelevant to the Orthodox.

Fr. Harakas cites Orthodox teaching that the Incarnation gives "special meaning to human life and culture and even ethnic identities." He readily concedes, however, that "Orthodoxy, ... as it is incarnated in multiple ethnic and cultural traditions, faces a new kind of challenge in the cauldron of American multiculturalism." Fr. Harakas illustrates this theme by utilizing the "three-sided typology" of Orthodoxy in America, developed by Fr. George P. Liacopulos, a typology that includes the Old Calendarists, the Greek Orthodox Archdiocese, and the Evangelical Orthodox Mission of the Antiochian Archdiocese. The Old Calendarists exemplify the sharp distinction between Orthodoxy and what is perceived as American culture, an alienation reminiscent of the identification of the Russian Orthodox Church Outside Russia with a largely imaginary nineteenth-century Russia. For its part, the Greek Orthodox Archdiocese, in striving to determine the appropriate mix of religious and ethnic identities, features tensions among "The Ethnocentric/Traditionalist Approach," the Americanizing "Orthodox Christian Laity Movement" and "The Archdiocesan Mission Center as an Instrument of Evangelistic Renewal in the Church." Finally, the Evangelical Orthodox Mission, wholly anchored in the American context and persuaded that "the watered-down religious life of America provides an arena for Orthodox missionary activity" necessarily evaluates Orthodox ethnic particularism negatively. The position of the Evangelical Orthodox, although surely understandable, remains uncongenial to Fr. Harakas who keeps ever before us the vision of the matryoshka dolls, the religious umbrella hovering over ethnic diversity, and the different hats worn by Fr. Vaporis.

What, then, does it mean to be an Orthodox Christian in America, allegedly the "first universal nation" whose people, it is argued, cannot define themselves by appeal to real or imagined "blood, kinship, language and belief"? But is this characterization entirely accurate? Surely the vast majority of Americans would consider English basic to their identity, and the minority who do not *will*, as the realization grips those enamored of such self-defeating devices as bilingual education that their economic future depends upon firm control of the English tongue. Even in ethnically homogenous nations, after all, the categories of "blood" and "kinship" that underpin ethnicity are usually inseparable from language. And if "belief" here denotes not religious faith but, rather, that credence, evinced by the vast majority of Americans in their nation's political institutions and system of law, the case for an authentically American identity seems to me immeasurably strengthened. As for Sheldon Hackney's notion that the idea of democracy is "the most powerful popular conception of America," it is to be emphasized that American democracy is not simply an abstraction but a concept grounded concretely in law and political definitions. What is American, I would insist, is not merely the "constantly changing and modulating cultural pluralism" to which Fr. Harakas alludes. Cultural pluralism assuredly pervades American life but within boundaries dictated by common language, law and political institutions. Otherwise, cultural pluralism would likely resolve itself as chaos. Fr. Harakas and some of the commentators he cites seem to me to shroud American identity in a mystery not wholly justified by objective assessment.

Fr. Harakas relies on the hypotheses I have just questioned to countenance the cultural diversity prevalent in American Orthodoxy today. The multiple cultures in which "Orthodox Christian truth was incarnated" have been transported to America where an Orthodox doctrinal and sacramental umbrella came to loom over "multiple ethnic, language and cultural identities." (I shall soon defend my preference for an umbrella that is jurisdictional as well as doctrinal and sacramental.) Fr. Harakas calls our attention to the several liturgical languages used in the five Florida parishes of which he is a member. I accept his argument that "these varied practices are valid expressions of ethnic and Orthodox religious identities in the American scene" but *only* if they are considered transitional practices in the evolution of American Orthodoxy toward English as the dominant liturgical tongue and, most important, toward a united autocephalous American Orthodox Church. I grant, of course, that "the critical issue for the Orthodox Church in America [or anywhere else, for that matter] is that it remain committed to the True Faith" but the True Faith is ill served by perpetuating a plethora of liturgical tongues and ethnic jurisdictions. The changing hats of Fr. Vaporis and the matryoshka dolls of Slavic invention inhere in the human condition but the Orthodox umbrella under which lurk various ethnically-defined jurisdictions should be dispatched as soon as circumstance allows.

Fr. Harakas appears to edge toward the same conclusion. For while he argues that it is not un-Orthodox to foster cultural (read "ethnic") diversity, he admits that demographics "point to either a consolidation of Orthodox Christianity in this country, or its eventual dissolution." He ponders the fate of the Lutheran churches in America, originally ethnically-based but driven by sheer desire for survival gradually to merge into larger and larger bodies. Fr. Harakas underscores "the fact that the process took almost two centuries to accomplish even partially." Even assuming that Orthodoxy in America could survive two centuries of jurisdictional disunity, there exists no compelling ecclesiological or canonical reason to do so. And whatever the duration of ethnic diversity, it is possible, if not probable, that jurisdictional diversity might outlast its original ethnic rationale. I'm reminded of the artificial states created in the Middle East by Great Britain and France after World War I, the borders of which states corresponded to no discernible geographic, ethnic, linguistic or, for the most part, religious division. Yet these states are with us still, for if one leaves borders, however artificially conceived, long intact they tend to assume permanence. Each state develops its own symbols and substance of statehood: flag, anthem, passport, army, currency, educational system, vested economic interests and vested elites. Each state becomes a nation, albeit often weak and vulnerable, almost in spite of itself and often in defiance of the wishes of its people. Orthodox Churches in America have thus far eschewed armies but they have certainly developed vested economic interests and vested hierarchical elites. At least one jurisdiction even sponsors an educational system designed to serve ethnicity quite as much as the faith.

Fr. Harakas ends his paper with a set of cogent pastoral guidelines bearing upon ecclesial and ethnic identities of the Orthodox in America. Several deserve special emphasis. There is particular wisdom in Fr. Harakas' insistence that "however American identity is defined and understood, Orthodoxy must ... work to affirm the American identity, into which we must seek to incarnate the True Faith." One wonders whether this can be accomplished while Orthodoxy in America languishes in ethnic and jurisdictional diversity. I believe that Fr. Harakas finally concedes as much when he calls for a collective Orthodox theological response to what in American society and culture "is contrary to the True Faith, what can be affirmed and endorsed, what can be ... incarnated with the Spirit of Orthodoxy and what must be vigorously rejected and condemned." Is such a collective response conceivable outside the perimeters of an autocephalous American Orthodox Church? I do not believe that Fr. Harakas thinks so, for his penultimate paragraph reminds the Orthodox hierarchy, here and abroad, that implicit in Christ's command to "feed my sheep" is "a call ... to unify the flock of Christ here in the United States, regardless of how difficult and how long it will take." I would most gently fault Fr. Harakas for failing to urge more vigorously the forging of jurisdictional unity among the Orthodox Churches that dot the American landscape. As I suggested at the outset, too much of his admirable presentation could be interpreted not only as explanation but also as apology for the persistence of ethnic and jurisdictional diversity. Allow me now to advance arguments in favor of a more urgent approach to the creation of an autocephalous American Orthodox Church.

The Orthodox mission in America is (1) to preserve Orthodox believers in their faith and (2) to represent to all Americans what Orthodox deem the True Faith. To serve best this twofold mission clearly calls for jurisdictional unity among America's various Orthodox Churches – it calls for nothing less than creation of an autocephalous American Church.

As we know, the genesis of Orthodoxy in America had no precedent in the Church's history. Never had so many believers from so many different jurisdictions descended, more or less at once, upon a non-Orthodox land. Under the circumstances, it was altogether natural that these immigrants would develop their own ethnically-based Churches with strong ties to their Mother Churches in Eastern Europe and in lands along the eastern Mediterranean. Ethnic diversity demanded jurisdictional diversity. Immigrants simply felt most comfortable amid their own. I would also suggest that jurisdictional diversity was initially salutary for, without it, I doubt that the Church would have retained as many souls as it did. Three imperatives, however – the spiritual, the canonical, and the pragmatic – render jurisdictional diversity anachronistic. The spiritual dimension is revealed in the Church's own self-definition as "One, Holy, Catholic and Apostolic." Despite the sacramental unity prevailing among the Orthodox in America, their jurisdictional separation along ethnic and national lines casts a shadow over oneness. And in inhibiting each Church from subordinating its particular interests to those of the whole Church, jurisdictional separation also compromises catholicity.

The situation of Orthodoxy in America is also canonically anomalous, for the canons of every Orthodox Church prohibit parallel ecclesiastical organizations in the same area. In each particular place, only one bishop is to preside in unity of faith with the entire Orthodox episcopate. Orthodox Christians in each particular place are mandated to live as a single Church, jurisdictionally as well as sacramentally, and to worship in the tongue or, when occasion demands, the tongues of the worshipers.

Pragmatic necessity also impels American Orthodox toward unity, for who can deny that Orthodox witness to non-Orthodox Americans – that second aspect of Orthodox mission in America – is seriously impaired by jurisdictional disunity? One can hardly blame non-Orthodox Americans for regarding the Orthodox Churches around them not as the One True Church but as an aggregate of mutually exclusive and occasionally fractious ethnic enclaves. I say this despite the substantial muting of the ethnic emphasis in recent decades, notably in the Orthodox Church in America (OCA) as well as in the Antiochian Archdiocese. But Orthodoxy still seems to many to be bound to the cultures of Greeks, Arabs, Russians, Serbs, et al., thereby denying converts the richness of catholicity as well as compromising their right to remain fully American in their own land. Orthodox in America must ask themselves whether Churches organized, in contravention of their own ecclesiology and canons, along different and non-indigenous ethnic lines can acquit themselves of their apostolic obligation to preach to all nations.

Nor does pragmatic necessity leave untouched Americans of traditional Orthodox background. A substantial majority of marriages celebrated in Orthodox Churches in America are mixed and one can only guess the number of marriages involving one Orthodox spouse which are not blessed by the Church.[1] Not every non-Orthodox partner is anxious to assimilate to the ethnic mores of his or her spouse. For many an Orthodox spouse, moreover, the ways of the forebears gradually recede into irrelevance. For him or her, the local ethnically-defined church no longer represents quite the haven in an alien America that it was for the original immigrants. And what of the even more pronounced ambivalence felt by many children of mixed unions? Orthodox in America generally acknowledge the unreality of the dream of many of their fathers to return "home." There is no Orthodox diaspora in the classical sense of "dispersion" pending return to a fixed sacred homeland.[2] America is all the home the descendants of immigrants are likely to see, and this fact should be reflected in jurisdictional unity – a unity which would also help end the wasteful redundancy of clergy, buildings, educational facilities, media resources and monastic houses. In too many cities and towns, churches under different jurisdictions, and even under the same jurisdiction, stand cheek by jowl, both half empty. We often boast of the converts who have come to adorn our churches in America (usually with little assistance from native Orthodox, we might add) while gliding silently over losses due, in some measure, to our ethnic and jurisdictional disarray.

But while I regard as urgent and inevitable the creation of an autocephalous American Orthodox Church, such a Church must be ushered into existence with due regard to ethnic sensitivities. The first step ought to be unity of the episcopate in one synod, the redundancies there to be eliminated through attrition rather than through more aggressive means. Dioceses could retain their existing organizations and parishes and as many of their old national traditions, including liturgical languages, as they consider necessary to preserve their flock in the faith. I am confident that adoption of English as the main liturgical tongue, a process well underway, will continue, but it is best to allow it to proceed with minimal extra-parochial pressure. The influx over recent decades of especially Greek, Arab and Russian immigrants surely dictates patience on the linguistic front. Let American Orthodox see cultural and linguistic diversity *within* a united, autocephalous Church as a sign of catholicity. Has the incorporation into the OCA of people of non-Russian extraction: Romanians, Carpatho-Russians, Albanians, Bulgarians, Alaskans and Mexicans led to their Russification? Similarly, has the inclusion of the Evangelical Orthodox and many others into the Antiochian Archdiocese wrought the Arabization of these largely Anglo-Saxon converts?

How is the jurisdictional unity favored by a substantial majority of American Orthodox clergy and laity to be brought about? One, alas, can hardly look to the Standing Conference of Canonical Orthodox Bishops in America (SCOBA), for this organization merely reflects and exacerbates existing divisions. Never to my knowledge, except perhaps at its meeting in Ligonier, Pennsylvania in 1994, has SCOBA seriously broached the issue of an autocephalous American Church. And the tentative accord reached at Ligonier quickly foundered on objections raised by the Ecumenical Patriarchate of Constantinople. Herein the rub! Because the See of Constantinople commands four Churches with voting rights in SCOBA,[3] among whom only the Greek Archdiocese features substantial numbers, the topic discussed more than once in the past has been not creation of an autocephalous American Church but, rather, creation of a pan-Orthodox American synod under the jurisdiction of Constantinople – a consummation devoutly to be avoided by the great majority of non-Greek jurisdictions.

The reluctance of other Mother Patriarchates to countenance formation of an autocephalous American Church offers, I believe, no insurmountable obstacle. Not so the adamant refusal of the Ecumenical Patriarchate whose case rests upon Canon 28 of the Council of Chalcedon, promulgated in A.D. 451, which accords Constantinople the right to appoint bishops in "barbarian" lands (i.e. those unhappy climes beyond the imperial sway of the Eastern Roman Emperor). Unfortunately, this Greek Christian sovereign yielded, almost 550 years ago, to the Ottoman Muslim Sultan, while "barbarian" lands now cover 99.9% of the globe. But releasing the Greek Archdiocese into an autocephalous American Church would likely be followed by the demand of other Greek jurisdictions in the misnamed "diaspora" for analogous status, the end product of which would be devolution of the jurisdiction of the venerable See of Constantinople upon a dwindling handful of faithful in modern Turkey.

It is Constantinople's insistence upon retaining its self-assigned prerogatives that lends to the notion of comprehensive jurisdictional unity among American Orthodox, at this juncture, a phantasmal quality. And given the numbers and resources, human and material, of the Greek Archdiocese in America, its exclusion from an autocephalous American Church would render that Church woefully incomplete and gravely impaired. An American Church that includes all of today's jurisdictions will one day be a reality but the road thereto will, for many years to come, remain hard and fraught with frustration. American Orthodox, having arrived at a consensus in favor of unity, can only urge their Mother Patriarchates to honor their own ecclesiology and canon law and their divinely-bestowed mandate to serve and augment the flock of Christ.

This is not at all to say that an autocephalous American Church that dissolves existing jurisdictions will usher in the millennium (the pun is intended). It is certainly not earnest of "putting on Christ." The old ethnic differences will for a time continue to divide; the often antithetical claims of the secular order, as Fr. Harakas rightly insists, will yet have to be confronted and answered in an authentically Orthodox Christian voice; and the nature of American Orthodoxy's place in America's political and cultural order will still have to be defined. But without an autocephalous American Orthodox Church, these issues will neither be faced nor even fully recognized.

NOTES

[1] Editor's note: According to Fr. Charles Joanides, elsewhere in this book, a conservative estimate places intermarriage rates within the Greek Orthodox Archdiocese at 67%.

[2] The term "diaspora," borrowed from Jewish tradition, implies a specific point of return – in the Jewish case, Palestine. The Orthodox boast no point of return that enjoys the sanction of doctrine or Tradition.

[3] One Greek, one Ukrainian, one Carpatho-Russian and one Albanian.

ORGANIZATION, COMMUNITY, CHURCH:
REFLECTIONS ON ORTHODOX PARISH POLITY IN AMERICA

JOHN H. ERICKSON

What is a parish? According to the Uniform Parish Regulations (UPR) of the Greek Orthodox Archdiocese:

> The Parish is the local body of communicants of the Church in a given locality, organized under the jurisdiction of the Archdiocese, whose ecclesiastical authority is its canonically consecrated Bishop. Locally, the Parish is headed by a canonically ordained Priest heretofore duly appointed by the Archbishop or hereafter duly appointed by the Bishop in the Diocese in which the Parish is located. (Art. I Sec.1)[1]

Much the same definition can be found in comparable documents of other Orthodox jurisdictions in America. For example, the Sample Parish By-Laws of the Orthodox Church in America (OCA), suggest wording along the following lines:

> This parish, which is under the Diocesan Authority [of the bishop of such-and-such a diocese of the Orthodox Church in America], is a local community of the Church having at its head a duly appointed Priest and consisting of Orthodox Christians who live in accordance with the teachings of the Orthodox Church, comply with the discipline and rules of the Church, and regularly support their parish. (para. 3)[2]

Of course, these documents set forth the official policies and regulations of our churches in America. Their apparent consistency and clarity is somewhat deceptive. Over the centuries, whether in the Old World or in America, the parish has not always conformed to the definitions and norms of our current attempts at uniform regulation. Far from it! In fact documents such as those just quoted represent simply the latest stage in the evolution of the Orthodox parish.

A few years after the Greek Orthodox Archdiocese initially adopted its Uniform Parish Regulations (Denver Clergy-Laity Congress, 1964), Archbishop Iakovos gave this brief account of the history of the parish in America (Athens Clergy-Laity Congress, 1968):

67

Our parishes in America began as organizations and developed into religious communities. Today they are churches. Around them our whole life is entwined and is developed. Thus we have accepted what St. Paul states with these words: "Whether we live or die, we are the Lord's" (Rom 14.8).[3]

Our parishes began as organizations – and in many respects they still are organizations, corporate entities with legal status. They developed into communities – religious communities perhaps, but also ethnic and cultural communities. Yet they are called to be churches, more important to their members than earthly ties of whatever sort. The Uniform Parish Regulations of the Greek Orthodox Archdiocese and the comparable documents of other Orthodox jurisdictions in America were formulated, at least in part, in response to earlier tendencies to reduce the parish to a self-sufficient and self-satisfied corporation or ethnic club. They were formulated, at least in principle, in order to allow our parishes truly to be churches, canonical in their organizational aspect and religious in their communal aspect. How well have they succeeded? The purpose of this paper is three-fold: to examine some of the more striking features of older parish bylaws and the attitudes behind these bylaws; to indicate how the Uniform Parish Regulations and comparable documents attempted to address perceived ecclesiological distortions in these older bylaws; and finally to suggest what remains to be done if our Orthodox parishes in America are truly to live as churches.

The parish as corporation and ethnic club

When Greek, Russian, Serbian, Romanian, Arab and other Orthodox immigrants began to stream into America in the late nineteenth century, they quickly formed organizations of various sorts – social clubs and patriotic associations in order to maintain a sense of cultural identity, mutual aid societies and brotherhoods for support in times of distress and need. And almost as quickly they set about establishing parish churches, very often as a direct outgrowth of their cultural or fraternal organizations – the Society of Athena, the Sts. Cyril and Methodius Brotherhood, the Soudie Syrian Brotherhood Society, or what have you. These immigrants were not necessarily deeply religious people, but, as one immigrant put it, "there couldn't be any Greek life" – Serbian life, Russian life, or Romanian life – "without the church." In their Old World villages, the local parish church, standing from time immemorial on the same consecrated ground, had been a self-evident and organic part of life. Its daily and annual cycles of worship determined the patterns for work and leisure, fasting and feasting. Its moral teaching provided a common point of reference for behavior. Its sacraments and other rites gave the faithful tangible experience of the holy.

Immigrants to America – whether Greeks or Slavs, Romanians or Arabs – wanted such a church for themselves and for their children. But in America the parish church could not be taken for granted as it was in the Old World. They themselves would have to build these churches. And while these immigrants wanted a church, they wanted something more as well. They wanted a place where they could be with their Old World compatriots, where their very particular social, cultural, linguistic and spiritual heritage could be affirmed, where they could find some shelter from the pressures of New World life, where some semblance of the community they had left behind could be recreated. As a result, the relationship between church and community underwent a subtle change. In the Old World, it was the Church that determined the shape and tone of community life. In America, this relationship comes to be reversed. Now it is the community that determines the shape and tone of church life. The interests and concerns of a particular natural community – of this or that nationality, of this or that village, of this or that political faction – take precedence over the wider demands of the Church understood as a community of faith, a community open in principle to all nations and all peoples.

It should come as no surprise that many older parish bylaws tend to define the parish in national or ethnic terms. For much of its existence, a certain parish in Connecticut in effect was a wholly-owned subsidiary of "American Sons and Daughters of Carpatho-Russia, Inc." The lands, buildings, church and hall of another parish were owned by the "Russian Orthodox Society of the City of Vancouver," which had as its stated purpose "(a) The bringing together of the Russian people of the City of Vancouver and its surrounding areas. (b) To serve their spiritual, religious and cultural needs."[4] Typical is the way another parish approached the question of membership: "A member of the Church shall be any person of Ukrainian origin, of good moral habits, who recognizes the Faith, including all the Holy Sacraments and rites of the Church, pays the established membership fees, and fulfills all the other obligations of a parishioner, and abides by the Church Constitution and its By-Laws."[5] And of course for many years this tendency to link church membership with ethnicity was not limited to parish bylaws. According to its 1922 Charter, the purpose of the then newly-established Greek Orthodox Archdiocese was "to nurture the religious and moral life of American citizens of the Orthodox faith, who are either themselves Greek or of Greek ancestry."[6]

As those acquainted with the history of parish formation in America can attest, this tendency toward particularism has not always stopped at the level of ethnicity or nationality. Many American cities can boast of not one, but of two or more Orthodox churches of the same national background, in many cases dating from the same period and often even located in the same neighborhood. Why? In some cases political allegiances have been determinative. In the course of struggles in the Greek community between Royalists and Venizelists, some parishes – typically named for St. Constantine or for Sts. Constantine and Helen – were dominated by supporters of King Constantine, while others were dominated by the Venizelists. When St. Eleftherios was formed in the Bronx in 1918, there was no question where the loyalties of its parishioners lay – it was named for Venizelos' patron saint. In other cases, regional animosities have played a decisive role. The early history of the Greek community of Chicago offers a striking example. Around 1892 a group of immigrants formed the Society of Lycourgos, which in turn organized Annunciation parish and obtained a priest from the Holy Synod of the Church of Greece. As its name suggests, the Society of Lycourgos was dominated by immigrants from Sparta, and their chosen priest hailed from the same region. But the parish also included a growing number immigrants from the rival region of Arcadia, who resented Spartan domination of parish affairs. In 1897 some of these Arcadians went off to fight in the Greco-Turkish war. They arrived too late for the war, but while in the old country they met a priest from their own region who was eager to visit his two sons in Chicago. With a congenial priest so conveniently at hand, the Chicago Arcadians quickly established a parish of their own, this one dedicated to the Holy Trinity.[7]

National, political and regional loyalties often have determined actual parish membership, but – apart from ethnic references – we see relatively few traces of this in actual parish bylaws. St. Eleftherios in the Bronx or St. Constantine in Brooklyn did not have to write a political test into their bylaws – their very names proclaimed their loyalties! The same, however, is not true of financial requirements for membership. Invariably older bylaws carefully specify requirements for being a "member in good standing" or "voting member" of the parish: a certain minimum age, fulfillment of "religious duties" (in older Slavic parishes this being the "annual obligation" of confession and communion), and above all payment of "annual church dues and assessments." Someone who meets these requirements "shall be a voting member of the Corporation and thereby shall have the privilege of signing duly authorized petitions and to be present and vote at all Corporate meetings." Such a person also "shall be entitled to the services of the Rector-Priest, and to the Holy Sacraments and other Church and spiritual needs."[8] The message conveyed by such bylaws – and one can find them in the closets and attics of all practically all our older churches – is that this parish is governed by those who have a financial stake in it and that it exists in order to serve their particular cultic and cultural needs.

The parish becomes introverted, turned in upon itself, with virtually no sense of mission and outreach and only a minimal sense of responsibility towards anyone outside its own immediate membership. Here again, older parish by-laws illustrate this point very vividly. A member in good standing, i.e., one who has paid his annual church dues and other assessments in full, "is entitled to all Church Rites and ministrations which the Priest of said parish administers" – at least at a very reasonable price! "Baptism $5.00, Matrimony $20.00, Funerals (Adults) $20.00, Funerals (Children) $10.00," etc. On the other hand, a member who is suspended because of non-payment of dues "loses all rights to church services such as Baptisms, Weddings and Funerals." "Any non-member who desires the services of the Church for Baptism [his own? his child's?] must declare his intentions of becoming a member of this Parish, [and] shall be assessed the sum of Fifty ($50.00) dollars plus the cost of services." "Any non-member who desires the services of the Church for a Wedding must declare his intentions of becoming a member of this Parish, [and] shall be assessed the sum of Fifty ($50.00) dollars plus the cost of services." "Any expelled or non-member desiring the services of the Church for funerals shall be required to donate the sum of Two Hundred and Fifty ($250.00) dollars in addition to the cost of such services performed."[9] Such provisions in effect reduce the sacramental life of the Church to a series of commercial transactions intended to satisfy the private religious needs of individual members and to insure the financial stability and material well-being of the parish corporation. Absent is any sense of the parish as church, with a responsibility in and for the world – or even for Orthodox Christians who happen not to be dues-paying members of the parish in question. Absent also is any real sense of community, since the most significant and truly necessary "rites and ministrations" are, in effect, privatized. We see here the parish reduced to organization, a corporation without a corporate life, a community in name only, a church in appearance only.

Let us turn from the question of parish membership to the question of parish governance and roles within the parish. Here again, many of the peculiarities of older parish bylaws can be traced to circumstances surrounding early parish formation and life. With little knowledge of Orthodox canon law but great awareness of how most American Protestants organized their church life, the immigrants tended to emphasize the independence of the local parish corporation. Older bylaws show a preoccupation with organizational details. Offices multiply far beyond what state laws governing religious corporations require – parish assembly, board of trustees, president, first vice-president, second vice-president, treasurer, secretary, recording secretary – perhaps in order to give the new immigrants a sense of importance and self-worth in the midst of a society which valued them at most as a source of cheap labor. But noteworthy is (a) the absence of any reference to episcopal authority and supervision, and (b) the tendency to view the priest simply as a hired employee of the parish corporation, along with the cantor or choir director, the janitor, and the gravedigger for the parish cemetery.

In the late nineteenth and early twentieth century, this was particularly true in parishes whose founding members came from Old World churches that at the time lay outside what might be called the "Russian sphere of influence" – the Romanians, some Bulgarians, but especially the Greeks. In practice these parishes were independent of any authority beyond the local community. Some might ask the Church of Greece to supply a priest. Others turned to the patriarchates of Constantinople, Alexandria, or Jerusalem. Some simply relied on the recommendations of friends and relatives back home. It is little wonder that a few parishes were misled into hiring impostors, usually vagrant monks who pretended to be ordained priests in order to obtain the fees customarily paid for performing baptisms, marriages, and other vital "rites and ministrations." But whatever arrangements were made, the lay board of trustees continued to view itself as the ultimate authority within the parish, particularly when the parish's finances and property were involved.

In the same period, immigrants coming from homelands within the "Russian sphere of influence" – Syro-Arabs, Serbs, Albanians, as well as those who identified themselves as "Russian" – generally turned to the bishops of the Russian Orthodox Church's North American mission diocese, who assigned priests for their nascent parishes, in some cases paid all or part of their priest's salary and pension, and in many cases also held title to their parish properties. But in the wake of the communist revolution in Russia, dramatic changes affected the archdiocese as a whole and the parishes under its jurisdiction. With financial support from Russia cut off, the central church administration resorted to various stopgap measures, including the mortgaging of parish properties – a move that proved to be as unpopular as it was imprudent from a financial perspective. In addition, representatives of the communist-backed "Living Church" tried to gain control of the assets of the Russian Orthodox Church in America. In responding to this crisis, ordinary parishioners showed little inclination to associate with the "Living Church" or with other rival claimants to hierarchical authority. With very few exceptions, parishes remained loyal to the archdiocese, the "Russian Orthodox Greek Catholic Church of America" or "Metropolia," as it came to be called. But neither did they want to leave their parish properties vulnerable to lawsuits or to ill-advised financial moves on the part of the central church administration. In response to this grim situation, they responded by effectively severing the administrative and financial life of their parishes from the wider concerns of Orthodoxy in America, becoming in practice every bit as independent as their counterparts in other ethnic parishes. Consider, for example, the "protective clauses" that many parishes introduced into their bylaws during this period:

> The Russian Orthodox Greek Catholic Church [name], of [city and state], hereinafter referred to as the "Church" or as the "Corporation," as an ecclesiastical corporation organized and existing under and by virtue of the laws of the state of [state], hereby recognizes and will honor the canons of the Russian Orthodox Greek Catholic Church of North America for spiritual guidance and, accordingly acknowledges its authority in all matters of a purely religious or spiritual nature as distinguished from all matters of administrative, or temporal, or secular nature, which have been, are, and will be governed and administered in accordance with the charter, the by-laws, and the rules and regulations of the Corporation.
>
> No patriarch, archbishop, metropolitan or bishop, or any ecclesiastical authority of the North American diocese or any other diocese shall have any authority, claim or right to manage, or in any way to control or affect, the real or personal property of the Corporation.
>
> No unincorporated or incorporated diocese, sobor, diocesan convention, diocese council, or any ecclesiastical authority of the Russian Orthodox Church, or any other church, shall administer and/or dispose of the real or personal estate of the Corporation for the benefit of any church, corporation, society, or institution....
>
> No bishop of the Orthodox Church or any convention, or any sobor of the Orthodox Church, or any other church, shall have the right to assess the Corporation or its members without the permission of the Corporation membership.[10]

Such clauses may have helped save parish properties, but in the process they set up a false dichotomy between the spiritual and the material, between religious matters and financial matters – a dichotomy alien not only to the Orthodox canonical tradition but also to the most basic principles of Orthodox theology. They also focused attention more than ever on the financial independence and self-sufficiency of the parish. Parishioners might be very generous in supporting their parishes in various ways, but their parishes – as corporate entities – were less inclined to be generous. Even after the hardships of the Great Depression gave way to the relative affluence of the post-World War II era, as parishes accumulated substantial reserve funds and embarked on grandiose building projects, money raised in the parish only very grudgingly went beyond the parish.

The parish as Church

Older parish bylaws give a rather dismal picture of the Orthodox parish in America: an organization self-consciously independent of hierarchical authority in all but "spiritual" matters, dominated by the interests and concerns of this or that natural community, of this or that ethnic group or political faction or clique, an organization that has become – to quote Fr. Alexander Schmemann – "an end in itself... whose whole efforts and energies are aimed at advancing its own good," an organization that "lives by standards and principles which, when applied to an individual, are condemned outright by Christianity as immoral: pride, gain, selfishness, and self-affirmation," an organization that "represents the very victory of secularism within American Orthodoxy."[11] Fortunately much has changed since the bylaws cited thus far were originally formulated. Energetic hierarchs like Archbishop Athenagoras in the Greek Orthodox Archdiocese and Metropolitan Antony Bashir in the Antiochian Archdiocese induced all but the most wayward of parishes in their jurisdictions to accept a higher level of hierarchical supervision and financial accountability than heretofore. Influential theologians like Fr. Schmemann expounded the sacramental basis for church order. A new generation of seminary-trained priests began to see themselves as more than just hired chaplains to the ethnic community. The fruit of their labors, translated into legal form, can be seen in the Uniform Parish Regulations of the Greek Orthodox Archdiocese and the comparable documents of other jurisdictions. The documents in question merit further examination. In what ways have they succeeded in making Orthodox parish polity in America more "canonical"? In what ways have they fallen short?

One of the more conspicuous changes has to do with the relationship between the parish on the one hand and the (arch)diocesan authority and other extra-parochial agencies on the other. According to the Uniform Parish Regulations, which here may be regarded as typical of the documents under consideration, the parish is "organized under the jurisdiction of the Archdiocese" (Art. I sec.1). It is bound by "the decisions of the Clergy-Laity Congresses irrespective of whether it was represented thereat, the administrative determinations of the Archdiocesan Council, and such interim legislation as may be adopted between Archdiocesan Clergy-Laity Congresses by the Archdiocesan Council" (Art. I sec. 2). On pain of suspension, it "shall remit monthly to the Archdiocese the portion of its total commitment allocation for Archdiocesan and Diocesan needs as determined by the Clergy-Laity Congresses" (Art. XVI sec. 3). "In the event of heresy, schism, or defections from the Archdiocese, that segment of the Parish which remains loyal to the Church and the Archdiocese shall retain title to the Parish property" (Art. III sec. 6). And in the event of dissolution, the parish's properties "shall devolve to the Archdiocese" (Art. XVIII sec. 1). In short, the parish's ties to the Archdiocese – the jurisdiction – are strongly emphasized. It cannot, for example, withhold assessments on the grounds that it was not represented at a given council or assembly.

The parish is not an independent entity. This point is emphasized most forcefully when the Uniform Parish Regulations and comparable documents turn to the subject of roles within the parish, and above all to the role of the priest within the parish. According to the Uniform Parish Regulations, "The Priest, by virtue of his canonical ordination and episcopal appointment, heads the local parish of the Church..." (Art. IV sec.1) "...as head of the parish, by virtue of the ecclesiastical authority vested in him," he "shall guide and oversee the total parish program...." (Art. V sec.1). He and other clergy "are assigned or transferred by the Bishop within his Diocese by virtue of the authority of his office and in accordance with the canons, ecclesiastical procedure and the needs of the Diocese. In accordance with the aforementioned canons and ecclesiastical procedure, neither the Parish Council nor the Parish Assembly is authorized to dismiss a Parish Priest" (Art. IV sec. 2).

The Model Constitution for Parishes of the Antiochian Archdiocese and the Sample Parish Bylaws of the Orthodox Church in America (OCA) are equally forceful on this point. The local parish is subject to the ecclesiastical authority of the diocesan bishop; locally it is headed by a priest, not by the president of the parish council or any other local figure or body; and authority to appoint and dismiss this priest lies exclusively with the bishop, not with parish council or parish assembly. But several additional features in these texts and their derivatives should be noted in passing. According to the Antiochian Model Constitution, "The Parish Council shall consist of the Pastor and three (3) members of the Voting Membership to be appointed by him," an additional unspecified number of members elected by and from the Voting Membership, and the heads of various parish organizations *ex officio* (Art. VI sec.1).[12] In other words, the Model Constitution tries to assure that the priest will have at least a few sympathetic members on the parish council. Within the OCA, newer parish bylaws and the uniform bylaws in force in some dioceses generally correspond in substance to the Sample Bylaws, but sometimes they expand upon them, enhancing the priest's authority in various other ways. In the one-page preamble to the bylaws of one parish we read: "The Orthodox Church is a hierarchical Church, having the special ministry of canonically-ordained males: bishop, priests and deacons. The bishops are appointed to guide, rule, and teach the flocks committed to their charge. The bishop is the living image of God upon earth and the fountain of all the sacraments. The priests and deacons are representatives of their bishops...."[13] Some practical implications of these basic principles are spelled out in the body of the text, not only in the three long pages which these bylaws devote to the competence of the parish rector, but also in its treatment of other entities within the parish. For example, "No [Parish] Meeting may be held without the permission of the parish rector, for it is his sacred duty to guide the whole life of the parish for which he is responsible before God. Being the representative of the bishop, the Parish Rector presides at all Parish Meetings" – though "with the permission of the Parish Rector the Senior Warden may preside." In addition, "The Parish Rector, being the representative of the bishop, is the presiding officer at all meetings of the Parish Council" – though again, with his permission, "the Senior Warden may preside."[14] And according to these bylaws as well as many others in the OCA, "The Parish Rector serves as intermediary in dealings of the diocesan authority with the parish and vice versa on all parish matters."[15]

Other less conspicuous provisions of the Uniform Parish Regulations and comparable documents should be mentioned, at least in passing. For example, the linking of membership with ethnicity, so striking in some older parish bylaws, virtually disappears. In the Uniform Parish Regulations we do find that "educating in the Orthodox Faith and in the language of the Church" is one aspect of the parish's "diakonia" (Art. II sec. 2) and that having "a Greek Language School" should be "a concern of each parish" (Art. XVII sec. 3). But such provisions are relatively inconspicuous. Certainly most of the parishes in our Orthodox jurisdictions in America are now more inclusive, or at least less exclusive, than they used to be. Indeed, sometimes we even find expressions of concern for mission and outreach. According to the Uniform Parish Bylaws of the OCA's Diocese of the South, "The Parish must strive to maintain an apostolic zeal and a missionary spirit to draw new souls to the Orthodox Faith.... The Parish, likewise, must be ever ready to accept into its fellowship all persons who desire to follow the Orthodox way...." (Art. II sec. 3).[16] To facilitate this, "The languages of worship in the Parish shall be those that meet the needs of the membership, so that the people may understand..." (Art. II sec. 2) – this meaning Spanish as well as English in the diocese in question.

Nevertheless, broadly speaking, if we compare the documents now under consideration to the older parish bylaws reviewed earlier, major and substantive changes all revolve around one crucial point: The Orthodox Church is hierarchical, not congregationalist in its polity. The parish therefore is not an independent entity. It is obliged to conform to jurisdictional standards; it is subject to the ecclesiastical authority of the diocesan bishop; and its local head is a priest appointed by that bishop. By means of the Uniform Parish Regulations and comparable documents, our churches tried to correct a major ecclesiological deviation, one that had warped and distorted Orthodox parish life in America for much of the twentieth century. But now, as we enter a new century, it may be worthwhile considering whether these documents themselves may be in need of emendation. Do they leave unaddressed any critical ecclesiological issues? Do they become one-sided or unbalanced at any point? In a word, do they fully succeed in their goal of helping our parishes truly to be churches?

One issue that does not seem to have been addressed yet is the relationship of the parish with other Orthodox parishes, particularly with other Orthodox parishes in the same geographic area. The documents under consideration regularly speak of the parish as "a local body of communicants of the Church in a given locality," and they make it sound as though only one parish is operating in a given locality, in splendid isolation from all others. In fact, in many parts of America several Orthodox parishes, even of the same jurisdiction, are located in close proximity to each other. Members of these parishes may be spread over an entire region; on Sunday morning they may drive past several other parishes in order to reach their own. Historically, Orthodox canon law has emphasized the importance of the principle of territoriality, and it has applied this principle not only to diocesan and supra-diocesan structures but also to the parish. Newer parish bylaws, like many older parish bylaws, pay lip service to this principle. But in fact it is ignored in practice, and perhaps for very good reasons. Would it not be appropriate for parish bylaws today at least to attempt to address this issue, and not just by rhetoric about the desirability of cooperation but in concrete ways, e.g., by providing guidelines for the establishment and funding of shared ministries or joint philanthropic, social and cultural projects?

A more critical issue, however, has to do with the role of the laity in church life. Back in the 1960s and '70s, the Uniform Parish Regulations, Model Constitution, Sample Bylaws, and related documents tried to correct a widespread problem in Orthodox parish life in America: rampant laicalism. They did this by emphasizing the dependence of the parish on the diocesan authority and, still more, by reevaluating the role of the priest within the parish. Some devote many pages to describing the way in which the priest's position as head of the parish is to be actualized in practice. "He is responsible before God and the diocesan authority for the whole life and activities of the parish...." Besides fulfilling "his pastoral and liturgical duties," he – among other things – is "to fight religious superstition and ignorance, and to forbid marriages, parish functions – socials and the like – on all Saturday evenings and on the eve of Major and Great Holy Days." He "is responsible for the inside and outside of the church edifice, seeing that it be in strict accordance with the rules and architecture of the Orthodox Church" and that "the iconography of the church be in strict Byzantine style...." He "must organize and supervise a church school..., establish and have under his supervision a parish library..." etc.[17] Unfortunately the documents in question did not devote comparable attention to the role of the laity. In general, the laity are treated simply as the passive element in the Church. For example, this is what the OCA's Sample Bylaws have to say:

> The religious, moral and social duties of the parishioners are: complying in their life and activities with the Orthodox Faith; attending the Divine Liturgy and other services on Sundays and holy days; keeping the rules and fasts of the Orthodox Church; at least once a year making Confession and receiving Holy Communion; bringing up and teaching their children according to the Orthodox faith and in the spirit of the Church; respecting the clergy, the Diocesan Authority and all of the other hierarchs and governing bodies of the Church; obeying in matters of faith and ecclesiastical order; cooperating in every way toward good results in the work of the parish and directing their personal activity towards the welfare and prosperity of the parish. (para. 13)

The substance and wording of the Uniform Parish Regulations of the Greek Archdiocese are virtually identical at this point (Art. VI sec. 6), and both documents then go on to discuss the financial obligations of parishioners. The message seems to be this: A good Orthodox layperson is one who pays, prays, and obeys.

Of course there are occasional passages that emphasize the need for mutual accountability and for active cooperation between clergy and laity. In the Uniform Parish Regulations, for example, we find: "Each Parish shall be administered by the Priest and a Parish Council cooperatively" (Art. V sec. 2). Here is a more extended example from the Uniform Parish Bylaws of the OCA's Diocese of the South:

> Since the priest must answer to God for the lives and the salvation of those who are entrusted to his pastoral care (Hebrews 13:17), nothing in the Parish can be initiated without his approval and blessing, neither must he do anything

pertaining to the life of the Parish without the knowledge of the Parish Council and the parishioners, so that always there may be unity, mutual trust, cooperation and love. (Art.V)

But very seldom are such exhortations translated into specific and concrete measures. Instead, generally speaking, the documents under consideration take for granted and perpetuate that pernicious opposition of clergy and laity which characterized the older parish bylaws analyzed earlier, simply replacing laicalism with clericalism. They insist upon the accountability of parish and laity to hierarchical authority, to the bishop and to the priest as his local representative, but there is no comparable insistence upon hierarchical accountability.

Consider the question of appointment and transfer of parish clergy. The Uniform Parish Regulations of the Greek Archdiocese say tersely, "Prior to the assignment or transfer of a Priest, the Parish Council of the respective Parish shall be informed by the Bishop regarding his decision" (Art. IV sec. 2). The Sample Bylaws of the OCA make the process at least seem less arbitrary: "Members of the clergy are appointed to parish churches by the Diocesan Authority, which takes into consideration the life and needs of the parish in question." (para. 5) The Model Constitution of the Antiochian Archdiocese goes a step further: "All clergy of this parish shall be appointed or removed the Metropolitan Archbishop with the advice of the Parish Council" (Art. V sec.1). How is this advice to be obtained? How are "the life and needs of the parish" to be determined? Surely greater attention should be given to the role of the parish membership – or at least of the parish council – in the selection process.[18]

How are we to transcend the polarization of clergy and laity that has characterized – and in many respects still characterizes – our Orthodox church life in America? There are no easy answers to this question. But we might begin by reflecting more attentively on the experience of the early Church, in which all the baptized faithful constituted God's "portion" (*kleros*) and "people" (*laos*), in which ordination was understood as a setting apart for ministry rather than as induction into a pyramidal power structure, in which due recognition was given to the diversity of gifts – gifts both of treasure and of talent – that are essential to the catholic being of the local church. In our parishes today, we have a wealth of talent. We have well-educated and spiritually sensitive priests, but we also have a multitude of lay men and women with expertise not just in finance (thus equipping them to serve on the parish council) but also in medicine, the arts, education, and even theology. These lay men and women often have a well-developed life of prayer, they participate eagerly in the Church's liturgical life, they regularly receive Holy Communion, and very possibly they keep "the rules and fasts of the Orthodox Church" as rigorously as their priest does. They are not unwilling to fulfill their financial obligations to the parish, and indeed they gladly give much more. They are even willing to obey the priest and diocesan authority "in matters of faith and ecclesiastical order," though in general they do not believe in blind obedience. Are we making adequate use of the diverse talents of such people? Are their manifold gifts being appropriately acknowledged and pressed into service for the enrichment and edification of all? Or are we subtly suggesting to them that their talents are somehow profane, that only the priest is competent when it comes to sacred matters?

Metropolitan John Zizioulas has observed that the emergence of the pres-byter-centered parish "destroyed the image of the Church as a community in which *all* orders are necessary as *constitutive* elements," ultimately making both deacon and even bishop, not to mention the so-called "lower orders" and laity redundant.[19] Certainly many of our recent efforts to establish the parish on a "canonical" basis, as exemplified in documents like the Uniform Parish Regulations, simply confirm the accuracy of his observation. The modern presbyter-centered parish in America may be an improvement on the older parish council-centered parish, but it still does not conform to that "image of the Church" which we find in the most ancient stratum of our canonical tradition. But how is the true "image of the Church" to be restored? According to Zizioulas, the proper solution would be "creation of small episcopal dioceses," which "would enable bishops really to know their flocks and be known by them" and thus "automatically improve the pastoral quality of the episcopate."[20] This solution may be too simplistic. It anachronistically takes an idealized second-century church order as normative in every detail for all ages and situations, ignoring the many ways in which our present situation differs from that of the early Church. At any rate, the "problem 'parish-diocese'" that Zizioulas criticizes has been around since the third or fourth century and shows no signs of disappearing. But, even within the "problem parish-diocese" of modern America, it should be possible to recapture some sense of the rich diversity of gifts and ministries that characterized the local church in antiquity. "Our parishes began as organizations and developed into religious communities." But are they today in fact churches in the full sense of that word? They will be able to fulfill that high calling only if the gifts of all the faithful are dedicated to God's service.

NOTES

[1] In *Special Regulations and Uniform Parish Regulations* (New York: Greek Orthodox Archdiocese of North and South America, 1984).

[2] "Sample Parish By-Laws in Accordance with the Statute of the Orthodox Church in America" (pamphlet, Syosset, NY: Orthodox Church in America, n.d.).

[3] Quoted by George Nicozisin, "The Mission of the Greek Orthodox Parish in America," in *Agape and Diakonia: Essays in Memory of Bishop Gerasimos of Abydos*, ed. Peter A. Chamberas (Holy Cross Orthodox Press: Brookline MA, 1998), p. 246.

[4] Russian Orthodox Society of the City of Vancouver, "Constitution and By-Laws" (Vancouver, 1956) Art. I sec. 2.

[5] St. George's Ukrainian Orthodox Church of Minersville, Pennsylvania, "Constitution and By-Laws" (1974) Art. III sec. A. In fairness it should be noted that the by-laws in the next section go on to explain how "a person of other than Ukrainian origin" may join the church.

[6] Art. 2, cited by Lewis J. Patsavos, "History of the Charters: The Structure of the Archdiocese According to the Charters of 1922, 1927, 1931 and 1977," in *History of the Greek Orthodox Church of America*, ed. Miltiades B. Efthimiou and George A. Christopoulos (Greek Orthodox Archdiocese: New York, 1984), pp. 67-92 at p. 78.

[7] This episode and others from the early history of Orthodoxy in America is recounted in John H. Erickson, *Orthodox Christians in America* (Oxford University Press: New York, 1999), p. 72 et passim.

[8] The Russian Orthodox Greek Catholic Three Saints Church, Ansonia, Connecticut, "By-Laws" (mimeographed, ca. 1968) Sec. VI art. 2 and art. 5.

[9] St. Mary's Russian Orthodox Church (Church of the Holy Assumption), Pittsburgh, Pennsylvania, "Parish By-Laws" (mimeographed, ca. 1967) Art. II cf. Art. XIV.

[10] The Russian Orthodox Greek Catholic Three Saints Church, Ansonia, Connecticut, "By-Laws" (mimeographed, ca. 1968) Sec. I and Sec. IV, art. 12-14. The same provisions can be found in the older bylaws of at least six other parishes. Fortunately all are now superseded.

[11] "What is a Parish?" on The Alexander Schmemann Home Page, www.concentric.net/~Kyinsman/Schmemann.html

[12] In *The Priest's Guide* (Antiochian Orthodox Christian Archdiocese of North America: Englewood, NJ, 1977).

[13] Saints Peter and Paul Orthodox Church, Manville, New Jersey, "The Parish Bylaws" (mimeographed, ca. 1974) Preamble.

[14] *Ibid.* Art. VII sec. 1a, Art. VIII sec. 2a and b.

[15] *Ibid.* Art. V sec. 2b; cf. Sample Parish By-Laws para. 9e.

[16] (mimeographed, 1981).

[17] Saints Peter and Paul, Manville, Art. V sec. 2b and 2c.

[18] An exception to this general tendency should be noted in the *Constitution and*

Laws of The American Carpatho-Russian Orthodox Greek Catholic Diocese of the United States (1970), according to which "The right to appoint and institute Pastors belongs to the Bishop. However, the parishes of the Diocese, as a special privilege, may present their candidates." (para. 64e) The appropriate procedure for exercising this "privilege" is then detailed: "The Parish shall present the names of one, or not more than three candidates to the Bishop.... If the Bishop and his Consistory be satisfied that the candidate or one of the candidates so selected by the Parish is duly qualified for the pastorate, and that he shall accept the office, the Bishop shall grant his jurisdiction." "If none of the candidates is acceptable, a new candidate or set of candidates shall be presented..." (para. 65a-b). It could be objected that these provisions represent a regrettable concession to "older" attitudes, but at the same time these provisions do offer a clear and orderly way for the parish to make its preferences known.

[19] In *Being as Communion* (St. Vladimir's Seminary Press: Crestwood, NY, 1985), p. 250.

[20] *Ibid.* p. 251, n. 6.

Clergy and Laity in Late Byzantine Canon Law: Reflections on the Past and Perspectives for the Future

Patrick Viscuso

This paper will examine the relationship between clergy and laity in late Byzantine canon law. The main sources examined will consist of commentaries, nomocanons, and canonical answers from approximately the twelfth to the fifteenth centuries. On the basis of this examination, theological insights will be derived for application to the parish life of the contemporary Orthodox Church existing in the United States. Since a major portion of contemporary parish life concentrates on the family, this brief study will concentrate on family law and marriage.

The main canonical sources examined will include the major jurists of the twelfth century, Alexios Aristenos (mid-twelfth century), Theodore Balsamon (ca. 1130 and 1140, died after 1195), and John Zonaras (died after 1159), who wrote commentaries on the received corpus of Byzantine church law.[1]

The *Nomocanon of Fourteen Titles* and the *Alphabetical Collection* of Matthew Blastares will be examined as representative of nomocanons. Nomocanons were legal handbooks incorporating ecclesiastical and civil legislation often used in the late Empire's court system, which included clerical membership in its judiciary, and in patriarchal tribunals, whose importance in civil matters increased especially during periods of turmoil. The *Nomocanon of Fourteen Titles* was an evolutionary document produced by a number of hands over several centuries and includes a commentary by Theodore Balsamon. Its traditional authorship is attributed to the patriarch Photios the Great (ca. 810-died after 893). The *Alphabetical Collection* was the work of the hieromonk Matthew Blastares (ca. 1335) and is an encyclopedia organized topically with separate sections devoted to ecclesiastical and civil legislation.[2]

Canonical questions and responses are works often reflecting contemporary needs and concerns. The main canonical answers considered will be those of Theodore Balsamon and Ioasaph of Ephesos (d. 1437). Ioasaph was St. Mark Eugenikos' predecessor to the see of Ephesos in the fifteenth century. His writings capture an image of diocesan or parish life during the last century of the Empire and cover topics ranging from burial to superstitions concerning vampires as well as animated corpses.[3]

While these sources are separated by time and space, in general they are dealing with the same body of ecclesiastical law. This body of legislation consists of canons or laws produced by local and ecumenical councils, as well as certain patristic writings viewed as possessing legal authority. When discussing similar topics such as marriage impediments, these sources often use the same chain of citations or framework of canons. Their comments reflect common theological presuppositions and demonstrate mutual dependence, particularly in the case of later works.

One of the key characteristics of these late Byzantine canonical writings is the structuring of relationships. In their discussion of marriage, impediments of kinship, whether created through affinity, consanguinity, or by spiritual relationship, are often set forth in detail. There is an elaborately structured system of marital degrees with its own technical vocabulary used in describing a complex social structure, within which individuals are assigned specific positions and associations.

The roles of persons in the Church are specified in a ranking that approaches the hierarchical formation of an army. One of the main characteristics of this hierarchical ranking is the assignment of particular law. Parish priests, deacons, subdeacons, chanters and readers are governed by different laws regarding marriage, and perhaps even a different theology and definition of matrimony, than the laity. Among the clergy, the lives of bishops, monks and married clergy are governed by distinct regulations and theological ideals. Women and men are also treated diversely, whether clergy or lay.

In attempting to explain the construction of this hierarchy of bishop, monk married clergy, laity, male and female, one approach might be to seek the rationale for the structure in its purpose. The major concerns expressed in late Byzantine texts are for sanctification within this life, assurances for the life to come, and protection from evil within both. The writings of Ioasaph of Ephesos reveal that among the common concerns of the late Byzantine parish were beliefs in the existence of demons that destroy infants and superstitions concerning diabolically-possessed corpses that terrorize the living through nocturnal risings. There is a strong belief in necromancy and the use of amulets to protect against satanic forces. The inadvertent summoning of Satan through the misuse of incantations is a subject of serious canonical directive and response.[4]

Within this context, frameworks or citations of canonical texts are constructed in the nomocanons, responses and commentaries that concentrate on preserving the character or fundamental nature of the sacerdotal person, the bishop and the priest primarily, as a mediator between God and man. The most used term in describing this role is the word "vessel" or "σκεῦος." In the late canonical texts under consideration, the priest is not understood as the icon of Christ or as taking a role similar to the person of Christ. He is fundamentally seen as a means through which a divine reality is conveyed to the recipient of mysteries. The "σκεῦος" is meant to partake of divine grace, to handle holy things, and to transmit or convey the divine blessing or presence. In turn, the receiver of divine things from the clergyman is also governed by a framework of canons meant to assure the reception.[5]

In both cases, for the sacerdotal vessel and the lay partaker of the sacrament, there is a theological presupposition that purity is necessary in order to convey and receive holiness. There is a converse assumption that clergy and laity can also be debarred from sacramental participation. Spiritual pollution is possible through specific acts or contact with certain objects and persons. This pollution results in a state of impurity and consequent defilement that prevents ritual participation in divine mysteries.

When placed within this context, clergymen, especially bishops and priests, stand at the top of an ecclesiastical hierarchy between God and the laity. Their role is to sanctify and baptize the society surrounding them either through sacramental ministry or canonical decisions. On the other hand, in the texts under consideration, the laity are described as being in the "world." One of the main theological assumptions made is the layman's susceptibility to the passionate life, which is frequently associated with sexuality, women, marriage and children.

Often the same canonical problem is solved variously for clergy and laity based on these different presuppositions concerning their orientations. For example, when discussing expulsion of spouses as a canonical problem, in other words, how it is penanced and remedied, the commentaries assume that the motivation for clergy committing such actions is based on false piety. The canons cited are concerned with theological errors leading to disdain for the drinking of wine, consumption of meat, and conducting of licit marital relations. In contrast, the same documents when dealing with similar expulsions by laymen ascribe to laity motivations based primarily on infidelity and the pursuit of licentiousness.[6]

However, there are also commonalities in approach, especially regarding married clergy and laity. The fact of marriage appears to join both to similar canonical legislation calling for fasting from the passionate life, associated with otherwise lawful marital relations, prior to administration and reception of Holy Communion. For example, Balsamon discusses the subject of fasting from nuptial relations in his fifty-second canonical response:

Question 52: If during the forty-day fast spouses did not live in chastity will they be worthy of the divine hallowed elements of Communion on the world-saving feast of Pascha, or not?

If we have been taught neither to eat fish nor even animal products throughout the whole holy forty-day period, and on every Wednesday and Friday, much more will they be required to refrain from sexual intercourse. At any rate, spouses who transgress in this manner, and who transform into satanic incontinence the salvific penitence springing from fasting and deliverance from fleshly desires (as if the rest of the entire year did not suffice them for the fulfillment of their fleshly desires), will not be deemed worthy of divine and holy Communion on the feastday of the holy and great Pascha, but will be chastened by penances.[7]

Likewise, the canonical sources share a common explanation for the changing of earlier legislation, regarded as Apostolic, that permitted married bishops. The prohibition of such marriage and the mandatory tonsuring of spouses formerly married to candidates for the episcopacy are described by the late canonical texts as meeting a requirement for greater chastity in order that episcopal petitions to God on behalf of the Church might be heard.[8] The texts thus link the requirement of celibacy directly to the bishop's sacerdotal role as mediator with the divine and as "σκεῦος" or vessel for the transmission of holiness.

The role of monk and nun stands between clergy and laity. They are not vessels to transmit holiness to the laity, but are governed by a framework of canons distinct from laypersons. In general, they are prohibited sponsorship at weddings and baptisms, the mysteries or sacraments establishing kinship relationships for the unmarried. They are forbidden to adopt. Monastics are not permitted "ἀδελφοποιία" variously translated "brother adoption" or "same-sex union" depending on one's contemporary point of view.[9] When married persons enter monastic life, which is described by one source as traversing "the road towards better things" and choosing "the better life," late commentaries and collections of laws provide for death benefits to the remaining spouse.[10] In this sense, the monastic in canonical texts is governed by regulations setting forth as his or her role to live a life divorced from the passionate world, dominated by kindred ties and family, and to be dead to the earthly life. Monks and nuns are described as married to the "heavenly Bridegroom" and heirs of blessedness. Consequently, monks are recognized as an appropriate source for candidates to the episcopacy by their separation from the sensual life and their orientation to the world to come.[11]

Among the laity, the distinction between male and female becomes apparent in their assignment of different roles, even forms of humanity. Using the Trinitarian terminology of his time, Theodore Balsamon described husband and wife as possessing a common human nature realized in different modes of existence as male and female hypostases, two different realizations of humanity, with distinct characteristics that at once unite and distinguish them in their hypostatic relations. In describing the union brought about by marriage, Balsamon states, "we believe and confess that the spouses are, on account of marriage, reckoned to be one humanity having more or less the same soul, which is perceived in two hypostases." The hypostases of male and female after the marital union manifest their continued existence by a difference of sexual roles and functions, different modes of existence for the same humanity; and yet are united by these very same functions through their marital relations in which they mutually partake of their common human nature.[12]

There are negative and positive assumptions made in late canonical discussions of problems facing men and women. In general, women appear to be viewed as sources of temptation for men, in the words of one author as a "snare not easily stepped over by unguarded eyes" and possessing an "easily erring nature of female thought."[13] When discussed in terms of appointment as deaconess or in the order of widows, concern is expressed for the susceptibility of women to the passionate life. The texts link the setting of high age requirements for entrance into these positions and ranks as a necessity so that the flame of female passion might be lessened for avoidance of scandal; "since the Fathers distrusted their easy deception and slipping toward evil, they thought it fit to ordain women at this age."[14] In late Byzantine descriptions of the purpose for deaconesses, their office is portrayed as a reward for perseverance in the monastic life with the requirement, in the words of one canonist, that her σχῆμα must be "perfect...that during her life, she must contend for virtue with the most excellent of men."[15]

Women are viewed as a source of birth through the contribution of blood, but also of defilement through corrupt blood when the seed of man is not joined to them. Regulations and commentaries restrict their access to the mysteries and even church buildings on account of pollution associated with their bodily functions. In the case of deaconesses, the late jurists, in dealing with earlier received documents describing their handling of the chalice and placing it upon the altar table, explain their contemporary prohibition from the altar due to their "monthly distress."[16] In the words of the second canon of St. Dionysios (d. 264/265) which forbade reception of Holy Communion: "Indeed, the woman with a flow of blood did not even dare to touch the Lord, short of the border of His outer-garments." Consistent with this view of blood and women, Ioasaph of Ephesos provides for the following in his twenty-seventh response:

> Whether a menstruating woman is able to sponsor a child at holy baptism, be blessed with a husband, or be anointed with holy oil?

> This has been entirely forbidden. If it is not permitted for her to enter the Church to any extent, how will she do any such thing?[17]

In summary, late Byzantine canonical texts describe a hierarchical Church with defined roles for clergy and laity determined by theological concerns for the transmission and reception of sanctification. Theological presuppositions in these texts existed concerning the necessity for purity and definitions of defilements. Abstinence from the passions was viewed as an attribute necessary for mediatorship between God and man as well as reception of the divine blessings. Passions were associated with sexual life, even lawful marital relations. Kinship relations were associated with the earthly life. In this context, the monastic and the celibate bishop occupied the highest ranks within the religious hierarchy. In this ranking, married clergy followed and were viewed as effective mediators or vessels when practicing abstinence. Laity were subdivided into male and female, each viewed as living within the world and striving under specific conditions to receive divine grace and protection from diabolical influences.

Given these theological viewpoints, certain insights can be applied to present parish life, especially regarding family law in the contemporary Church. The Church is an incarnational reality with its truth articulated within historical circumstances. Canons and regulations, opinions and commentaries, with relevance for the late Byzantine period, may no longer have application for the changed conditions of contemporary parish life. Nevertheless, there are theological principles that remain constant.

The divine mediatorship of the clergy is a necessity for a sacramental Christian in need of sanctification. For parish life in the American context, highly influenced by other models of the Church, the notion of the bishop and priest as part of a hierarchy between God and humanity is an idea from a foreign land separated by time and culture. However, for Orthodox of the twenty-first century, this mediatorship and participation in the Church's mysteries is integral to Christianity.

In the American context, the idea that laws and regulations derived from early, middle and late Byzantium might be used to address present-day realities literally appears medieval. Nevertheless, the United States is a country founded on the tradition of living documents from the eighteenth century, inspired by an historical legal inheritance from antiquity. The Orthodox Church's legal tradition is also derived from antiquity, but inspired to use classical civilization in new ways. This tradition remains vital for the specific circumstances of parish life, whether applied with strictness or economy. As shepherds and teachers, the hierarchy continues to make use of the canons as living documents for Church.

As articulated by Theodore Balsamon, the Trinitarian model for the understanding of marriage remains a powerful theological image, especially for a contemporary society in which the institution of marriage is changing and the roles of men and women appear ill-defined. The affirmation of nuptial relations and matrimony as an image of the hypostatic union provides a positive model and standard. The question must be asked whether celibacy is a "better way" and whether family life is inherently passionate and earthly? The late Byzantine canonical sources examined in this paper theoretically viewed monks and nuns as spiritually superior to married clergy and laity.

There are other aspects of late Byzantine canonical thought that are obviously based on the historical culture of the time. Certain regulations concerning purity, pollution and ritual defilement, particularly those addressing involuntary contamination, are derived from late Byzantine culture.

The views on menstruation and women are related to Byzantine science with its mistaken notions concerning anatomy, birth and medicine. Much is also owed to Classical and Hellenistic philosophy regarding beliefs in inherent female feeble-mindedness.[18] Although inapplicable for our culture and civilization, the purity regulations often illustrate respect and reverence for the sacred mysteries encountered in the Church. Nevertheless, the position of women within the Church cannot be based on canonical thought and legislation derived from mistaken ideas regarding the "monthly distress" and its contaminating qualities.

The recruitment of bishops from monastic ranks was based in late Byzantine canonical thought on the spiritual superiority of monasticism and notions concerning the need for greater chastity. If these assumptions are likewise historical in nature and founded on cultural presuppositions, perhaps a fundamental change is necessary to allow married priests the possibility of service to the Church in the episcopacy.

In conclusion, late Byzantine canonical texts, when discussing the relationship between clergy and laity emphasized sacerdotal mediatorship between the divine and human, a spiritual hierarchy between God and the laity, and purity requirements set forth in particular frameworks of canons governing specific ranks and categories of persons. The late Byzantine canonical tradition is a living inheritance for contemporary Orthodox parish life in the American context, but should not be accepted uncritically and without historical examination. In the words of the late Byzantine canonist

Matthew Blastares, the canons remain "guides and leaders of a pious commonwealth that show the way to eternal life, a reward and gift of God, a dogma of noble and God-bearing men, a new covenant of the Church, and a correction of voluntary and involuntary sins."[19]

NOTES

[1] Theodore Balsamon's canonical writings are contained in the first five volumes of the canonical collection, G.A. Rhalles and M. Potles, Σύνταγμα τῶν θείων καὶ ἱερῶν κανόνων, 6 vols. (Athens: G. Chartophylax, 1852-1859), as well as in P.G., 137 and 138. For additional information and bibliography, see Patrick Viscuso, "Marital Relations in the Theology of the Byzantine Canonist Theodore Balsamon," Ostkirchliche Studien 39 (1989): 281-288. For a summary of information on Zonaras, see H.G. Beck, 656-657; and A. Kazhdan, The Oxford History of Byzantium, 3: 2229. Regarding Alexios Aristenos, see H. G. Beck, 657; and A. Kazhdan, The Oxford Dictionary of Byzantium, 1: 169.

[2] For general information on nomocanons, see A. Kazhdan et al., ed., The Oxford Dictionary of Byzantium, 3 vols. (New York: Oxford, 1991), 3: 1490-1491; H.G. Beck, Kirche und Theologische Literatur im Byzantinischen Reich (München: C.H. Beck'sche, 1959), 140-147; J.A.B. Mortreuil, Histoire du Droit Byzantin, 3 vols. (Paris: E. Guilbert, 1843; reprinted, Osnabrück: Otto Zeller, 1966), 1: 199-200; C. de Clercq, "Byzantin (Droit Canonique)," Dictionnaire de Droit Canonique 2 (Paris: Letouzey et Ané, 1937): 1170-1176; H.J. Scheltema, "Byzantine Law," in The Cambridge Medieval History, ed. J.M. Hussey, vol. 4: The Byzantine Empire, part 2: Government, Church, and Civilization (Cambridge: Cambridge at the University Press, 1967), 61-62. The full title of Blastares' nomocanon is Σύνταγμα κατὰ στοιχεῖον τῶν ἐμπεριειλημμένων ἁπασῶν ὑποθέσεων τοῖς ἱεροῖς καὶ θείοις κανόσι πονηθέν τε ἅμα καὶ συτεθὲν τῷ ἐν ἱερομονάχοις ἐλαχίστῳ Ματθαίῳ (An alphabetical collection of all subjects that are contained in the sacred and divine canons, prepared and at the same time organized by Matthew the least amongst hieromonks). This handbook of theology and canon will be referred to as the Alphabetical Collection throughout this study. A text of this nomocanon occupies the sixth volume of Rhalles and Potles. For basic secondary material on Blastares and his canonical work, see my article, "A Late Byzantine Theology of Canon Law," The Greek Orthodox Theological Review 34 (1989): 203-219. A listing of Greek manuscripts for the Alphabetical Collection is found in Robert E. Sinkewicz and Walter M. Hayes, Manuscript Listings of Authored Works of the Palaeologan Period (Toronto: Pontifical Institute of Medieval Studies, 1989), H 07 - K 08.

[3] For insights on Balsamon's canonical responses, see V. Grumel, "Les réponses canoniques à Marc d'Alexandrie, leur caractère officiel, leur double rédaction," Échos d'Orient, 38 (1939): 321-333. A text of the work (Canonical Questions of the Most Holy Patriarch of Alexandria the Lord Mark and the Answers for them by the Most Holy Patriarch of Antioch, the Lord Theodore Balsamon) may be found in Rhalles and Potles, 4: 447-496. Information on Ioasaph is covered in my recent article, "Vam-

pires, not Mothers: The Living Dead in the Canonical Responses of Ioasaph of Ephesos," *St. Vladimir's Theological Quarterly* 44 (2000): 169-179. Since the publication of this article, I have obtained a copy of a critical edition and study of Ioasaph's works, see Alexander Kordakides, Ἰωάσαφ Ἐφέσου (Athens: Nektarios Panagopoulos, 1992).

⁴ See my article, "Vampires, not Mothers: The Living Dead in the Canonical Responses of Ioasaph of Ephesos," *St. Vladimir's Theological Quarterly* 44 (2000): 169-179.

⁵ A discussion of ritual defilement, clergy and laity occurs in my study, "Purity and Sexual Defilement in Late Byzantine Theology," *Orientalia Christiana Periodica* 57 (1991): 399-408. For references and treatment of marriage and clergy, see my article, "Late Byzantine Views on Marriage and Ordination," *Byzantine Studies/ Études Byzantines*, New Series 1-2 (1996-1997): 134-150.

⁶ See my article, "Late Byzantine Canonical Views on the Dissolution of Marriage," *The Greek Orthodox Theological Review* 44 (1999): 273-290.

⁷ Rhalles and Potles, 4: 485-486.

⁸ According to canon five of Holy Apostles, the bishop is prohibited divorce of his wife on account of piety. For the later requirement of a married candidate for the episcopate to divorce, see my study, "The Prohibition of Second Marriage of Women Married to Priests," *Orientalia Christiana Periodica* 66(2000):441-448.

⁹ See my article, "Failed Attempt to Rewrite History," *The New Oxford Review* (December, 1994): 29-31, and Claudia Rapp, "Ritual Brotherhood in Byzantium," *Traditio* 52 (1997): 285-326.

¹⁰ Justinian, *Novel* 22.5; *Epanagoge* 21.1, see I. Zepos and P. Zepos, *Ius Graecoromanum*, 8 vols. (Reprint, Darmstadt: 1962), 2: 300; *Basilika* 28.7.4, H.J. Scheltema, N. van der Wal, and D. Holwerda, eds., *Basilicorum libri LX Series A*, 8 vols. (Groningen: 1955-88), 4: 1362-1363; *Nomocanon of Fourteen Titles* 13.4, Rhalles and Potles, 1: 297.

¹¹ For discussion of the monastic life, see my article, "Purity and Sexual Defilement in Late Byzantine Theology," *Orientalia Christiana Periodica* 57 (1991): 399-408.

¹² For a discussion of the Trinitarian definition of marriage, see my study, "Marital Relations in the Theology of the Byzantine Canonist Theodore Balsamon," *Ostkirchliche Studien* 39 (1990): 281-288.

¹³ See Balsamon's commentary on canon forty-six of the Council in Trullo, Rhalles and Potles, 2: 415; and Matthew Blastares, *Alphabetical Collection* M 11, Rhalles and Potles, 6: 390.

¹⁴ Matthew Blastares, *Alphabetical Collection* Γ 11, Rhalles and Potles, 6: 171; John Zonaras' explanation is almost identical in his commentary on the fifteenth canon of Chalcedon, Rhalles and Potles, 2: 254-255.

¹⁵ Matthew Blastares, *Alphabetical Collection* Γ 11, Rhalles and Potles, 6: 172. Blastares' description of the ordination of deaconesses and its relationship to his thought on menstruation will be discussed in my forthcoming study, "Menstruation: A problem in Late Byzantine Canon Law," in *Byzantine Studies/Etudes Byzantines*.

[16] See for example the thirty-eighth canonical response of Balsamon, Rhalles and Potles, 4: 477:

Question 38 - The divine canons have made mention of deaconesses, therefore, we seek to learn what was their ministry?

Response - Long ago orders of deaconesses were recognized by the canons, and these also had a rank in the altar. But the monthly distress excluded this service from the divine and holy altar. Deaconesses were appointed by the most holy Church and Throne of Constantinople who did not have a participation in the altar, but usually attended church services and maintained order in the women's part of the Church consistent with ecclesiastical principles.

[17] For the Greek text see Alexander Kordakides, Ἰωάσαφ Ἐφέσου (Athens: Nektarios Panagopoulos, 1992), pp. 228-229.

[18] See the excellent study by Lesley Dean-Jones, "Medicine: The 'Proof' of Anatomy," which appears in Elaine Fantham et al, *Women in the Classical World* (New York: Oxford University Press, 1994), pp. 183-205.

[19] Rhalles and Potles, 6: 5.

Between Ecumenical Councils: The Orthodoxy of the Body of the Faithful

Jaroslav Pelikan

At the risk of seeming to be playing games with titles, it could be said that while most of the discussions of the theme "The Orthodox Parish" in this symposium are concentrating, and properly so, on the term "parish," I want to consider the term "orthodox" in that theme – with both an upper-case and a lower-case "O." One reason for this concentration comes out of my current scholarship. As some of you know, I am, for six years now and God willing for the next two or three, working on the preparation, in four massive volumes, of *Creeds and Confessions of Faith in the Christian Tradition* from the New Testament to the twentieth century, with a companion volume entitled *Credo*, which will serve as a historical guide to the set. The second of the five parts of the work, under the general rubric "Affirmations of Faith in Eastern Orthodoxy," will bring together, for the first time in English translation, all the Eastern texts bearing the title "Confession [*Homologia*]" as well as other such materials; indeed, because all the collections of these texts in their original languages seem to be out of print, it will be the only edition of them in any language. To this audience it is not necessary to expatiate on the ambiguity of their status, which I have discussed elsewhere.[1] "The West incessantly asks us for the symbolical books of Orthodoxy," the Bulgarian Orthodox New Testament scholar Nikolaj Nikaronovic Glubokovsky once observed, with some annoyance. "We have no need of them. The faith of the seven first councils is sufficient for us."[2] And the Greek Orthodox theologian Christos Androutsos in his *Dogmatike*, while acknowledging their authoritative standing, prefers to characterize them as the "so-called [*ta kaloumena*] symbolical books" of Orthodoxy,[3] although in his *Symbolike*, he was willing simply to head the chapter: "*Ta symbolika biblia tes Anatolikes ekklesias.*"[4]

But that view of how orthodoxy is affirmed and preserved – which it is easy to caricature and which indeed can easily become a caricature of itself – may just as easily overlook the historic role that was played, between ecumenical councils and since the last ecumenical council, by the entity to

93

which this conference on "the Orthodox parish" is being devoted. For the title "*Orthodox* parish" cannot simply designate a denominational affiliation or an ethnic identity or a jurisdictional structure. What, we are compelled to ask, makes the "Orthodox parish" in that title truly Orthodox? The beginnings of a historical basis for an answer – and the subtitle of my paper – were provided in a seminal essay of 1859 by John Henry Newman, by then a Roman Catholic priest: "The Orthodoxy of the Body of the Faithful During the Supremacy of Arianism." It was based on Newman's truly masterful knowledge of the works of St. Athanasius, in which arguably he had no peer in the nineteenth century, and was originally published in *The Rambler*, then reprinted as an appendix to the later editions of Newman's first book, *The Arians of the Fourth Century* (which had originally come out in 1833, while the author was still an Anglican).

The striking opening sentences of the article – which carries, throughout, some marks of what Stephen W. Sykes, speaking about Newman's *Essay on Development* of 1845, once called "enough confusion, perversity and sheer prejudice, along with profound originality and brilliance, to keep controversialists occupied for decades"[5] – read as follows:

> The episcopate, whose action was so prompt and concordant at Nicaea on the rise of Arianism, did not, as a class or order of men, play a good part in the troubles consequent upon the Council; and the laity did. The Catholic people, in the length and breadth of Christendom, were the obstinate champions of Catholic truth, and the bishops were not.[6]

Newman did go on to concede the presence on both sides of certain "exceptions" to these sweeping generalizations. And in a carefully-framed postscript that he felt obliged to add to the article later, he responded to Roman Catholic critics who had charged him with having underemphasized the doctrine of papal infallibility (which had meanwhile been promulgated, to mixed reactions from Newman, by the First Vatican Council on 18 July 1870):[7]

> In drawing out this comparison between the conduct of the Catholic Bishops and that of their flocks during the Arian troubles, I must not be understood as intending any conclusion inconsistent with the infallibility of the Ecclesia docens, (that is, the Church when teaching) and with the claim of the Pope and the Bishops to constitute the Church in that aspect[8] – though even here, it should be noted, he was still attributing the infallibility to "the Pope *and the Bishops*," whereas *The Dogmatic Constitution on the Catholic Faith of the First Vatican Council* had overtly declared that "such definitions of the Roman pontiff are *of themselves, and not by the consent of the Church, irreformable* [*ex sese, non autem ex consensu ecclesiae irreformabiles*]."[9]

To a degree that church histories based upon a view of the Church "from the top down" have oversimplified or just overlooked, it was "the orthodoxy of the body of the faithful" that preserved the faith between ecumenical councils. In one of the relatively few bits of genuine humor that I came across when I worked through all the writings of all Four Cappadocians – St. Basil the Great of Caesarea, St. Gregory of Nazianzus the Theologian, St. Gregory of Nyssa, and St. Macrina, the principal speaker in the dialogue *On the Soul and the Resurrection* written down by her brother, who called her his "sister and teacher [*adelfe kai didaskalos*]" – in preparing my Gifford Lectures of 1992 and 1993 at the University of Aberdeen, Gregory of Nyssa (speaking, according to the dating by Johannes Quasten, in May 383, two years after the First Council of Constantinople[10]) described how truly involved the faithful on all sides were in the century of the Council of Nicaea and the First Council of Constantinople:

> People swarm everywhere, talking of incomprehensible matters, in hovels, streets and squares, marketplaces and crossroads. When I ask *peri ton hobolon*, they answer with philosophical disquisitions about the Begotten and the Unbegotten. If I inquire *peri timematos artou*, I am told that the Father is greater than the Son. I call the servant to tell me *To loutron epitedeion estin*, and he rejoins that the Son was created out of nothing.[11]

A parallel characterization is the statement of St. Gregory the Theologian:

> Every square in the city has to buzz with their arguments, every party must be made tedious by their boring nonsense. No feast, no funeral is free from them: their wranglings bring gloom and misery to the feasters, and console the mourners with the example of an affliction graver than death. Even women in the drawing-room, that sanctuary of innocence, are assailed, and the flower of modesty is despoiled by this rushing into controversy.[12]

To make my point (or their point), let me briefly identify four historical case studies from Orthodox history where it was "the Orthodoxy of the body of the faithful" that expressed itself between ecumenical councils, or in place of the action of an ecumenical council.

1. The most immediate instance, and the one about which both Gregories as well as Newman were speaking, was the First Council of Constantinople in 381 and *The Niceno-Constantinopolitan Creed* that came out of it. Clarifying both the doctrine about the Father and the doctrine about the Son, *The Creed of Nicaea* had specified that the Son was "God from God, light from light, true God from true God, begotten not made, *homoousios* with the Father."[13] But there was nothing about the Holy Spirit to correspond to these clauses, simply the five words: "and in the Holy Spirit [*kai eis to hagion pneuma*]."[14] The consequence was – to quote not the judgment of some

modern historian of doctrine, but the quite surprising statement of St. Gregory of Nazianzus the Theologian himself, in his *Oration on the Great Athanasius* – that between the Councils of Nicaea and Constantinople, "to be only slightly in error [about the doctrine of the Holy Spirit as God] was to be orthodox."[15] But it is clear that in its orthodoxy, lay spirituality knew all along that when believers experienced the gifts of the Holy Spirit, they were receiving the presence not of some demigod but of none less than the one true God, as the council's creed finally confessed in 381. In endeavoring to explain why it was that the cardinal Christian doctrine of the Trinity, and specifically the doctrine of the Holy Spirit within the Trinity, had not been revealed and set down all at once, Nazianzen in another of his orations contrasted that development with the historical development of the requirements of the divine law from Moses to the New Testament, as both of these developments had been not only studied by the scholars but experienced concretely in the life and prayer of orthodox believers in the Church:

> In the case by which I have illustrated it [the development of the requirements of the divine law from Moses to the New Testament] the change is made by successive subtractions [for example, of circumcision and of the dietary regulations]; whereas here perfection is reached by additions. For the matter stands thus: The Old Testament proclaimed the Father openly, and the Son more obscurely. The New [Testament] manifested the Son, and suggested the Deity of the Spirit. Now the Spirit Himself dwells among us, and supplies us with a clearer demonstration of Himself. For it was not safe, when the Godhead of the Father was not yet acknowledged, plainly to proclaim the Son; nor when that of the Son was not yet received to burden us further (if I may use so bold an expression) with the Holy Ghost; ... but that by gradual additions, and, as David says, 'goings up,'[16] and advances and progress from glory to glory, the light of the Trinity might shine upon the more illuminated. For this reason it was, I think, that he *gradually* came to dwell in the Disciples, measuring Himself out to them according to their capacity to receive Him.[17]

As Georges V. Florovsky has summarized this passage, "The spiritual experience of the Church [and by this, as those of you who knew Father Georges are well aware, he meant the total Church, not only its bishops or theologians] is also a form of revelation."[18]

Or to put it another way: as the historical events of the life and teachings of Jesus that were recorded in the four Gospels had provided the Church with empirical information concerning the earthly career of the Second Hypostasis of the Trinity, on the basis of which *The Creed of Nicaea* could formulate its confession about Him and about the relation of the Son to the Father as *homoousios*; so it was the events experienced by the history of the Church from the first to the fourth century – missionary growth, persecution and martyrdom, apostasy and sainthood, fidelity and heresy, discipline and worship, and the consolation of the Holy Spirit in life and in death – that vindicated "the orthodoxy of the faithful" by providing a kind of "database" concerning the earthly career of the Third Hypostasis, on the basis of which *The Niceno-Constantinopolitan Creed* could frame its confession about the Holy Spirit and about the Spirit's functioning in the Church.

2. But there was an even more fascinating example – and, judging on the basis of the state of the surviving primary sources, one that is probably more verifiable – in the following century. It was not until the third ecumenical council, the Council of Ephesus in 431, that the Church by decree made the teaching official "that the holy Virgin is the Mother of God [Theotokos];" and Nestorius, bishop of Constantinople, "New Rome," was condemned as a heretic and deposed from his throne for denying that title to the Virgin Mary and for refusing to call her more than "Mother of Christ [Christotokos]."[19] So it was brought about that this Marian title became part of the rule of faith, remaining so even for some Protestant confessions.[20] All of that was going on at the official level of authoritative conciliar and creedal dogma, to which, as to every dogma, the beliefs and prayers of ordinary believers forever after were obliged to conform, under threat of dire punishments, both temporal and eternal. But the doctrine of the Virgin Mary as Theotokos cannot be treated as simply yet another example of a dogma imposed from above on popular religion.

On the contrary: from an extremely unsympathetic source, which may for that reason be regarded as an objective source, namely, Emperor Julian "the Apostate," who had once been a church member but had rejected Christianity, we know that almost a century before the Council of Ephesus and without the pressure from above of any authoritative conciliar and creedal dogma or any imperial edict, Christians – not, it would seem from the context of Julian's remarks, priests and prelates, or at least not only they, but lay Christians – "would not desist in calling Mary the Mother of God [*Theotokon de hymeis ou pauesthe Marian kalountes*]," in their private prayers and perhaps in their public hymns, though they and the Orthodox Church were not yet doing so in their official dogmas.[21] This is, moreover, perhaps the earliest uncontested instance of the word "Theotokos," its appearance in other places, including the writings of Athanasius, being textually dubious.[22] Apparently, then, the title moved upward rather than downward, from the practice and prayer of the faithful in the fourth century, or even earlier than the fourth century, to the agenda of an ecumenical council in the fifth century, following the principle that "the rule of prayer should lay down the rule of faith" and toppling even the bishop of New Rome while it was on its way up.

Some modern scholars have even attempted, on considerably shakier grounds, to use this title to document a still longer continuity in the popular religion of the city of Ephesus, starting with devotion to Artemis the Mother Goddess and ending with devotion to Mary the Mother of God.[23] For during the missionary journeys of the apostle Paul, Ephesus had been the site of a popular uprising against him, stirred up by the goldsmiths and artisans of idols, who felt their livelihood threatened if idolatry was abolished and who therefore raised the cry, "Great is Artemis of the Ephesians!" (Acts 19.23-41). Less than four centuries later, the double Church of Saint Mary in Ephesus (whose ruined walls can still be seen) was the site for the vindication of the cult of the Blessed Virgin Mary as Theotokos.

3. For Eastern Orthodoxy, the reinstatement of icons by the Second Council of Nicaea in 787 ratified the devotion of the laity as an argument in favor of images, and it interpreted images as "confirmation that the becoming man of the Word of God was real and not just imaginary." On that basis the council decreed that "like the figure of the honored and life-giving cross" (of which the iconoclasts, too, had continued to approve), images were to appear not only in churches and on priestly vestments, but "in houses and by public ways." For, as it declared concerning the images of Christ, Mary, and the other saints, "the more frequently they are seen in representational art, the more are those who see them drawn to remember and long for those who serve as models, and to pay these images the tribute of salutation and respectful veneration."[24] Quoting these canons of the Second Council of Nicaea as having "established and confirmed to all ages the worship of holy and venerable images," *The Orthodox Confession of the Catholic and Apostolic Eastern Church* by Peter Mogila made it a point to emphasize that there was a vast qualitative difference between such a worship of icons by the Christian faithful and the pagan worship of idols.[25] Similarly, *The Christian Catechism of the Orthodox Catholic Greco-Russian Church* of 1839 explained that it was not contrary to the Ten Commandments "to honor icons as sacred representations, and to use them for the religious remembrance of God's works and of his saints; for when thus used, icons are books, written with the form of persons and things instead of letters," and therefore a fundamental component in Christian education at all levels.[26]

Interpreters of *lex orandi lex credendi*, the principle I quoted earlier from Prosper of Aquitaine, that "the rule of prayer should lay down the rule of faith,"[27] have been careful to emphasize that it was not to be applied indiscriminately, so as to elevate every vagary of poetic language or lay piety or popular superstition (any more than every vagary of theological speculation and erudition) to the status of doctrine and the rule of faith.[28] Therefore, even as the iconodule Second Council of Nicaea in 787 was decreeing that it was legitimate "to pay these images the tribute of salutation and respectful veneration [*aspasmon kai timetiken proskynesin*]," it simultaneously felt it necessary, presumably because of abuses both potential and real, to insist that "certainly this is not the full adoration in accordance with our faith [*ten kata pistin hemon alethinen latreian*], which is properly paid only to the divine nature" and therefore not properly paid to icons or to saints, not even to the Virgin Mary as Theotokos.[29] Therefore East and West were agreed that, in the distinction later formulated by Thomas Aquinas, not such "adoration [*latria*]," but only "veneration [*dulia*]" (or in the case of the Virgin, *hyperdulia*) was appropriately addressed to the saints.[30] That Eastern Orthodox and Roman Catholic caution about the possibility that the popular religion of "the faithful" might ignore and blur the edge of such orthodox distinctions between the "full adoration" that pertained only to the Holy Trinity and the "salutary and respectful veneration" that pertained to the saints – or that at times it had already been guilty of doing so – would be sharply intensified in the polemics of the confessions of the Protestant Reformation.[31]

4. The most dramatic case study, though it may be harder to prove that it was as directly attributable to popular reaction, did involve "the orthodoxy of the body of the faithful:" the rejection of *The Confession of Faith* that had been issued in 1629 by the enigmatic Cyril Lucar (Loukaris). He was elected patriarch of Constantinople in November 1620; and, as one historian has pointed out, "though he was four times deposed from and restored to the throne, he was Head of the Greek Church for fifteen out of the next eighteen years."[32] His *Confession* was published not only in his own name (which, in the light of the office he held, would already have been a prestigious credential), but "in the name and with the consent of the patriarchs of Alexandria and Jerusalem." Thus its espousal of Protestant doctrines of the sole authority of Scripture rather than the authority of Scripture *and* Tradition[33] and of only two Sacraments[34] appeared to carry the presumed canonical authority of three of the five ancient patriarchates that constituted the principle of "pentarchy" – Constantinople, Alexandria, and Jerusalem, though not Antioch, and of course not Rome – as well as the intellectual force and the prestige of one who has been rightly called "the first important theologian of the Eastern Church since the fall of Constantinople in 1453…, the most brilliant and politically outstanding Greek Patriarch and national leader ('ethnarch') of the seventeenth century."[35]

Amid all the politics and church politics at work, the complex phenomenon of Uniatism among the Slavs, in a curious way, corroborates the thesis of "the orthodoxy of the faithful" during the controversy over Cyril Loukaris. For there is much to be said in favor of the historical suggestion that the willingness of Orthodox believers during the seventeenth century in Ukraine, Ruthenia and Eastern Slovakia to give their allegiance to the Union of Brest of 1595/1596 and the Union of Užhorod of 1646, reuniting them with Rome but seeking to preserve Eastern spirituality and liturgy, can be traced to their more or less clear perception that the Orthodox faith had been compromised by its most prominent official spokesmen – so that, paradoxically, the only way to remain Byzantine seemed to be for them to break with Byzantium![36] But the confession was condemned, and so was the patriarch who had been identified as its author, coming to a tragic end; and it seems fair to view several of the seventeenth-century Eastern Orthodox "confessions [*homologiai*]" as (borrowing a phrase from the physics of Isaac Newton) "an equal and opposite reaction" to this quixotic effort at an *Orthodox Confession*, as well as to the Protestant confessions themselves.

One direct implication of this emphasis on "the orthodoxy of the body of the faithful" is to reject out of hand any understanding of our theme of "the Orthodox parish" that would reduce the popular religion of Christians to mere morality, relegating questions of doctrine to the clerical and theological professionals, as though the common people cared only about how they behaved but not about what they believed and how they worshiped. For because "doctrine" has been the particular form that "faith" or "beliefs" have taken when they were articulated or defined, the difference between the clergy and the laity could be taken to be, not that the laity were occupied only with the moral consequences of beliefs and did not concern themselves with the content of the beliefs, but rather that the content of their beliefs was often the content as it was prayed and celebrated – a difference not in content but in idiom. As the Eastern Orthodox patriarchs insisted in their response to Pope Pius IX in 1848, "The guardian of religion is the very body of the Church, even the people themselves [*ho hyperaspistes tes threskeias estin auto to soma tes ekklesias, etoi autos ho laos*]."[37] And if there is any firm conclusion to be drawn from the social history of popular religion, it is that the ordinary people of the church do care, not only about conduct but about matters of their "faith" or "beliefs," even though the modality of such caring in prayer and liturgy may sometimes be dismissed as superstition by the condescension of the skeptic, the snobbery of the elitist, the cynicism of the Grand Inquisitor. For the Church has never been – or, at least, has never been *only* – a school, and the teaching of the Church has never been only the business of scholars or theologians, or even only of the clergy and the bishops in council assembled. Because Christian doctrine is and must be the concern of the Church, of the entire Church, creeds and confessions of faith do claim to be speaking for their entire church, indeed, for all Christians.

Analogously, not all of the delegates from the thirteen colonies who attended the fateful deliberations that produced the American Declaration of Independence at Philadelphia on 4 July 1776 – much less all of the citizens of the colonies, who had sent them there – could have written what Thomas Jefferson wrote; and it would be a fatuous kind of populism to suppose otherwise on the basis of Ralph Waldo Emerson's poetic language about the Battle of Concord (which was fought about fifteen miles from here), when

> By the rude bridge that arched the flood,
> Their flag to April's breeze unfurled,
> Here once the embattled farmers stood,
> And fired the shot heard round the world.

But Jefferson insisted very strongly that when he wrote, he was consciously speaking not in his own name but in the name of all, including those "embattled farmers." What these delegates said in the conclusion of their Declaration of Independence about their political situation, therefore, the lay Christians who have been faithful to the creeds and confessions of faith of the Church in different ages could have said (and, using somewhat different words, often did say) about their doctrinal declarations: "And, for the support of this declaration, with a firm reliance on the protection of Divine Providence, we mutually pledge to each other our lives, our fortunes, and our sacred honor."

For every time an early creed opened by declaring its faith in "one God," as one after another of them did and as creeds and confessions would go on doing throughout Christian history, echoing *The Shema* of the Book of Deuteronomy, (Dt 6:4-9, 11:13-21, Num 15:37-41) it was also defining the monotheism that distinguished Christian belief (as well as Jewish belief) from the idolatry of Greek and Roman polytheism, of which the worship of Caesar was seen as a particularly virulent expression. One of the underlying issues at stake, whether theological or political, was what Erik Peterson called "monotheism as a political problem."[38] When, in the first postbiblical account of a Christian martyr who "pledged his life, his fortune, and his sacred honor," *The Martyrdom of Polycarp*, the Roman proconsul Statius Quadratus, the political and spiritual descendant of Pontius Pilate and the representative of Emperor Antoninus Pius, ordered the aged Polycarp, "Swear by the fortune of Caesar!" Polycarp instead confessed "with boldness, 'I am a Christian. And if you wish to learn what the doctrines of

Christianity are, appoint me a day, and thou shalt hear them;'" and so St. Polycarp went to his death, vindicating "the orthodoxy of the faithful."[39]

NOTES

[1] Jaroslav Pelikan, "The Eastern Orthodox Quest for Confessional Identity: Where Does Orthodoxy Confess What It Believes and Teaches?" James W. Cunningham Memorial Lecture, *Modern Greek Studies Yearbook* 14/15 (1998/1999), pp. 21-30.
[2] Nikolaj Nikaronovič Glubokovský, quoted in S. Herbert Scott, *The Eastern Churches and the Papacy* (London, 1928), p. 351.
[3] Christos Androutsos, *Dogmatike tes Orthodoxou Anatolikes Ekklesias* (2d. ed.; Athens, 1956), p. 20.
[4] Christos Androutsos, *Symbolike ex epopseos Orthodoxou* (2nd ed.; Athens, 1930), pp. 37-45.
[5] Ian Ker and Alan G. Hill, eds., *Newman after a Hundred Years* (Oxford, 1990), pp. 355-56.
[6] John Henry Newman, "The Orthodoxy of the Body of the Faithful During the Supremacy of Arianism," *The Arians of the Fourth Century* (4th ed.; London, 1901), p. 445.
[7] *The Dogmatic Constitution on the Catholic Faith of the First Vatican Council*, in Norman P. Tanner, ed., *Decrees of the Ecumenical Councils* (2 vols.; Washington, 1990; hereafter abbreviated as "Tanner"), vol. 2, pp. 815-16.
[8] Newman, op.cit., p. 464.
[9] Tanner vol 2, p. 816.
[10] Johannes Quasten, *Patrology* (4 vols.; Westminster, Md., 1951-86), vol 3, p. 280.
[11] Gregory of Nyssa *Oratio de deitate Filli et Spiritus Sancti* (*Patrologia Graeca* 4:557). Adapted from the translation in Bertha Diener, *Imperial Byzantium*, translated by Eden and Cedar Paul (Boston, 1938), p. 167
[12] Gregory of Nazianzus *Orations* XVII.2 (*Patrologia Graeca* 36:13A).
[13] *Faith of the 318 Fathers* (Tanner vol. 1, p. 5).
[14] *Faith of the 318 Fathers* (Tanner vol. 1, p. 5).
[15] Gregory of Nazianzus *Orations* XXI.33 (*NPNF*-II vol. 7, p. 279).
[16] Quoting Ps 83:6 (LXX).
[17] Gregory of Nazianzus *Orations* XXXIV.26 (NPNF-II 7:326).
[18] Georges V. Florovsky, *Collected Works* (14 vols.; Belmont, MA, 1972-89), vol. 7, p. 156.
[19] *The Definition of the Council of Ephesus* (Tanner vol 1, p. 59).
[20] *Formula of Concord. Epitome* 8.12, *Bekenntnisschriften der evangelisch-lutherischen Kirche* (11th ed.; Göttingen, [1930] 1992), p. 806.
[21] Julian, *Against the Galileans* 262D (*Loeb Classical Library* vol. 3, p. 399).
[22] W. H. Lampe, ed., *Patristic Greek Lexicon* (Oxford, 1961), pp. 639-41.
[23] Theodora Jenny-Kappers, *Muttergöttin und Gottesmutter in Ephesus: Von Artemis zu Maria* (Zurich, 1986).

[24] *The Decrees of the Second Council of Nicaea* (Tanner vol. 1, pp. 135-36).

[25] *The Orthodox Confession of the Catholic and Apostolic Eastern Church* by Peter Mogila 3.55-56, in Ioannis Karmiris, ed., *Ta dogmatika kai symbolika mnemeia tes Orthodoxou Katholikes Ekklesias* (2 vols.; 2d vol. revised. Athens and Graz, 1952-68), [761]-[762].

[26] *The Christian Catechism of the Orthodox Catholic Greco-Russian Church*, p. 521, in Philip Schaff, ed., *Bibliotheca Symbolica Ecclesiae Universalis: The Creeds of Christendom* Reprint edition (3 vols.; Grand Rapids, 1990), vol. 2, p. 527.

[27] Jaroslav Pelikan, *The Christian Tradition* (5 vols.; Chicago, 1971-89), vol. 1, p. 339; vol. 2, pp. 34-35; vol. 3, pp.66-80.

[28] See, for example, Johann Adam Möhler, *Symbolik, oder Darstellung der dogmatischen Gegensätze der Katholiken und Protestanten nach ihren öffentlichen Bekenntnisschriften*, edited by Josef Rupert Geiselmann (2 vols.; Darmstadt, 1958), vol. 1, pp. 22-23.

[29] *The Decrees of the Second Council of Nicaea* (Tanner vol. 1, p. 136).

[30] Thomas Aquinas, *Summa Theologica* 3a, p. 25.

[31] For example, *The Second Helvetic Confession* 5:3; 23:1; *The Westminster Confession of Faith* 25:2.

[32] Colin Davey, *Pioneer for Unity: Metrophanes Kritopoulos (1589-1639) and Relations Between the Orthodox, Roman Catholic and Reformed Churches* (London, 1987), 98.

[33] *The Orthodox Confession of Cyril Lucar* 2 (Karmiris 2:[645]).

[34] *The Orthodox Confession of Cyril Lucar* 2 (Karmiris 2:[647].)

[35] *The Oxford Dictionary of the Christian Church*, edited by F. L. Cross and E. A. Livingstone (3rd ed.; Oxford, 1997), p. 1001.

[36] Oskar Halecki, *From Florence to Brest (1439-1596)* (Rome, 1958), pp. 199-419; Michael Lacko, *The Union of Užhorod* (Rome and Cleveland, 1966).

[37] Karmiris [1000].

[38] Erik Peterson, "Der Monotheismus als politisches Problem," *Theologische Traktate* (Munich, 1951), pp. 45-147.

[39] *The Martyrdom of Polycarp*, p. 10 (*ANF* 1:41).

Parish Management: Managership and Leadership
A Perspective from the Laity

Thomas C. Lelon

Understanding the Orthodox Christian parish in twenty-first century America in terms of current management theory and practice is an unusual exercise, to say the least, and for some may even appear a bit unseemly. After all, the parish is a religious endeavor, not a corporate business venture. Nevertheless, at times, it is helpful to perceive the parish as a managerial organization with all its attributes. Such a perception provides an insightful frame of reference for understanding the parish's operating dynamics. This knowledge enables clergy and laity to develop and execute practical plans of action designed to fulfill the parish mission.

Parish mission

In my view, our parishes have a twofold mission: extrinsic and intrinsic. It is fair to say that our parishes are fulfilling the extrinsic aspect of their mission. By and large, the parishes are satisfying the parishioner's fundamental needs of worship, religious education and social interaction. However, our parishes are falling short in pursuing and fulfilling their intrinsic mission.

Our parishes need to create a deeper sense of a community of faith and heritage, one that is the dynamic manifestation of Orthodox Christian theology and mysticism. Furthermore, our parishes need to focus on cultivating a more spiritual environment with three objectives in mind:

1) to deepen the parishioner's understanding of his or her relationship to God and to others;
2) to strengthen the parishioner's ability to deal with the challenges of existence; and
3) to enable the parishioner to live a life in Christ that ultimately leads to union with God.[1]

Admittedly, it is an extremely difficult task for the Orthodox Christian parish in America to achieve its intrinsic mission. Parish management, as here presented, is a starting point in taking on this crucial challenge.

Some definitions

The Orthodox Christian *parish* is a community of laity under the spiritual care of one or more priests guided by the diocesan bishop or metropolitan. In the administrative affairs of the parish, clergy and laity are engaged in a partnership that is characterized by a synergistic relationship. Synergism is working together, clergy and laity, in concert with the Holy Spirit to create outcomes that are greater than those generated by a priest or by a parishioner, acting individually on his or her own accord.

This partnership is founded on mutual trust, open communication, and reciprocated teaching, learning and helping.[2] But even more, this managerial collaboration is built, as St. Paul wrote in his First Epistle to the Corinthians (12:31-13:13), on *a more excellent way*, the way of love. It is this love, and all that *love builds up* (1 Cor 8:1), that fortifies and enhances parish management. It is this love, this grace of Christ that unites us in mind, heart and spirit, heals our disagreements and conflicts and enables us to endure and overcome whatever the challenge.[3]

Parish management is the process of planning, organizing, managing, leading and controlling the resources of the parish so as to achieve the parish mission. Parish resources include the Holy Scripture, Sacred Tradition,[4] the faithful (clergy and laity), prayer, the sacramental life, worship, the facilities, the parish programs and the funds. Overall, the parish effort is directed toward the parishioner, be that person a child, a teen, an adult, a senior, a native, or an international.

Furthermore, parish management is participatory. Input is sought from all parties with the aim of reaching a consensus on a given issue and/or course of action. Under this managerial arrangement, the parish is viewed as a democratic enterprise, not in the sense that the parish is ruled by parishioners, but in the sense that the laity and the clergy share in the decision-making process of the parish. The claim that "*the Church is not a democracy*" is haughty and misleading. Such declarations do a disservice to American Orthodox Christians. The fact is that over the centuries, imploring the Holy Trinity, hierarchs, presbyters and the laity have participated in a process of shared decision-making.

Parish culture

Parish management operates in a context or environment, namely: the parish culture. Parish managerial decisions are effective and efficient to the degree that they fit within the parish culture.

Parish culture may be viewed as an organic collection of *shared meaning, ideas and thought*. It guides the priest's and the parishioners' perception and understanding of the parish, and shapes their behavior within the parish setting.[5] Parish culture is an intricate sociological, psychological and spiritual phenomenon with intellectual, artifactual, ethnic, ecclesial and societal dimensions.

Dimensions of parish culture

Intellectual parish culture evolves from the pattern of shared assumptions and values that govern the way the priest and the parishioners think about and act on the issues facing the parish. On the one hand, assumptions are the shared view of what the parish looks like and how it operates, the mental models or "theories-in-use" that the faithful hold and rely on to guide their perceptions, decisions and behaviors.[6] On the other hand, values are enduring beliefs that are shared and that help determine what is right and what is important, and what is wrong and unimportant. These shared assumptions and values constitute the core of parish culture.

Artifacts. Beyond this intellectual core are the external artifacts that also shape parish culture. Artifacts are the observable symbols and signs operative in the parish. Parish artifacts include the physical structure, the stories and legends, the rituals, the ceremonies and the language.

Physical structure. The physical structure of the parish consists of the church, the church hall, the school, the gymnasium and the grounds.

Stories and legends. Parishioners pass on stories and legends to one another about the parish's heroes, personalities and defining moments. Providing a historical perspective and a sense of continuity with the past, these tales perpetuate the parish culture.

Rituals and ceremonies. Rituals and ceremonies provide parishioners with a common experience, which reinforces values espoused by the parish culture. Here are two examples: the ritual of the social hour in the church hall following the Sunday celebration of the Divine Liturgy and a ceremonial presentation of Holy Bibles to college-bound high school seniors in June.

Language. The language artifact includes the extent to which English and other languages are used, the phrases and metaphors that are expressed and the nature of the conversational interaction. For example, "Do I address you as 'Reverend Doctor Pappas' or as 'Father John,' or simply as 'John'?"[7]

As parishioners interface with these artifacts on ongoing bases, they reaffirm their sense of parish belonging and authenticate their conceptualization of the parish – its nature, scope and meaning.

Ethnicity. In addition, ethnic identity influences parish culture. Be they immigrant or native, ethnic constituents share a common heritage with their own set of assumptions and values. These ethnic-oriented parishioners are somewhat assimilated, and yet remain somewhat apart from the parish culture. Some of these folks are more assimilated than others. Some even actively promote a subculture. At times, particularly if they are in the majority or are a highly vocal minority, these ethnic-minded parishioners superimpose their values and their way of doing things on the parish culture.

Ecclesial and societal factors. Perhaps as important, parish culture is impacted by ecclesial and societal factors. Voiced through the archbishop, metropolitans, bishops, chancellors and professional staffs, diocesan, archdiocesan and patriarchal policies and procedures (the Holy Canons, the Charter, the Uniform Parish Regulations and the Typikon) impact the local parish culture. And of course, American assumptions and American values permeate the entirety of our parish life. Clearly, parish management functions in a multifaceted parish culture.

Parish orientation

A close examination of this culture reveals that our parishes hold a conservative orientation. This is not surprising. After all, conservatism is our natural disposition. As Orthodox Christians, we believe that we hold the fullness of the true faith of the Apostles. Furthermore, we are deeply conscious of the fact that our Holy Tradition has been preserved from generation to generation through monumental devotion and sacrifice, "fundamentally without change and interpolation."[8] As Orthodox Christians we have been in the business of preservation for a very long time. Indeed, we have been faithful to the past. Yet, this conservatism is reflected in our approach toward parish management.

Some of the research findings on national culture may partially explain our conservatism. Geert Hofstede, a noted Dutch management scholar, studied several thousand IBM employees working in fifty different countries. He found that Greeks ranked 28th in power distance and first in uncertainty avoidance. In contrast, the USA ranked 38th in power distance and 43rd in uncertainty avoidance. Hofstede's cultural dimensions of power distance and uncertainty avoidance dominate the managerial environment of the typical Greek Orthodox Christian parish[9].

Power distance is the degree to which the faithful accept an uneven distribution of power. Bishop, priest and parishioner alike accept the hierarchy of status and power. In interactive activity, clergy and laity are more apt to play out their designated positions, and show respect and deference to those in authority.

Uncertainty avoidance is the degree to which the faithful seek to evade ambiguous or risky situations. Bishop, priest and parishioner alike prefer to live and act in situations of certainty while emphasizing continuity and stability. Basically we are risk-averse. Clergy and laity are reluctant to try new ways of doing things. Essentially, the tone is "Don't rock the boat!"

Thus, in our parishes, management functions in a culture characterized, in part, by significant power distance and strong uncertainty avoidance. And these manifestations do not always serve the best interest of the faithful or the parish. The parish needs to face up to this reality. At times it may be less costly and more beneficial to be a parish community of risk-takers with minimal concern for authority and maximum emphasis on equity in participation. Under such environmental dynamics, parish management would do better adhering to strategies and tactics that are both flexible and practical.

Managerial continuum

Under such a set of cultural factors, the parish is best served by viewing parish management as a managerial continuum. The continuum is perceived as a managerial line of behavior where at one end is managership and at the other end is leadership. Both are vital. Each problem-situation is unique, each having its own set of particular influencing factors. Some situations call for managership while others require leadership, and still others demand a certain combination of both. In short, the situational requirements determine which approach is best. Hence, the priest and/or layperson need to move back and forth on the management continuum, acting as a manager or acting as a leader or acting as some combination of both, depending on the demands of the given situation.

Managership is concerned with parish maintenance. It is essentially conservative. Managership focuses on ensuring that the spiritual and administrative systems and processes of the parish work well. As manager, the priest or layperson influences others through the use of the formal authority allocated to the given position held in the parish. In making things happen or getting things done, managership relies on the power of the position to reward (acceptance) and to punish (rejection). Under managership, the priest-manager or lay-manager is viewed as an authoritarian decision-maker and implementer. Under this approach, task-directedness, reactivity, continuity, stability, conservation and status quo are dominant themes.

Leadership is concerned with parish change and growth. It is risk-taking. Leadership focuses on moving the parish from where it is to where it ought to be. As leader, the priest or layperson influences others through witness, martyrdom, persuasion, inspiration and personal power, that is, the force of his or her vision, personality and situational expertise. Under leadership, the priest-leader or lay-leader is viewed as a democratic/participatory decision-maker and implementer. Under this approach, people-directedness, proactivity, innovation, continuous improvement, reformation, vision and change are the foci.

The use of leadership in parish management is especially conducive to the current population of our parishes. Our parishes are replete with educated and/or accomplished men and women, native and immigrant. In their chosen professions and civic life, these parishioners are involved in an array of collaborative endeavors. They are activists and are accustomed to voicing their views and offering their good will, talents and expertise. Their norm for collaboration is participation in the decision-making process. The managership approach that tends to dominate our parish culture is a turn-off to these good souls. Consequently, using the strategies of leadership, we need to persuade these dedicated and extraordinary parishioners to fully participate and join in the efforts to create a vision and a plan of action for achieving the parish's intrinsic mission.

An admonition

Parish life must be made relevant to the parishioner, regardless of his or her particular predisposition. If parish relevancy is enhanced through change, we need to embrace change. We need to change our current conservative mind-set. We need to be more innovative. We need to be risk-takers. In short, we need to be true leaders. If we are to intensify our relationship with the Lord and with all those whom we interact with, if we are to endure and overcome our existential adversities, and if we are to live a life in Christ leading to union with our Triune God, the parish must be the place in our lives where we experience the Divine, where we are spiritually fortified and encouraged to stay the course towards Christ.

Too often, we stigmatize the proactive approach as destructive to the life of the Church. We unthinkingly declare that attempts at innovation, continuous improvement and change are a betrayal to our sacred beliefs and practices rather than the manifestations of the Holy Spirit. Proactivity in parish management is acting in the Holy Spirit and ensures the survival and perpetuation of our Holy Faith. We need to be more discerning in our application of managership and more assertive in our use of leadership.

Finally, it is imperative that parish management strives to ensure that all its efforts are worthy of the meaning of *parish*, that is, *ecclesia*. *Ecclesia*, as conceptualized by St. Paul in his First Epistle to the Corinthians (12:27): *Now you together are the body of Christ.*

NOTES

[1] Vladimir Lossky, *The Mystical Theology of the Eastern Church* (London: James Clarke & Co. LTD, 1957).

[2] R.M.Kanter, "Collaborative Advantage: The Art of Alliance," *Harvard Business Review*, July-August, 1994, pp. 96-108.

[3] John Short, "Exposition 12:31, The First Epistle to the Corinthians," *The Interpreter's Bible, Volume X* (New York: Abingdon Press, 1953), p. 165.

[4] Maximos Aghioroussis, "The Dogmatic Tradition of the Orthodox Church" in *A Companion to the Greek Orthodox Church* (New York: Greek Orthodox Archdiocese of America, 1984), pp. 148-168.

[5] Adapted from Philip M. Rosenweig, "National Culture and Management." A note for class discussion dated March 24,1994 and numbered 9-394-177, Harvard Business School, (Cambridge, Massachusetts).

[6] P. N. Johnson-Laird, *Mental Models* (Cambridge, England: Cambridge University Press, 1984). J. L. Aronson, "Mental Models and Deduction," *American Behavioral Scientist* 40 (May 1997), pp. 782-97.

[7] Steven L. McShane & Mary Ann Von Glinow, *Organizational Behavior* (Boston: Irwin McGraw-Hill, 2000), pp. 498-500.

[8] Leonidas Contos, "Introduction to the Orthodox Church" in *A Companion to the Greek Orthodox Church* (New York: Greek Orthodox Archdiocese of America, 1984), pp. 1-6.

[9] Geert Hofstede, *Culture's Consequences: International Differences in Work-Related Values* (Beverly Hills, California: Sage Publications, 1980).

LEADERSHIP IN THE PARISH: A THEOLOGY OF MINISTRY

GEORGE C. PAPADEMETRIOU

Parish leadership is of enormous importance to the growth and welfare of the Church, especially in the context of today's complex social and technological changes. The task of this paper is: to examine the past, the Traditional understanding of leadership in the parish; to offer some thoughts on the contemporary situation; and to offer comments and theological guidelines for leadership in today's parish, keeping in mind that the Church of Christ has been maintained through two thousand years with our roots firmly embedded in the nourishment of the Holy Gospel. Externally, appearances have changed; internally, in the domain of the Holy Spirit, the emphasis is on continuity.

Parish

In the early Church there is no mention of "parish." In the New Testament, when reference was made to a geographical unit of the Church the term used was *ecclesia*. This referred to what we know today as "diocese." Later, in the fourth century when the Church was expanding rapidly, we first encounter the term *enoria* – parish. This appears in the writings of St. Gregory of Nyssa.[1] At about the same time we also find reference to *enoria* by Epiphanios of Cyprus.[2] *Enoria*/parish had become distinct from diocese.

The parish is the smallest unit of the community life of the faithful. As a Eucharistic community every parish is in communion with a diocese of the "catholic church" in a concrete place and time. The faithful live the mystery of the Church as practiced in the Church. One purpose and mission of the Church, as the Body of Christ, is the illumination and perfection of the faithful in Christ. Those who exercise leadership have a primary responsibility to seek, to attain and to maintain this goal for the faithful and for themselves. Included is the derivative responsibility of maintaining the unity of the community, of struggling against division, which is of the Devil.

The Church is the "body of Christ" (1 Cor 12:27), that is, the unity of the faithful – the holy people of God – illuminated and guided by the Holy

113

Spirit. The parish is a place where the faithful members of the body of Christ live in holiness and struggle constantly to always be and live in Christ. When we speak of the parish we, the Orthodox, refer to an entity that is an integral part of the Church and its presence in the world. Christ and His Church exist in an unbroken and undivided bond of unity. As Saint John Chrysostom states, the Church is "one *genos* – race – of God and humanity."[3]

Effective leadership in New Testament times and subsequently clearly resulted from the diversity of gifts – *charismata* – with which leaders were endowed. The ministries of prophesy and service – *diakonia* – make their appearance early. In his first epistle to the Corinthians Saint Paul states: "There are varieties of gifts, but the same spirit. There are varieties of service, but the same Lord. There are many forms of work, but all of them in all men, are the work of the same God" (1 Cor 12:4-6). These gifts of service are bestowed for the common good: "In each of us the spirit is manifested in one particular way, for the same useful purpose" (1 Cor 12:7). The purpose of prophetic ministry is to build up the church. St. Paul tells us that "… when a man prophesies … his words have power to build" (1 Cor 14:5), and he urges the community leaders: "You are, I know, eager for the gifts of the spirit: then aspire above all to excel in those which build up the Church" (1 Cor 14:12). Saint Paul also addresses *diakonia*/service in discussing the collection of financial resources to support the Church of Jerusalem. He says, "I am on my way to Jerusalem, on an errand to God's people there. For Macedonia and Achaia have resolved to raise a common fund for the benefit of the poor among God's people at Jerusalem" (Rom 15:25-26. See also 2 Cor 8:4,19; 9:1).

The Church (including the parish) is the community of the people of God. It is not divided into "clergy" and "laity." All are members of the Body of Christ. Saint John Chrysostom clearly points out that it is inappropriate to distinguish between "sheep" and "shepherds." Under Christ "we are all sheep." Both the shepherds and the shepherded are shepherded under the One, Heavenly Shepherd.[4]

Since at least sub-apostolic times, the Church has recognized three orders of leadership in the clergy: bishop, presbyter and deacon. However, in accordance with the statement of Saint John Chrysostom, above, all the people of God, without distinction, "are under the Great Shepherd Christ," including those who function as parish leaders.

The Church as people of God: clergy-laity and the ministry of leadership

The concept of "the people of God" is based on the Old Testament affirmation that a divine covenantal relationship exists between God and His people Israel. A quick look at some terminology provides insightful background into this concept. The Hebrew *am* – and its Greek equivalent *laos* – refer to the socio-cultural dimensions of the people of Israel, which, of course, include religion. (This is in marked contrast to the terms for "nation" – in Hebrew *goy* – and its Greek equivalent *ethnos* – which refer to political dimensions.) *Quahal* is the Hebrew word for the congregation of God's people. In the New Testament and subsequently we find the Greek word *pleroma* used in a functionally similar manner – to refer to the congregation of the people of God. Furthermore, the Scriptures clearly make a distinction between *laos* (the people of God) and *ethne* (the "nations" which have not yet come to God). The insights deriving from this brief linguistic look at the concept of the people of God are very important. Carefully examined, the religio-cultural aspects of this concept show it to be totally devoid of either racism or nationalism. The differentiation is only between those "of God" and those "not yet of God."

The people of God in the New Testament are portrayed as *hagioi* – holy people – saints. They lived in the world. But they were separate, under God, from much of the world in which they existed. So the term "holy people" designates the Church, which is open to all, transcending all barriers of race and nationalism.[5]

The people of God in the Old and New Testament were governed according to a set pattern. The leadership in Scriptural times was one of charismatic order. There were people set apart by the Holy Spirit for leadership in the community of God, to maintain the appropriate order and unity. In a list that many will recognize from an apostolic reading, Saint Paul tells us about the *charismata* of the leadership of God's people: "first the apostles, second the prophets, third teachers, then workers of miracles, then healers, helpers, administrators, speakers in various kinds of tongues" (1 Cor 12:28). In a similar vein he states: "Having gifts that differ according to the grace given to us, let us use them: if prophecy, in proportion to our faith; if service, in our serving; he who teaches, in his teaching; he who exhorts, in his exhortation; he who contributes, in liberality; he who gives aid, with zeal; he who acts of mercy, with cheerfulness" (Rom 12:6-8).

These *charismata* of ministry imply, certainly in Saint Paul's mind – and I would suggest in all our minds – that all people are to serve the Lord according to their own particular gifts. Please note: the concept of "clergy" as distinct from "laity" – and the unacceptable aberration that is unfortunately encountered at times – "clergy" *versus* "laity" – is non-existent in the New Testament, especially so in the writings of Paul. All who are baptized in Christ are "God's people" – the Body of Christ – the Church. All who are committed to the "one faith" are the *pleroma* of the Body of Christ. "All, clergy and laity, those who lead and those who are led, men and women, all make up the *pleroma*, the fullness of the Church, the Body of Christ."[6]

The *pleroma*, that is, the people in the Church, are the fullness of Christ's Body and have a primary role in the ministry of leadership in the Church. The term *laikos* – layperson – etymologically is derived from the term *laos* – people. The Scriptures refer to "the people of God."[7]

The Church, here *Ecclesia*, is the congregation, the assembly, or simply the convocation, of the people of God – for worship, fellowship and administration of the life of the congregation in a particular locality. Each baptized person is a member of the Body of Christ, the Church. All who are baptized are ordained into the order of the "people of God" – *laos tou Theou*. St. Peter makes this perfectly clear: "… you are a chosen race, a royal priesthood, a holy nation, God's own special people, that you may declare the wonderful deeds of him who called you out of darkness into his marvelous light" (1 Pet 2:9).[8] The lay people participate in the preparation for the Eucharist with their gifts and offerings – *prosphora*. They bring the bread, wine and other necessities.[9] The Church is the people of God, both clergy and laity.

Through baptism one becomes an icon of Christ. Once baptized and chrismated, the Christian belongs to Christ and the Holy Spirit.[10] St Gregory the Theologian speaks of this same truth when he tells us: "Chrism is a sign of the holy and royal" priesthood, and that "all those being anointed… become both priests and kings."[11] Saint John Chrysostom asks: "What does anointed (chrismated) and sealed mean?" And he answers: "The Spirit… through these gifts … made them … at the same time, priests and kings."[12] And Saint Basil the Great adds – now we have testimony from all three of the great hierarchs – "All of you – *pantes* – shall be called to be priests and *liturgoi* of God."[13] He emphasizes "all" – *pantes*. Laity and clergy are all of the royal priesthood.

Traditionally, lay people were expected to "pray and pay." At this point, I would like to share an anecdote that Cardinal Aidon Gasquet relates in his essay "The Layman in the Pre-Reformation Parish," written in the nineteenth century. In the Middle Ages, he says, an inquirer asked a priest: "What is the place of the layman in the Church?" The priest answered "The layman has two positions: he kneels before the altar and sits below the pulpit." Cardinal Gasquet added that he overlooked the third position: "The layman also puts his hand in his purse."[14] These "positions" of the layman have been seriously questioned by today's people of God – and especially here in America – where lay people have been heavily involved in all aspects of the governance of parishes since the beginning. Indeed, in the early immigrant decades, lay men and women established and led many Orthodox parishes, before there was a significant clergy presence in America.

The people of the early church viewed themselves "as an elect race" who resided in the Roman non-Christian society.[15] This situation changed, however, especially in the later Roman Empire after the Edict of Milan in 313.[16] The duality in the Church of clergy and laity is a later development that did not always benefit the Church; indeed, at times it became detrimental. People in the Church are led to God by spiritual guides or spiritual fathers and are governed by those possessing gifts – *charismata*. The clergy are elected by the "people of God," by both clergy and laity, to minister in the Church.[17]

The work of the "people of God," clergy and laity, must be based on the vision and goal set forth by Christ Himself, that is, the Kingdom of God. The Pastoral dimension is a common mission of both clergy and laity. They share in the Church's ministries of teaching, sanctification, worship, administration and mission. In all these areas clergy and laity participate jointly, to expand the church and to lead God's people to holiness.[18]

Each baptized Christian participates in the royal priesthood of Christ. St. John Chrysostom, in addressing the lay people, states: "You are yourselves made priests in Baptism ... priests in that you offer yourselves to God" (On 2 Cor. P.G. vol. 61C.417). The faithful who are baptized are incorporated into the Body of Christ and share the priestly, prophetic and kingly office of Christ.[19] All the people of God share in the leadership of the Church for the expansion of the Body of Christ and the greater glory of God.

The three orders of clergy – bishop, presbyter, and deacon – had developed by the end of the first century or the beginning of the second. However, it appears there were no monarchical bishops with absolute authority over the church.[20] The bishop is inseparably related to the Eucharist and his primary mission is to maintain peace and unity in the community. The emphasis of the clergy, as leaders in the Eucharist, is to unite God's people against the forces of evil. John Romanides points out that St. Ignatius exhorts the Christians to do "all things pertaining to the church corporately with the bishop, presbyters and deacons." But "the faithful are not saved through the bishop as an individual who has some sort of magical power." In the Church, as the Body of Christ, God is working salvation through Christ and the Holy Spirit in the corporate mysteries. The bishops are the image of Christ and the presbyters are the image of the apostles as liturgical functionaries. The altar as center of worship is inseparable from the bishop and is necessary for salvation. The bishop does not have his own authority independent of the community. As further noted by Romanides, "The Bishop is not something independent of the ministry of the faithful. The Bishop obtains 'the ministry which belongs to the community (or people...), not of himself, neither by men, nor through vainglory, but the love of God the Father and the Lord Jesus Christ.' The representatives of one community to another are not appointed by the bishop, but elected by a council."[21]

In the early Church the *chorepiscopos* or village-bishop functioned without the authorization to ordain, or to consecrate church buildings, which are the only difference between bishops and priests in Orthodoxy today. Of importance to Orthodoxy is the collegiality of the priests, with the bishop presiding. The clergy do not "have any individual power to administer the mysteries as intermediaries between God and man, for they are but part of the whole community as the body of Christ in which God Himself works salvation in the corporate mysteries. What did characterize the clergy was their responsibility of keeping the Body united in the love of Christ and keeping the power of the Devil and division outside the Church."[22]

In the past, the people of God – clergy and laity together – elected their leaders in the community. Professor Trempelas makes reference, as an example, to the election by the clergy and laity of the successor to Bishop Augustine of Hippo.[23] Even today the practice of popular election of bishops still persists in Cyprus. Priests in Greece, until the first part of the twentieth century, were elected as pastors in a particular community to lead them in their spiritual journey.[24] The leadership of the parish is in the hands of the "people of God."

Management and leadership in the parish

In the contemporary parish in America leadership is unclear, and consequently conflicts often arise. The parish leadership is comprised of a council (which includes men and women) and the pastor as spiritual counselor. The bishop of the diocese by extension exercises leadership over the parish but from a distance, becoming directly involved, usually, when there is conflict between priest and parish council. Conflicts often arise relative to who manages the parish and who exercises leadership in the community, the priest or the parish council and its president. At times a superficial division of duties is created, that is, the priest is in charge of the "spiritual" aspect of the parish and the president of the "secular" affairs of the community. In cases where there is overstepping of the boundaries, conflicts may arise, and the bishop may become involved to resolve the issues.

Let me speak briefly of management and leadership in the parish. Modern experts speak of leadership as being broader than management and sometimes they overlap. "Leadership is a broader concept than management. Management is a peculiar kind of leadership."[25] There is a difference between leadership and management. "Management is thought of as a special kind of leadership in which the accomplishment of organizational goals is paramount."[26] The emphasis here is on management that achieves the "organizational" goal. Management is directed toward attaining a goal of the individual or group such as the diocese or the parish. Management also has a social responsibility. This dimension of management is to manage the "social impacts and the social responsibilities of the enterprise."[27] This is very useful to the bishop and the pastor as well as to every Christian leader. There is an obvious need to take social impact into account. The parish does not exist in a vacuum. Significant decisions ripple into the lives of others. Desirable management skills on the part of leaders include those related to planning, organizing, motivating and controlling. But it must be emphasized that these skills are to be exercised by the Christian leader with a strong focus on the Gospel-mandated objective – bringing souls to Christ. Hopefully there is no need to point out that the misdirected use of management skills related to motivation and control invite disaster.

There are four styles of management that leaders develop. The traditional one often involves a strong commitment to the organization but reluctance to take risks. The entrepreneurial style can have little commitment to the organization but can be quite willing to take risks as challenges. The purposeful style of management can have great commitment to the organization, and still be quite willing to experiment and take risks. The fourth type, labeled crisis management, has little concern for the organization and resists taking risks. It is like the firefighter making decisions impulsively, "off the top of his or her head," without planning. This type of crisis management must be avoided by the Christian leader because it only brings spiritual harm to the community.[28]

Sociologists of religion suggest that "participatory congregations" are the most beneficial for growth of the Church. They advise that "member involvement and shared involvement in congregational governance and leadership... seem most likely to flourish."[29]

Modern methods of organization and leadership are potentially very beneficial to parish leadership for spiritual growth. As Bishop Lesslie Newbigin says, "Industrial management is far ahead of the Church."[30] The theology of ministry of the parish, which includes leadership, is an important aspect of life in Christ in contemporary society.

Power, authority, diakonia and leadership in the parish

Leadership in the parish, as we traditionally know it here in America, consists of a parish council. The council is made up of baptized, chrismated and practicing Orthodox men and women. The priest is a member of the council by virtue of his ordination and having been canonically assigned to the parish by the diocesan bishop, who has the added responsibility of approving the election of the members of the parish council. This practice is found only in the life of the Church in America. The traditional governance of the Church in Constantinople consisted of a "mixed council" of both clergy and laity until 1923, when the "mixed council ceased to exist."[31] Participation of the laity in the governance of the Church in Constantinople was eliminated and the clergy now exercise exclusive leadership and management of the Church there.

In America, Orthodox lay people are very active in the life and governance of the Church. Parish councils, in concert with the clergy, exercise leadership and hold legal authority within their parishes. But questions frequently arise regarding the precise power and authority of the parish council. Who exercises leadership in the parish? Is it a majority of the lay members of the council, or is it the clergy? Conflict often arises in seeking a Christian resolution to this question. Sometimes we encounter a dualistic dichotomy of separation of powers between clergy and laity. The roots of this idea seem to go back to the early nineteenth century, before the Ecumenical Patriarchate reorganized its affairs. Until 1860 lay leaders were involved in various synods of the Ecumenical Patriarchate. This practice existed before the fall, in 1453, and continued afterward. The situation changed when "... the promulgation of the General Regulations (1860) ... gave the administration of spiritual matters to a twelve-member synod of metropolitans and left the rest of the temporal character to the care of a mixed national council of metropolitans and laymen."[32] As noted above, this also changed – in 1923 – when laymen were excluded from the governance of all Church affairs in the Patriarchate of Constantinople.

The voice of the people is expressed in the ordination of the clergy by the acclamation of *Axios* – He is worthy – in the service of ordination. The parish, however, is governed by a lay and clergy council. Quoting Istavrides, "In each local parish an ecclesiastical committee, elected by its members or appointed by the bishop, takes care of the financial and other temporal affairs of their community."[33] The Orthodox Church, it must be noted, is hierarchical as well as conciliar. This is true in all aspects of the life of the church. The conciliar expression of parish leadership and authority lies in the local community's parish council of clergy and laity. This is expressed as 'hierarchical' and 'synodical' administration of the Church.

When we speak of a hierarchical system we point to the fact that there is a vertical scale, wherein authority and power accrue to bishops and patriarchs, with Christ as the highest authority. But the Church is also synodical in that it has a horizontal expression, where the people of God, both clergy and laity, are engaged in the leadership of the Church, including the parish.

'Synod' is derived from two Greek words *syn-odos*, 'together' and 'road.' It expresses the view that we walk "together on the road" seeking spiritual perfection in Christ. The view that the Orthodox Church is 'synodical' and 'hierarchical' goes back to New Testament times, when the *proestos* – the presiding presbyter or bishop – led the people in worship. The *proestos/* bishop was the liturgical and spiritual leader of the community, admitting candidates to baptism and presiding at the Eucharist. He was the lead teacher and moral guide of the community. He received guests from other *ecclesies*, and maintained his *ecclesia* 'in communion' with others. "He ordained presbyters and deacons and, therefore, controlled who was ordained. Finally he participated in the ordination of other bishops."[34]

Leadership in the parish, as any type of leadership, involves power and authority. However, power and authority are not synonymous. "Power describes the ability to compel others to do something, whether legitimately or not."[35]

In the early Church the spiritual man and often the martyr possessed great authority in the community. Those elected bishops were men of superior spiritual stature, whose purpose in leadership included the high-order objective of keeping the community united in the Body of Christ, the Church. "In the early Church authority was of men who were princes in the community which was wholly sanctified, *plebs sancto*, and who were overshadowed by the Spirit of God." And it has been noted: "Church leaders were all the more conscious of their authority in that they saw it as the vehicle of the mystery of that salvation, which God wishes to accomplish in the Church. They wanted to be, and knew that they were, moved by the Spirit, but they also knew that the Spirit inhabits the Christian community and the exercise of their authority; they remained closely linked to this community."[36] So, those in leadership positions exercised authority in the community then, as they should today, as stewards of our Lord Jesus Christ, the head of the Church.

Authority, administration, governance and leadership include power. Because power is inherent in the institution of the Church, possessing power may result in the abuse of power. Indeed, as we know in sadness, "history is replete with examples of the abuse of authority in the Church."[37] However, the abuse of power must be excluded from the Body of Christ, the Church. "Love is the supreme motivation both of the officers and of the other members of the Church. With this motivation, anything like power struggle is forever excluded from the Church. Love is the only power which the New Testament knows."[38] The Church is administrated by the motivation of love as the highest priority in the parish.

Father George Mastrantonis emphasizes that all who are incorporated into the Body of Christ through baptism become members of the Church as servants (1 Cor. 4:1). Harmony among clergy and laity is necessary for the attainment of the end – salvation – for all people. So he states: "The authority for administration of the Church is the ground where the laity plays the larger role by participating in the synods, election of the higher clergy, administration of all the properties of the Church etc."[39] The authority of the clergy in administering the sacraments is well founded in Scripture and Holy Tradition.[40]

The ministries in the Church are *charismata* – gifts received from the Holy Spirit. As Christ was apostle, prophet, teacher, evangelist, pastor and servant, He bestows these gifts to those who are baptized. "The obedience of all is due to God, Christ, the Spirit; only limited, and never unilateral obedience is due to other men in the community."[41] Hierarchs have authority and power inherent in their offices but these come as honors and dignities of the office for the purpose of *diakonia*/service whose objective is to attain the ultimate end of salvation. The relationship of the ruler (*arche*) and the ruled is that of synodical administration and of the *diakonia*/service of leadership.[42] In the early Church the differences between the *charismata* of the leadership were not in any way ontological but rather "the differences are in a pneumatical (i.e., spiritual) endowment."[43]

The leaders of the early Church included apostles, prophets and teachers, and also those who exercised administrative leadership. These leaders frequently became bishops, presbyters and deacons. Whether clergy or laity, their mission was always to lead the church and expand in the service of God and his people. These leaders were to inspire unity of the community, spiritual edification and ultimate union with God in Christ. Saint Paul speaks of the goal of leadership in the following way: "Leadership and Christian discipleship are fundamentally about Christ-likeness, about doing and teaching what Jesus taught and did ... a model that is to be passed on to the next generation."[44]

The ministry of leadership in the Greek Orthodox parish as manifested in America today involves lay and clergy alike. As pointed out earlier, the clergy lead the people to the sacramental worship with equal participation of the laity. The governing body of the parish council is in close relation with the diocesan bishop. The laity today, unlike the past, demand accountability and expect complete involvement in the affairs of the people of God, manifested in the parish leadership.[45] The leadership of the parish must be prophetic and completely devoted to Christ to solve the social problems of the day. As the late George Charles, a prominent layman, aptly stated: "We (people and clergy) cannot be eclectic and take or leave Jesus Christ on our own terms just because we have problems in our society or in our families. We can adjust the institutions, organization or agencies that serve the church (the body of Christ); in doing so we can help to deal with the problems of our society, the needs of our youth, the challenges for caring for our aged and the entire spectrum of the human rights. But we must first bring the essence of the church closer to our people so that the church means more to them spiritually."[46]

Parish leadership, as all Christian leadership, must be inspired by the Holy Spirit and a strong prophetic voice in today's world of the American society. Leadership in the parish must not be limited to administration. Foremost, it must be a clear voice for truth, love and Christ's servanthood for humanity. We cannot expect the laity to continue to "pray, pay and obey" as in the Middle Ages. We have to reach back further to the period of the New Testament, where love prevailed as the dominant element of ecclesial leadership – and followership. The prophetic voice of today's leadership speaks out for justice – for all people – in recognition of Christ as the ultimate leader in the Christian parish.

The parish is made up of the clergy and the laity and is governed by both. The people of God – all Christians – receive at baptism the gifts of prophecy, ministry and teaching and, as clearly stated by St. Paul, the Christian leadership of service (Rom 12:6 ff). This does not diminish the function of the ordained clergy of teaching and offering the mysteries (sacraments). Orthodoxy does not hold an "ontological difference between the clergy and laity because all the baptized make up the people of God."[47] The parish as a society needs organization and order, which is provided by cooperative leadership. However, the Orthodox Church differs fundamentally from other organizations, and its leadership must reflect the equality of the clergy and laity in relation to the life in Christ. St. John Chrysostom emphasizes that "all clergy and laity merit the same honor."[48] In Orthodoxy, there is no "absolute authoritarianism" since Christ "came not to be served but to serve" (Mt 20:28). Our Holy Orthodox Church manifests its divine-human reality in its servant leadership rather than by the authority and power claimed by the clergy, lay councils or any other authority. Servant leadership characterizes the authentic leadership and management of the Orthodox parish. Only secular government makes the claim of authority, administration and power. Chrysostom expresses the Christian spirit of authentic governance in the Church. The relationship of clergy and laity is properly one of fraternal relationship, not of dominance. He states that in the Church "there must not be the rule of the conceit of the ruler ... nor must there be servil-

ity of the ruled." In the Church there must be a spiritual authority, partnership and governance as given us by the example of the life and actions of
Christ.[49] As stated before, participatory style is the best possible administration and leadership in the parish. St. John Chrysostom makes this clear
when he compares secular (civil) governance and the Church. He says the
secular offices seem more attractive and important when only one is the
administrator (monarchy), but contrary to this, "the leadership is not a single
one person, but many (collective body or council of clergy and laity) who
have equal capacity, then precisely the honor is much more splendid, that
is, when the many preside"[50] in the community of the faithful. The practice
of parish governance must return to the authentic Christian and spiritual
way of leading the community to God with responsibilities of both clergy
and laity. The call of service is made to both clergy and laity in the Orthodox Church to follow Christ for a common spiritual goal, the salvation of
their souls. The question that contemporary Orthodox Christians pose is,
"How can we maintain that the Church is Orthodox when we live contrary
to the life of the Apostolic Church?" That is, "when in the Roman Byzantine Empire the secular state exercised monarchical governance, the church
opted for a democratic administration of church affairs. Today our church
has a monarchy or oligarchy, instead of democracy."[51] We must return to
the practice of parish leadership as discipleship. "It is not law or power,
knowledge or dignity, but service which is the basis of discipleship" and,
"the cost and the goal of service is love."[52]

The emphasis sometimes is on liturgical leadership by the priest and "administration of the secular affairs of the parish by the laity." This dichotomy
destroys the meaning and the goal of the authentic Christian parish, which
is to proclaim the Gospel to the world and establish God's kingdom, that is,
the ruling power of Christ. The *diakonia* of the priest must be balanced
between the cultic in its orientation and the prophetic dimension of the
ministries of parish leaders, both clergy and laity – which is to proclaim the
word of God and seek justice for all people. The present situation is that our
community leaders have "a strongly cultic and administrative character."[53]
But the church's leadership of service must pay heed to the word of God,
which emphatically states: "and what does the Lord require of you but to do
justice, to love mercy and to walk humbly with your God" (Mic 6:8).

The prophetic preaching of parish leadership must be centered on God
and the approach of God's reign. The prophets taught holiness and proclaimed righteousness (justice). They criticized moral corruption and
preached to establish a noble and moral society. They often talked about
the judgment, renewal and reconciliation of all people. They sought justice,
mercy and righteousness. They denounced evil and injustice in society re-

gardless of the price they had to pay as individuals. The prophets exercised extraordinary zeal to cure the social ills of the time, participated in politics, and even judged the private lives of secular leaders. This type of prophetic parish leadership is greatly needed today.[54]

Greek Orthodox parishes in America, in the early decades, were organized along secular lines, with one set of goals being to bring immigrant Greeks together for social and economic reasons – as well as for religious worship and fellowship. Archbishop Iakovos called this to our attention in his address to the nineteenth biennial Clergy-Laity Congress, in Athens, on July 22, 1968. He stated: "Our parishes (in America) began as organizations and developed into religious communities. Today they are churches. Around them our whole life is entwined and developed ... we have made the church the center of our life. The church is everything for us."[55] Implicit in the Archbishop's statement is the notion that the religious community warrants religious leadership that is able to fulfill its goal. The priest is a leader who shepherds the congregation to salvation through worship and spiritual guidance. "The priest is not a chaplain of a secular and social organization; he is a spiritual leader of a spiritual institution,"[56] and "so the parish remains one of the most visible places of hope and potential in our secular society."[57]

The Greek American Orthodox community, where baptized men and women serve in leadership capacities, needs to raise its level of consciousness to the Lordship of Christ and to service in the vineyard of the Lord. It is the Church's obligation, especially in the parish, to offer leadership that has a prophetic voice that speaks the truth on behalf of all people. Such leadership provides a voice of mission, that is, the proclamation of the Gospel, and also reconciles and heals those who are broken and suffering under the cross of oppression, hunger and prejudice.[58]

Conclusion

Leadership in the parish consists of clergy and laity, men and women. The clergymen are called by God and elected by the laity to lead God's people, the sheep (Jn 21:16). They are not lords and rulers but rather bearers of liturgical *charisma* bestowed on them through ordination. They are called to actualize Christ's love in the pastoral work of parish life by protecting and expanding His flock. The parishioners who are in Christ's flock have their own personalities and judgment. They know full well that they do not belong to the clergymen, but to Christ, to Whom they are committed at baptism.

The concept of authority and leadership in the Church is different from that of secular government. Church leadership is one of suffering – bearing the cross – and of servanthood – *diakonia*. The clergy, as liturgists, exercise the charisma of sanctification. But the gift of ordination "through laying on of hands" (1 Tim 4:14) does not separate the priest from the body of Christ and place him "above." He exercises the charisma of sanctification as part of the body of Christ. His position is not one of lordship but of spiritual father and shepherd.[59]

The priest is the father, healer and reconciler, not the overlord of the parish. The leadership of the priest is one of spiritual gifts, bringing the people of God to salvation and glorification. The priest and bishop gather the people of God at the Eucharistic table to unite in Christ. The leadership of the clergy in the parish is to preserve unity and struggle against the satanic forces that evoke division and conflict.

The parish council consists of people committed to Christ and his Gospel. They practice the faith, participating in the Eucharist and living as the disciples of Christ lived. Parish council members must be of the royal priesthood and not just good business people. They must be committed men and women with their vision focused on Christ and His work in the world.

The people of God, clergy and laity, live for Christ, in Christ and strive to be like Christ. Parish leadership must reflect Christ Himself, who is divine-human, and seek to transform the world into a society of brothers and sisters bound together in His blessed body. The improvement of leadership skills must expand into holiness, guiding and leading people to Christ, the Savior of the world.

NOTES

[1] P.G. Vol. 46C.1001A. See also John D. Zizioulas, *Eucharist, Bishop, Church: The Unity of the Church in the Divine Eucharist and the Bishop during the Three First Centuries.* Trans: Elizabeth Theokritoff. Brookline, MA: Holy Cross Orthodox Press (2001), pp. 197-217.
[2] P.G. Vol. 41C.677C.
[3] P.G. Vol. 53C.789.
[4] P.G. Vol. 52C.784. See also George D. Metallinos, *Parish: Christ in our midst* (in Greek), (Athens: Apostolike Diakonia, 1990), pp. 10-20.
[5] George C. Papademetriou, "The People of God," in the proceedings, *People of God, peoples of God: a World Council of Churches consultation on The Church and the Jewish people, Budapest, October 15-21, 1994,* ed. Leon Klenicki (Geneva: World Council of Churches, 1996). See also Yves M. J. Congar, *Lay People in the Church,* Trans. Donald Atwater, Rev. ed., (Westminster MD: The Newman Press, 1965), p. 3.
[6] P.N. Trempelas, *The Laity in the Church* (in Greek), (Athens: Soter publications, 1975), p. 99.
[7] Petros Vassiliades, "New Testament Ecclesiological Perspective on Laity," Aristotelian University of Thessaloniki School of Theology, *Epistimonike Epeteris,* 29

(1988), p. 348. Congar, *Lay People in the Church*, p. 3.

[8]Tertullian, "On Baptism, 7," *Anti-Nicene Fathers, Translation of the Writings of the Fathers down to A.D. 325*, eds. Alexander Roberts and James Donaldson (Grand Rapids: William B. Eerdmans Publishing Company, 1957), p. 672-73.

[9]Clement of Rome, *First Epistle to the Corinthians*, 41. See also *The Nature of the Church*, Faith and Order, Paper No. 181, Geneva (1998), p. 12-14.

[10]Cyril of Alexandria *Catechetical Mystagogy*; 3 A - G and E - S.

[11]Gregory the Theologian, "Discourse 4, On Holy Baptism, 4," P.G. Vol. 36C.364.

[12]John Chrysostom, "Commentary on 2nd Cor. 1, 21," P.G. Vol. 61C.411.

[13]Saint Basil, "Homily on the Beatitudes," P.G. Vol. 31C.1261-1264.

[14]This story is told in the book by Yves Conger, *Lay People in the Church*, xi.

[15] *The Layman in Christian History: A Project of the Department of the Laity of the World Council of Churches*, eds. Stephen Charles Neil and Hans Roedi Weber (London: SCM Press Ltd., 1963), p. 50.

[16]Neil and Roedi, p. 57 ff.

[17]Neil and Roedi, p. 59. See also Congar, *Lay People in the Church*, p. 79 ff.

[18]Konstantinos Mouratides, "The Bishop: Despotes or Diakonos: The divine-human significance of the episcopal ministry" (in Greek), *Koinonia*, 42:1 (1999), p. 9.

[19]Thomas Halton, "The Church," *Message of the Fathers*, No. 4 (Wilmington, DE: Michael Glazier, 1985), p. 146.

[20]John Romanides, "The Ecclesiology of St. Ignatius of Antioch," *Greek Orthodox Theological Review* 7:1-2 (1961-1962) 66ff. Patrick Burke, "The Monarchical Episcopate at the End of the First Century," *Journal of Ecumenical Studies*, 7:3 (1970) 500ff. John D. Zizioulas, "Episkope and Episkopos in the early Church: A brief survey of the evidence," *Episkope and Episkopate, Ecumenical Perspective* (Geneva: World Council of Churches, 1980) pp. 30-31.

[21]Romanides, 69. George Tavard, "The Function of the Ministry in the Eucharistic Celebration," *Journal of Ecumenical Studies*, 4 (1967), p. 634.

[22]Romanides, 69. Panagiotes E. Poulitsas, *Relation of State and Church: Especially in the Election of Bishops* (in Greek), Vol. 1, Athens (1940), pp. 372-375. Some theologians maintain that there are two types of priesthood, that of the Royal or Spiritual Priesthood and that of the Sacramental Priesthood. See Theophilos N. Simopoulos, "The place of Clergy and Laity in the Orthodox Church" (in Greek), reprinted from the *Epeterida* of the Theological School of the University of Athens, Athens: (1959), p. 61.

[23]Trempelas, *The Laity in the Church*, pp. 28-31. Also, Poulitsas, *Relations of State and Church*, pp. 274-326.

[24]My father, when he completed Seminary in Greece, was not automatically ordained a priest. He was elected by the people of his village (they cast votes) and requested the bishop to ordain him for this particular parish. This practice, to my knowledge, has been abandoned.

[25]Charles J. Keating, *The Leadership Book* (New York: Paulist Press, 1978), p. 88.

[26]Paul Hersey and Kenneth H. Blanchard, *Management of Organizational Behavior* (Englewood Cliffs, NJ: Prentice Hall, 2nd edition, 1972), p. 5.

[27]Peter Drucker, *Management* (New York: Harper and Row, 1974), p. 4.

²⁸Keating, *The Leadership Book*, pp. 88-95, an excellent guide for Christian leaders, written to help improve leadership skills in the church including the Parish Council, very helpful for understanding both modern management skills and a theological approach to leadership. Other useful texts: Norman Shawchuck and Roger Heuser, *Managing the Congregation* (Nashville: Abingdon Press, 1996); same authors, *Leading the Congregation* (New York: Harper Torchbooks, 1970), pp. 212-228.

²⁹William McKinney, "Parish," *Encyclopedia of Religion and Society*, ed. William H. Swatos, Jr. (Walnut Creek CA: AltaMira Press, 1998), p. 350.

³⁰Lesslie Newbigin, *The Good Shepherd: Meditations on Christian Ministry in Today's World*, (Grand Rapids: William B. Eerdmans Publishing Company, 1977), p. 55.

³¹Vasil T. Istavrides, "The Orthodox World," *The Layman in Christian History: A Project of the Department of the Laity of the World Council of Churches*, eds. Stephen Charles Neil and Hans Roedi Weber (London: SCM Press Ltd., 1963), p. 278.

³²Istavrides, p. 278.

³³Istavrides, p. 279.

³⁴Joseph T. Lienhard, "Ministry," *Message of the Church Fathers*, No. 8 (Wilmington DE: Michael Glazier, Inc., 1984) pp. 15-16. John D. Zizioulas, *Eucharist, Bishop, Church*, pp. 62-66.

³⁵Thomas Rausch, *Authority and Leadership in the Church: Past Directions and Future Possibilities*, (Wilmington DE: Michael Glazier, Inc., 1988), p. 38.

³⁶Yves Congar, *Power and Poverty in the Church* (Baltimore: Helicon, 1965) 46. "Authority in the Church is not the monopoly of the clergy, nor of juridically instituted offices." It is of a spiritual nature since the Church is God's "self-communication in Spirit, authority consists in the power of God's grace communicated to humans." See Menco A. Alfonso, *What is the Nature of Authority in the Church?* (Lanham MD: University Press of America, 1996) p. 64.

³⁷Rauch, *Authority and Leadership in the Church*, p. 39.

³⁸John L. McKenzie, *Authority in the Church* (New York: Sheed and Ward, 1966), p. 85. George H. Tavard, *A Theology for Ministry* (Wilmington DE: Michael Glazier, 1983), pp. 118-137. The bishop possesses the power or authority of love. The shepherds offer diakonia of leadership through sacrificial love. Hieronymos (Liapes), Metropolitan of Thebes and Levadeia, "Authority (Power) or Diakonia? Answers to Questions" (in Greek), *Synaxis*, 47 (1993), pp.7-12.

³⁹George Mastrantonis, *Administration and Authority within the Eastern Orthodox Church*, (St. Louis: O Logos, n.d.) 6. See the critical work by Philotheos Faros, *The Priesthood, Form and Deformation* (in Greek) (Athens: Publications Armos, 1994). Fr. Faros points out that the clergy do not take a position of leadership by election from those they lead. Following graduation from the Seminary the candidate is ordained and appointed by the bishop to a position of leadership. See "Leadership that was not won," pp. 138-139. The clergyman, however, received *charisma* from the Church to lead the parish, not in an "authoritarian" way, but with personal relations in love.

⁴⁰Ibid, pp. 5-6. See also Benjamin T. McKibben, *Oriented Leadership: Why all Christians need it* (Wayne, NJ: Orthodox Christian Publication Center, 1994), p.

188. See also Alex Bavelas, "Leadership: Man and Function," *Administrative Science Quarterly.* 4:4 (1960), pp. 190-198.

[41]Hans Kung, *The Church* (New York: Sheed and Ward, 1967), p. 401.

[42]Kung, *The Church*, 390. George H. Tavard, *A Theology of Ministry*, p. 119. For a discussion of the equality of all in the church, as the people of God, to lead and minister, see Sandra Schneiders, "Evangelical Equality: Religious Consecration, Mission and Witness," *Spirituality Today* 38 (Winter 1986), pp. 293-302.

[43]Bert Holmberg, *Paul and Power* (Philadelphia: Fortress Press, 1980), p. 101. See also Edward Shillebeeckx, *The Church with the Human Face* (New York: Crossroad Publishing Co., 1985), p. 44 ff.

[44]Steve Salton, "Leadership and Lifestyle: The Portrait of Paul in the Miletus Speech and 1 Thessalonians," *Society for New Testament Studies, Monograph Series 108*, Cambridge: University Press (2000), p. 184. See also the insightful article of Bishop Ieronymos (Liapes), Metropolitan of Thebes and Levadeia, "Authority and Diakonia in the Church: Answers to Questions," in *Synaxis* 47 (1993), pp. 7-12. See also "The Nature of Leadership in the Church" in *Report to His Eminence Archbishop Iakovos*, by the Commission Appointed to Establish the Theological Agenda for the Future of the Greek Orthodox Archdiocese (Brookline, MA: Holy Cross Press, 1990), pp. 15-16. The Church leadership and Christian discipleship is about "Christ likeness, that is, doing and teaching as Jesus did, that is passed on from generation to generation. Servanthood, which is a costly form of leadership service, is central to the Gospel. See Steve Walton, *Leadership and Lifestyle: The portrait of Paul in the Melitus speech and 1 Thessalonians* (Cambridge: Cambridge University Press, 2000), p. 184.

[45]Ibid., pp. 96-103. Schuyler Brown, "Apostleship in the New Testament," *Historical and Theological Problem in New Testament Studies*, 30:3 (1984), pp. 174-180. See the excellent study by Prof. Konstantinos Mouratides, "The Bishop: Despot or Servant? The divine-human Magnificence of the Episcopal Ministry," *Koinonia* 40:1 (1998), pp. 1-15; 41:2 (1998), pp. 141-154; 41:3 (1998), pp. 241-248; 42:1 (1999), pp. 9-14. Theodore Federoff, *Orthodox Parish Counseling Guide: Thesis presented to the faculty of the Graduate School, Indiana University of Pennsylvania*, (1975), p. 59. N. T. Bougatsos, "The Church and the Laity," *Synaxis*, 74 (2000), pp. 47-53. This is an excellent brief article on an Orthodox Christian view of "democratic" leadership and administration in today's Church.

[46]George G. Charles, "The Role of the Laity in the Orthodox Church in the Americas: The Role of the Priest and the Apostolate of the Laity," *Clergy Seminar Lectures*, ed. N.M. Vaporis, Brookline, MA: Holy Cross Press (1982), p. 38.

[47]John N. Karmiris, *The Status and Ministry of the Laity in the Orthodox Church*, Trans. Evie Zachariades-Holmberg (Brookline, MA: Holy Cross Orthodox Press, 1994), p. 8. "Thomas Hopko, What is a Priest? An Orthodox Statement," *To be a Priest: Prospective on Vocation and Ordination*, eds. Robert E. Terrwilliger and Urban T. Holmes, III, (New York: The Seabury Press, 1975), p. 25.

[48]P.G. Vol. 59C.527; Vol. 62C.4992, Vol. 62C.81; Vol. 51C.247. There is danger in emphasizing a democratic form of governance in the Church. The mistake would be similar to those made in medieval times, where the form of Church government

was that of the state. We tend to justify the 'democratic ideal' but that would conceive the Church after the 'likeness' of the state. The Church has its own concept of authority – that God is the source. The *demos* must be understood in political terms. The 'people of God' embody a totally different form of authority than that which the *demos* has of a political society. See Alfonso, *What is the Nature of Authority in the Church*, p. 51.

[49]*Commentary on 2 Cor., Homily 18.3.* See also Robert D. Dale, *Leadership for a Changing Church*, (Nashville: Abingdon Press, 1998), p. 56ff.

[50]P.G. Vol. 50C.509. Philip M Larcon, Jr., *Vital Church Management* (Atlanta: John Knox Press, 1977), p. 4.

[51]An excellent brief article by N. T. Bougatsos, "The Church and the Laity," p. 53.

[52]Hans Küng, *The Church*, p. 392. Metallinos, *Parish: Christ in our midst*, p. 108. Thomas Franklin O'Meara, *Theology of Ministry* (New York: Ramsey Paulist Press, 1983), p. 68.

[53]Thomas P. Rausch, *Priesthood: An Appraisal* (Mahwah, NJ: Paulist Press, 1992), p. 97. Archbishop Iakovos, *The Greek Orthodox Priest as Leader in America*, New York: Greek Orthodox Archdiocese of North and South America (1976), p. 7. The Archbishop speaks of the leadership of the priest in "well-defined goals" of spiritual orientation (soul-saving) rather than "all the fields of community activities." Archbishop John Shahovskoy, *The Orthodox Pastor* (Crestwood, NY: St. Vladimir's Seminary Press 1966), "The Spirit of the Parish Management," pp. 87-90.

[54]George C. Papademetriou, "The Prophetic Ministry of the Priest," *Theologia*, (1989), pp. 403-415. Alexander F. C. Webster, *The Price of Prophecy: Orthodox Churches on Peace Freedom and Security*, (Grand Rapids: Wm. B. Eerdmans Publishing Co., 1995). The entire book is a criticism of the lack of a prophetic voice for peace, freedom and justice in the Orthodox Church. The Orthodox need to be sensitive to justice, to proclaim it and to work for it in today's world.

[55] Archbishop Iakovos Address, July 22, 1968, to the 19th Clergy-Laity Congress of the Parishes of the Greek Orthodox Church of the North and South America, convened in Athens, Greece, July 20-27, 1968, Athens (1968), pp. 28-29. See *The Collected Works of Archbishop Iakovos, vol. 1: Visions and Expectations for a Living Church*, Demetrios Constantelos, ed. (Brookline, MA: Holy Cross Orthodox Press, 1998), p. 117ff.

[56]Eusebius Stephanou, *Meet Your Priest* (New York: Cosmos, 1962), p. 1934. The Greek Orthodox Archdiocese of the Americas produced a guidebook for parish council leadership. See *Welcome to the Parish Council: A Guidebook for Parish Council Members of the Greek Orthodox Archdiocese of North and South America* (New York: Greek Orthodox Archdiocese of North and South America, Department of Religious Education, Brookline MA, n.d.), p. 32.

[57]William J. Bausch, *Ministry: Tradition, Tension, Transition* (Mystic CT: Twenty-third Publications, 1983), p. 123.

[58]Anastasios (Yannoulatos) of Androusa (presently of Albania, "Address by the Conference Moderator," *San Antonio Report*, ed. Frederick R. Wilson (Geneva: WCC Publications, 1990), pp. 100-119. Metropolitan Emilianos (Timiades), *Priest, Parish, Renewal* (Brookline MA: Holy Cross Orthodox Press, 1994), pp. 160-172.

[59]Metallinos, *Parish: Christ in our midst*, p. 73ff.

INVIGORATING AND ENRICHING THE LITURGICAL LIFE OF THE PARISH

ALKIVIADIS C. CALIVAS

Creating a healthy liturgical environment

The need for worship is innate. Human beings, whether consciously or unconsciously, crave authentic worship. This craving is best fulfilled when "the experience of worship engages our minds, memory, imagination, feelings, body, heart, masculinity/femininity and other people."[1] Hence, each parish is responsible for providing suitable and effective liturgical experiences capable of inducing the inner and exterior involvement of the people.[2]

The forms of worship operate best when they stir the minds and the hearts of the people and engage them actively in the liturgical action. Worship becomes most attractive when it is performed with faith and is characterized by simplicity, beauty, clarity, directness, solemnity and joyful dignity. Thus we are obliged to pay special attention to the several essential elements that constitute the liturgical experience, namely: time, space, action, speech, art and song.

Many factors contribute to the creation of a healthy liturgical environment and a meaningful liturgical experience. An inspired priestly celebration and a coherent and persuasive homily are basic elements. The reading of Scripture lessons and other liturgical texts with care and conviction is another. The graceful and dignified performance of liturgical actions is also important. The prayerful attentiveness of the congregation and its ability to respond gracefully with voice and bodily posture is another. Finally, because singing is so central to our liturgical tradition, the quality of our liturgical music and singing is crucial. Songs intensify speech, heighten action, and evoke memories.[3] Therefore, the parish is obliged to both secure the services of qualified chanters and music directors, while at the same time efforts are expanded to return to the assembled worshippers their ministry of song.[4]

Liturgical reductionism – the 'Sunday Church'

A perplexing problem, at least for most Orthodox parishes in North America, is the fact that the rich liturgical tradition of the Church in many instances has been reduced, as Professor Paul Meyendorff observes, to the

131

Sunday morning Eucharistic liturgy.[5] "We have become a 'Sunday Church,' peopled by 'Sunday Christians.' The Eucharist," he notes, "has lost its connection to the Orthodox liturgical corpus, of which it is supposed to be the climax – something akin to reducing a fifteen-course banquet to dessert alone."[6]

Professor Meyendorff is certainly correct to lament the fact that we have reduced our liturgical experiences to a Sunday morning Liturgy. However, the greater problem – if not sin – is that in many places even this one experience is less than lofty and less than adequate to meet the spiritual needs of the people, let alone to sustain the vibrancy of their faith.

How and why have we become a Sunday parish? What has happened to make the parish lose the vibrancy of its liturgical life? We claim – and rightly so – that the Church is primarily a worshiping community. Why then do those in charge of parish life pay so little attention to the liturgical needs of the parish? How can this occur even when a parish has spent hundreds of thousands of dollars erecting a new beautiful church edifice or renovating an old one? To answer these and other related questions, I think, we must take into account several historical, social and cultural factors.

The early immigrant communities

To our immigrant forebears America appeared like a turbulent sea of opposing worldviews and lifestyles. To survive in such a situation, they organized themselves into communities or clubs with administrative forms that mirrored the realities of the political structures of their towns and villages. The community became the lifeboat that promised survival for cherished cultural values and institutions. One of those highly-valued institutions of the community was the Church. Thus, churches were established in order to help the community preserve its Orthodox faith and to help people in their spiritual and other needs. But the church was also viewed as the foremost instrument for the preservation of ethnic identity and the cultivation and transmission of the community's cultural heritage. Parenthetically, it must be remembered that the Church is respectful of ethnic identities and the cultural heritages of her people, because they are, after all, an integral part of human life and history. The Church, however, condemns all forms of phyletism, which idolizes and makes absolute individual identities conditioned by history. While the world tends to isolate people according to their identities, the Church welcomes all. In the Church, natural, social and spiritual divisions are transcended. Christ gives unity to all in his Body, the Church (Gal 3:28).

In time, as it matured and became integrated into the fabric of American life, the dynamics and the focus of the Orthodox community began to shift. Without losing its ethnic coloration or betraying the legacy of its heritage, the community gradually took on an ecclesial identity. The adoption of the new Uniform Parish Regulations of the Greek Orthodox Archdiocese by the Clergy Laity Congress in 1964 registered clearly the change in the primary identity of the community as an ecclesial entity.[7]

However, the sense of being a church is not always and fully operative in the parish. Its early beginnings linger on. Thus, for example, parish membership is often thought to be more of a commercial transaction rather than a faith commitment. One considers himself a member of the community and a good Christian, even if he does not share in the sacraments and attend church regularly, as long as he contributes to the financial support of the community.

The process of adaptation, acculturation and assimilation

As I have written elsewhere, Orthodox Christians in America need not abandon their roots nor be apologetic about the fact that they carry with them cultural values that have been hammered out in places and times other than their own.[8] Indeed, this very fact should remind us of our own responsibility and mission to be active and creative participants in the historical process. As heirs of an excellent legacy, we are compelled to understand and appreciate it. We are also required to define it and live it in accordance with our responsibility to the historical realities in which we find ourselves.

In America, no cultural tradition is able to remain completely autonomous or unaffected by the lure of the mainstream of American life. Indeed, acculturation becomes easier with each succeeding generation. All immigrant groups that come to America enter consciously into the stream of American life. They learn the language and the customs of the land and make the necessary adjustments that will allow them to preserve their cultural identity – and all that it entails by way of religion, values, ideals, language, customs and traditions – while adopting part of American culture. This is what sociologists call the process of *adaptation*.

The offspring of the immigrant and every succeeding generation – as well as the immigrant himself after prolonged contact – experiences the merging of cultures, the inevitable modifications that come as a result of the impact of one culture upon the other. This is the process of *acculturation*, which is inevitable, relentless and inexorable, but also acceptable and necessary.

Assimilation, on the other hand, is a matter of deep concern and every effort should be made to keep it at bay. Assimilation is that process by which an individual, for any reason, no longer identifies with his or her cultural group. As a result, all the advantages of an ecclesial, social or cultural influence are lost. Uprooted from such stabilizing influences, an individual is obliged to look for and restart a belief system, moral standards, values and ideals.

The best remedy against the corrosive inroads of assimilation is a vibrant community of faith, in which the religious values are not compromised by vague survival techniques but are enlivened by the transmission and practice of the true faith in all of its expressions. The high rate of mixed marriages makes it all the more necessary to strengthen the ecclesial ties of the Orthodox family member and to facilitate the acculturation process of the non-Orthodox family member in his or her encounter with the Orthodox Church, her rich history and unique Tradition.

Whenever the ecclesial identity of people becomes weak or dormant, the practice of the Orthodox faith is obviously uncertain and ambiguous, and the desire for worship is severely impaired. To address this and similar problems the parish must be willing to mount a broad-based, multifaceted evangelical endeavor to reach both those within and those who are outside the Church. Certainly, good pastoral work, strong liturgical preaching, inspiring liturgical services, and effective community-building and social justice programs can facilitate this process.

Changing cultural and social realities

Other factors that have contributed to the gradual decline of the liturgical life in many of our parishes are the changing cultural and socioeconomic realities of church life in America. The social mobility of vast numbers of Orthodox people has made the neighborhood urban parish almost a thing of the past. New suburban parishes have taken their place and are thriving. But in both the inner-city church and in the suburban parish, one notices a decline in liturgical life. For one thing, the suburban parish is usually located in an isolated place away from public transportation, not readily accessible even to those parishioners who care to experience a fuller traditional corporate prayer life. For many people who live in the suburbs, going to church has become a chore, especially for families with young children who have to travel long distances and for older folks who lack the means of transportation to get to the church. Also, the modern parish – and this is a crucial point – is no longer the foremost place for social gathering and interaction.

The modern family is not like the immigrant family. The families in today's parish are mostly nuclear and, in many instances, not ethnically or even religiously homogeneous. Mixed marriages have been on the rise, altering the character and composition of the parish. Traditional family structures have also been altered. Single-parent families and blended families are more common today then ever before. And oftentimes the parish has failed to recognize, let alone to meet, these needs and respond to the expectations and challenges of the modern family.

In times past, most families lived around or near the church. More often than not, the families that the parish catered to were extended families, with grandparents and other relatives living in close proximity to each other. Devotion to the Church was usually expressed by regular attendance at all – or most – of the divine services by at least one or more members of the family. Today, the extended family is a rare phenomenon. Today, both parents usually work and the pressures of work, of family commitments, and of school and after-school activities of children severely limit the family's leisure time. As a result, the time allotted to church attendance has been limited and devotion to the Church is often expressed differently than in the past. For example, increased monetary contributions or the offering of talents for special parish activities and projects often take the place of church attendance and worship.

The depreciation of worship

Clearly, however, as we shall see below, these substitutes for worship are not simply a radical departure from traditional practice but point to a fundamental misunderstanding of the meaning and role of worship in the life of the faith community and its individual members.[9] This loss of meaning leads finally to the depreciation of worship as an essential element of the Christian life.

In part, this is due to the fact that we have failed to educate and train the people adequately in the ways of Christian living, of which prayer and worship are constitutive elements. We think that people know the significance and the meaning of corporate worship, when in fact they don't. We think that they know the value and the power of personal prayer; or that they know how to pray, but they don't. How can we expect the people to practice consciously that which they do not know or cannot appreciate? We offer them precious little by way of authentic liturgical education and training. We are content to feed them pietistic trifle that has little to do with real life and real liturgy. Also, look at the way we deal with the children in our parishes. For decades the practice has been to exclude them from the liturgical assembly. To this day in many parishes children are whisked away from the Divine Liturgy to attend Sunday School classes, encouraging them to think that worship is, at best, a secondary component of church life.

Spiritless worship does not engender commitment

We are obliged to pose some serious questions. Can, in fact, our people worship in spirit and in truth, when the liturgical services they experience are often times spiritless or pretentious?[10] Can people be attracted to worship when the explanations we give for the sacred rites are woefully inadequate, the language of prayer is incomprehensible, the preaching of the word is uninspiring, and the music is mediocre? Can people relate to worship when the community's commitment to translate its devotional acts into works of justice and loving-kindness is lacking or lukewarm? Simply put, we must come to realize that an aesthetically, intellectually, and spiritually impoverished liturgy only alienates the people from the Church and her worship. This is especially true of the young. It does not take much to disaffect and estrange the younger generation from the Church. Highly mobile, today's young people – 'Generation X' – are less likely than the generations that preceded them to be faithful and loyal to an institution – even when the institution is the Church – unless they are convinced of its compelling excellence and value.

Examples of liturgical creativity and vitality

In spite of many obstacles, thanks to the vision and persistence of clerical and lay leadership, many parishes pursue a vigorous liturgical life where the Sunday Church syndrome is held at bay. While the traditional daily cycle of worship in these parishes may not be always and fully operative, there is nevertheless an array of divine services scheduled weekly. More importantly, the Sunday morning experience is so powerful that it carries into the activities of the week.

In addition to a modified daily Orthros, there are, for example, other services such as the Saturday night vespers, the feast day vespers and liturgies, the Wednesday or Friday Paraklesis, and the Monday night Compline. Often, the divine services – whether they are conducted in the morning or evening – are followed by some form of catechetical instruction for various constituencies of the parish.

In many parishes feast days are celebrated with an evening Divine Liturgy on the eve of the Feast, in order to accommodate working people and their families. Many times, a community dinner allowing for social interaction among the people follows the liturgical service. Various prayer services are also scheduled in the evenings or mornings prior to parish meetings and events. Also, other corporate services are scheduled to meet the special needs of parishioners, including such services as the monthly Agiasmos, periodic celebrations of the sacrament of Holy Unction, and other traditional services. Some parishes hold an early morning weekly service that brings people together on their way to work. A breakfast and an appropriate presentation follow the service.

In addition, many clergy schedule time and find the opportune moments to instruct the people in the ways of worship by teaching them the order and the meaning of the divine services. With the assistance of qualified persons they teach the people how to sing the hymns and how to read the prayers of the divine services and encourage congregational participation. Also, they provide texts of the Service of the Hours for use by the people in their daily devotions and meditations, whether in the privacy of their homes and or in the workplace.

The parish is neither a monastery, nor a laboratory, nor a museum

It is important at this point to make something clear. We cannot and must not turn our parishes into monasteries, or into liturgical laboratories, or for that matter into a Byzantine cathedral or village church frozen in some century long past. The parish is not a monastic community. Therefore any attempt to impose upon it a monastic liturgical model is, in the long run, doomed to failure. Neither is the parish a laboratory where subjective liturgical experiments are carried out. Subjective liturgical experiments usually produce trivial liturgy and result in the making of trivial Christians. Neither is the parish a museum, a place that attempts to replicate some idealized past that never was. The parish is a living organism, pulsating with life. Like any living person, it carries a history but it lives in the present and anticipates and works for a better tomorrow.

Revitalizing the liturgical life of the parish

The revitalization of the liturgical life of the parish requires hard work and long-term commitments. Its success depends on the ability of the clergy to identify the real needs of the people and to motivate qualified parishioners to accept liturgical ministries. Its success also depends on the willingness of the parish to support the liturgical programs through adequate funding. It means that funds are made available for the preparation, production and/or purchase of materials and, above all, for the training – and when indicated by local conditions the financial support – of lectors, singers, choirs and other ministries essential to a vibrant liturgical life.

On a broader scale, the success of the parish liturgical renewal program requires that the whole Church engage herself in the effort. It means, espe-cially, that the Church is able and willing to organize, authorize, support and otherwise empower a Liturgical Commission composed of competent theologians, pastors, philologists and church musicians to deal with the issues and tasks of liturgical renewal and reform. However good these ef-forts – whether on a parish or on a diocesan or on an archdiocesan level – may be, liturgical renewal will never be truly effective unless we understand and come to grips with the deeper underlying reason for the liturgical im-poverishment we are – or seem to be – witnessing in our times.

The deeper problem – a crisis of worship – a crisis of faith

This points us in another direction, where, in fact, we will find the more serious reason for the decline in the vitality of parish life in all of its varied expressions and manifestations. Orthodox theologians[11] have long cautioned us of the dangers of secularism. However, I am obliged to make note of the fact that secularism has also produced some very positive things. Indeed, as Olivier Clement notes, the Church should not be afraid of secularization, but work to preserve it from its exaggerations and seek to orient it in an-other direction by exposing the human being to the irreducible and the non-assimilable, to a God who is neither tameable nor consumable but is the very source of salvation;[12] by reminding society of its ethical traditions and the legitimacy of existence; and by speaking boldly in the public square of the antinomy of the cross and the glory, of a God "who comes alongside humankind in death and suffering to open up before him unexpected vistas of resurrection."[13]

However, this is neither the time nor place to talk about the beneficial effects of secularization in western societies, such as the curbing of militant clericalism, the appearance of the non-totalitarian state, the creative ad-vances in technology and medicine, and the acceptance of the other in his or her otherness in an authentic pluralism. Indeed, the very subject of secu-larism with its positive and negative effects is far too complex an issue to be dealt with properly in this context. Nevertheless, for our purposes it is im-portant that we examine some of the negative aspects of secularism, so that we may better understand the extent and meaning of the crisis of worship that some believe is now gripping the Church.

According to Metropolitan Anthony Bloom, a secular society is marked by two characteristics. First, in a secular society human beings have a blurred, weak and anemic sense of God. And second, in a secular society people develop an acute awareness of the temporal world. They tend to see the world and life essentially in material terms – inert, opaque, autonomous and self-sufficient, blind to their own depth. As a result, people in a secular society are inclined to "reject or ignore or be insensitive to the other dimension of the world, its transparency to the Divine Presence, its dimension of immensity and eternity."[14]

Herein lie the tension and the problem, since Christians view the world and life differently. For the Christian, the world is not a timeless self-sufficient entity of recurring cycles void of ultimate meanings; and life is not composed of competing chaotic forces where all forms of violence and death reign supreme and the struggle for the survival of the fittest is waged. Rather, Christians see the world and life in sacramental terms, as having "a calling, a destiny and a vocation, capable of being God-bearing, filled with divine Presence, without being destroyed or ceasing to be itself."[15] For the Christian, the world and every human being in it are deep enough to contain God. At the heart of the Gospel is the truth of God's solidarity with his creatures, of the Presence of his rule and of his gentle mercy and tender love which are the foundation both of salvation and of judgment.

Yet, if we think of it, even Christians can lose sight of God and ignore him. On our journey towards the Kingdom we are all susceptible to failure. Seduced by sin, we too can fall away from God, forsake and lose him. Sin is not only the denial and rejection of God but also an ignorance of him.[16] Therefore, the loss or the absence of the sense of God is a matter of deep concern for the Church.

The tragedy of secularism, which Father Schmemann insists is a Christian heresy, lies in the fact that it distorts, exaggerates and therefore mutilates something true.[17] "Secularism," he writes, "is above all a *negation of worship*. Not of God's existence, not of some kind of transcendence and therefore of some kind of religion. If secularism in theological terms is a heresy, it is primarily a heresy about man. It is the negation of man as a worshipping being, as *homo adorans:* the one for whom worship is the essential act, which both 'posits' his humanity and fulfills it."[18] Herein lies the great fallacy. No one is capable of eradicating the yearning for the wholly Other from one's soul. We have been made to worship, that is, to enter into communion with the living God. Therefore, we either learn to come before the true God in prayer and solemn feast or we delude ourselves with the worship idols.

While there is still much church-going and there are pockets where the dominant cultural tone is religious, modern American culture has freed itself from religious tutelage, values and authority. As the state of irreligion spreads and more people are drawn into its web, there is a tendency among a broad spectrum of the populace to dismiss worship as outdated, useless and unproductive.[19] When people – as a society or as individuals – lose sight of God and deny the sacramentality of creation, an air of unreality overtakes the world of faith. As God ceases to be relevant in the lives of people, the need for worship fades away and vanishes. Faith and worship are inseparable. When one withers and dies, so does the other. Worship is centered on God. It is "an epiphany of God, a means of his revelation, presence and power."[20] Hence, when there is little or no faith, we are faced with a crisis of worship, the product of the crisis of faith.

Creating a sound cultural context

Several years ago a commission of theologians, pastors and sociologists was established by the Greek Orthodox Archdiocese to examine the needs of the faithful and propose a theological agenda for the Greek Orthodox Church in America as the Church moved into the third millennium of the Christian faith. The Commission Report was published and gained wide circulation. In the first section, titled "The Faith Crisis," the Report maintains the following:

> Despite the resurgence of some religious affiliations, western society is on the whole marked by a cultural crisis of faith, that is, a wholesale drifting away from traditional religious and moral values which now has become a sociological condition affecting all religious groups... A tendency exists among bona fide Orthodox Church members to limit their religious participation to occasional church attendance. Such casual church membership often leads to a movement away from the Church, not so much in a sense of renunciation or joining another body, but in the sense that Orthodox Christianity no longer is a prime definer of one's identity.[21]

In the process of acculturation, doctrine and liturgy accentuate the separateness or particularity of the group, maintaining its identity. Therefore, to be true to its mission, the parish is obliged to provide for all of its people – both young and old – that cultural context in which faith and worship are vigorously dynamic, are rooted in life, and exemplify the meaning and impact of Christ upon the world. In such a cultural context clergy and lay leaders work hard to make the riches of our doctrinal, ethical and liturgical tradition available to the people in ways that fill their lives with meaning, purpose, hope and joy.

The creation of such a cultural context requires unfailing commitment and continuous monitoring. Parish leaders are obliged to evaluate regularly the life and activities of the parish. A parish that is organized in a manner that unites the faithful dynamically, makes Christian truths live in the hearts of people, and integrates these truths into life and acts upon them in concrete ways signifies that the liturgical, evangelical, educational, pastoral and philanthropic activities of the parish are well focused, vibrant and effective. However, where the secular mode of living and doing business has crept into the parish, where spiritual identities have been blurred and compromised, and where individual and communal activities have become ambiguous, the parish is obliged to reconsider its agenda, redirect its priorities, and revitalize the theological enterprise.

We must remember that the parish is, above all else, the fundamental eucharistic cell of the Church, where the saving work of the Church is actively pursued and enacted. The parish exists for one essential purpose to bring salvation to the world through the preaching of the Word and the celebration of the sacraments. Everything the parish is and does emanates essentially from the weekly celebration of the Divine Liturgy. At the Eucharist the new life in Christ is continuously advanced and the 'People of God' are inspired, enabled and emboldened to celebrate joyously the liturgy after the Liturgy, to become faithful witnesses of Christ in their everyday activities both at home and in the workplace, in the words of St. Gregory the Theologian to be "as instruments played by the Holy Spirit."

The times require that we work diligently and continuously to enrapture the people with the truth and power of the Gospel, in order to facilitate and effect the transformation of naïve religiosity into conscious Orthodox belief, practice and piety. In response to the moral and spiritual imperative of the Gospel, every parish must strive to remain faithful to the Orthodox spirit, vision and ethos, and accept the challenge to be truly the Church.

NOTES

[1] Charles Gusmer, *Wholesome Worship*. (Washington, DC, 1989), p. 17.

[2] My comments are based chiefly on my experiences as a priest of the Greek Orthodox Archdiocese and as a member of the faculty of Holy Cross Greek Orthodox School of Theology.

[3] Gilbert Osdiek, *Catechesis for Liturgy* (Washington, DC, 1986) pp. 167 - 79.

[4] Gilbert Osdiek, *Catechesis for Liturgy*, p. 178.

[5] Paul Meyendorf, "The Liturgical Path of Orthodoxy in America," in *SVTQ*, 40, 1&2 (1996), p. 54.

[6] Ibid. p. 54.

[7] Some of the issues that pertain to Orthodoxy in America are discussed in two previous articles, "The American Context: A Testing Ground for Orthodox Identity and Mission" and "Particularities of the American Context: Lessons and Responses." These essays are included in the second volume of this series, *Essays in Theology and Liturgy* (Brookline, MA 2001), pp. 51-68 and 69-92.

[8] See my article, "The American Context: A Testing Ground for Orthodox Identity and Mission," pp. 52 and 151.

[9] For a frank discussion on the liturgical problems that are facing the Church in the changing cultural realities of our times see *Passion and Resurrection* (a publication of New Skete Monastery, Cambridge, NY 1995), pp. xv-xli.

[10] For example, think of the mediocre rendering of the texts by celebrants, lectors, singers and choirs that we sometimes encounter.

[11] See for example, John Meyendorff, "Worship in a Secular World," in *SVTQ*, 12, 3&4 (1968), pp. 120-124. Alexander Schmemann, "Worship in a Secular Age," in *SVTQ*, 16, 1 (1972), pp. 3-16. Metropolitan Anthony Bloom of Sourozh, "Worship in a Secular Society," in Wiebe Vos, ed., *Worship and Secularization* (Bussum Holland 1970) p. 120-130. Olivier Clement, "Witnessing in a Secularized Society," in G. Lemopoulos, ed., *Your Will Be Done* (Geneva, 1989). p. 117-135.

[12] Olivier Clement, "Witnessing in a Secularized Society," pp. 120-132

[13] Ibid. p. 132.

[14] Metropolitan Anthony, "Worship in a Secular Society," pp. 121-123.

[15] Ibid. pp. 124-125.

[16] Ibid. p. 122.

[17] A. Schmemann, "Worship in a Secular Age," p. 11.

[18] Ibid. p. 4.

[19] See Charles Davis, "Ghetto or Desert: Liturgy in a Cultural Dilemma," in W. Vos, ed., *Worship and Secularization*, pp. 10-27.

[20] A. Schmemann, "Worship in a Secular Age," p. 5.

[21] "Report to His Eminence Archbishop Iakovos – Commission: Archdiocesan Theological Agenda," in *GOTR*, 34, 3 (1989), pp. 286, 301.

Paul Meyendorff

Nearly forty years ago, Fr. Alexander Schmemann wrote a series of three prophetic articles entitled "Problems of Orthodoxy in America."[1] The second of these was devoted to "The Liturgical Problem." It might be worth our time to review the observations he made back in 1964 to see how much or how little has changed since that time.

He begins by affirming the centrality of worship in Orthodoxy. Its primary function is "to immerse the man in the spiritual reality, beauty and depth of the Kingdom of God and to *change* his mind and heart."[2] He goes on to address the challenge posed in America by secularism, according to which the worship life of the community exists in isolation from all other aspects, administrative, financial, social, etc. He concludes his introductory section by stating that there is "a deep *liturgical* crisis."[3] He then goes on to address a number of issues and challenges.

Liturgical language

The first of these is what he terms "The Linguistic Reduction."[4] He argues against those who would say that simply translating all the services into English will resolve all problems. Schmemann certainly agrees that worship should be conducted in a language understandable to participants. At the same time, he is keenly aware that the translation of liturgical texts is no easy task, for it involves far more than translating Greek or Slavonic words into their English equivalents. That is because liturgical texts are first of all poetic texts, and any translation that fails to take this into account is inadequate. Many translations in his day "remain doubly 'alien': alien to the poetical power of the original and alien to the poetical possibilities of the English language." He concludes the section on liturgical language by complaining about the chaotic process of translation going on in his time – a process "without plan, without supervision, without qualifications and without even the discussion of the problems involved in translation."

143

Not much has changed since then. We have an ever-increasing number of translations and more appear every year. The chaos has only increased, and the discussion about translation often seems stuck on the neuralgic questions of whether we should use Elizabethan English ("Thee and thou") or a more contemporary style, and, increasingly, the question of inclusive language. Any new text is evaluated on the basis of these two issues alone. Credit should be given to the monastic community of New Skete, which has attempted to delve more deeply into the question of translation,[5] though their voice is largely ignored.

Largely as a result of disagreement over these two issues, we are presently in a state of paralysis. The recent attempt to create a unified liturgical translation committee under the auspices of the Standing Conference of Canonical Orthodox Bishops in America (SCOBA) has gone nowhere, and this group's new translation of the Liturgy of St. John Chrysostom has failed to obtain much acceptance or support from the hierarchy, who are even more divided on these questions than the clergy or the faithful.

The Typikon

Orthodox liturgical practice is regulated by a mysterious book called the *Typikon*. Never translated in its entirety into English, it is nevertheless constantly appealed to by self-proclaimed experts in liturgy, who place it on a par with the Ten Commandments and believe that it has been the norm since the days of the early Church. Reaching its final form in fourteenth-century Mt. Athos, the so-called "Typikon of St. Sabas" subsequently became the sole *Typikon* for all Orthodoxy and was the only one ever published.[6] It is a monastic book regulating the daily, weekly and annual cycles of worship. On a typical weekday, if one strictly follows the rules, services last over eight hours. The Saturday night vigil alone lasts nearly that long.[7] Difficult as it is to carry this out in a monastery, it is virtually impossible in a parish. As a result, services are always abbreviated, and, in the absence of any guidelines, these abbreviations are often arbitrary and haphazard, doing violence to the very structure and content of the liturgy.

In the early twentieth century, in response to a questionnaire, bishops of the Russian Orthodox Church called for large-scale reforms in church life and organization.[8] Regarding the *Typikon*, some twenty bishops (a third of the Russian episcopate!) called for the development of a parish *Typikon*, which would regulate and codify parish usage and eliminate abuses. The bishops also expressed considerable concern over the manner in which services were conducted. In particular, they called for greater participation on the part of the laity. Eleven bishops called for the introduction of congregational singing. They expressed concern that hymns and readings were, because of their mode of performance, incomprehensible to the people. Five bishops, including Archbishop (now Saint) Tikhon of North America,[9] recommended the recitation of the so-called "secret prayers" aloud. Many bishops called for the elimination of repetitious litanies on the one hand, and the expansion of scriptural readings and the restoration of liturgical preaching on the other.

The tragic events which followed derailed any possibility of bringing these reforms into reality. The projected council, which was to deal with these matters, was not called, and the Council of 1917-18, held in the midst of the Russian Revolution, was able only to reestablish the Russian patriarchate and elect Tikhon to the position. Communist oppression began immediately and precluded further discussion about the internal life of the church, particularly on liturgical matters. The subsequent adoption of many of the above reforms by the Renovationist Church after 1922 only made things more difficult. As the Russian Church battled for survival under the yoke of a militantly atheist regime, it was in no position to face the issue of liturgical reform. And even today, more than eighty years later, any suggestion concerning liturgical change usually leads to accusations of "Renovationism." But the questions raised by the Russian bishops in 1905 are as valid today as they were then, and the church, now freed from communism, is beginning, very tentatively and slowly, to address them. We in America, despite our own internal problems, have no such excuse.

Secularism – the real problem

Yet, Schmemann argues, the real challenge in America comes not from these inherited problems, but from secularism. Thus, resolving questions of liturgical language or the *typikon*, restoring frequent reception of Holy Communion as we have substantially done in recent years – all this by itself is insufficient and, in fact, misses the point. The real foe, he insists, is western secularism and the "American way of life." According to the secular worldview, the religious and the secular perspectives exist in separate realms and have little or no mutual impact. Thus, the contemporary, secular persons can attend church for one or two hours on Sunday and then live during the rest of the week as though "the fundamental religious realities of Creation, Fall and Redemption" did not exist. They see themselves primarily as self-sufficient or autonomous. Religion can be held in great honor and may supply ethical standards and provide help and comfort, but it does not transform our lives, does not make God and His Kingdom the very content of our life.[10]

It takes but one look at the liturgical life of the Orthodox parish in America to see the truth of his words. We have, for the most part, become a Sunday church peopled by Sunday Christians. Liturgy has lost that power to transform our lives, to refer every aspect of our lives to God and to His Kingdom. And it is clearly too much to ask the Sunday morning liturgy, which typically lasts little over an hour, performed in a way that is often incomprehensible to the average parishioner, to do all that. The liturgy has thus lost the power to challenge us to be what we are called. All too often, it functions like a placebo and gives us a false sense of security. As long as we fulfill our minimum obligation by paying our dues, coming to church on Sunday, receiving Holy Communion weekly, monthly, quarterly, or annually (all these patterns remain today), we are okay. We are perfectly happy in our little ghettos, be they Greek Orthodox, Antiochian Orthodox, Serbian Orthodox, Russian Orthodox, and even American Orthodox. But all this remains disconnected from our everyday life at home, at school, or in the workplace.

Clearly, and Schmemann is absolutely correct in this regard, the problem is not primarily liturgical. No amount of liturgical renewal and reform will by itself resolve this problem. What is needed is a spiritual renewal in all aspects of church life, including church organization, education and liturgical life. All must go together. It is not enough simply to make changes in the liturgy, for then the significant developments in eucharistic practice in recent decades should have produced far better results. Indeed, some have compared tinkering with the liturgy to rearranging the deck chairs on the Titanic. Nevertheless, few today would dispute the need for frequent reception of Holy Communion, the obvious value of celebrating the liturgy in the vernacular, or the theological rationale for reading aloud the so-called "secret prayers," particularly the anaphora. But it is evident that such reforms in themselves are not sufficient. They must be realized within the context of an evangelical and spiritual revival within the church.

Liturgical life, however, will remain the key. This is so both for theological and practical reasons: It is true for theological reasons because liturgy, the Eucharist in particular, lies at the center of Christian life. The Church is realized precisely when it gathers together to be the Body of Christ. There is no church in the abstract, only concrete assemblies gathered around the altar to celebrate the Eucharist and to be transformed into Christ's Body.[11] The eucharistic prayer itself affirms this when the Holy Spirit is called to descend "on us, and on the offered gifts." And, of course, what is true of the church is also true of every individual Christian, who through the Eucharist affirms his/her membership in Christ's Body, the Church.

It is true for purely practical reasons as well, because that one hour on Sunday is the one time that the people are there, and can therefore be reached. We have to begin with what we have. From the very beginnings of the Church, the liturgical assembly has been the primary, and often the only, place where instruction, formation, and ultimately transformation have taken place. What has changed in recent times is the amount of time our people spend in church. Worse yet is the still ongoing practice in some parishes of conducting church school for children during the Sunday liturgy, for not only does it transmit little content (how much can you teach in an hour a week?), but it teaches children not to go to church!

So where do we go from here? I have elsewhere pointed out several areas we Orthodox will need to address in the future.[12] I would like simply to outline them here, in the hope that they will serve as fodder for further discussion.

Lay participation: the priesthood of the laity

In the liturgy, the priestly function is exercised by *the entire community*, by virtue of their baptism. The primary function of the ordained clergy is to *preside* over the priestly community, to unite *their* priestly prayer. This is why liturgical prayers always use the first person plural. Nowhere is this clearer than at the very heart of the anaphora of St John Chrysostom:

> *Priest*: Remembering therefore this our Savior's command and all that has been done for us: the Cross, the Tomb, the Resurrection on the third day, the Ascension into heaven, the Sitting at the right hand, the Second and glorious Coming again; Offering your own of your own – in all things and for all things – *People*: We praise you, we bless you, we give thanks to you, O Lord, and we pray to you, our God.[13]

This is all one sentence, and the only active verbs are those which express the action of the gathered assembly and are sung by them: *We praise you, we bless you, we give thanks to you*. This is a sacrificial prayer, and the entire assembly is here performing its sacrifice of praise. Yet in both pagan and Jewish practice, only the priest offers sacrifices: here, it is evidently the whole assembly, the priestly people (cf. 1 Pet 2:9), which does this.[14]

Yet the way in which we celebrate the liturgy often obscures this fact, and few lay people are even aware that the anaphora is their prayer. For many centuries, already, the laity could not even hear the words of the eucharistic prayer, which was recited silently by the priest, who stood behind the closed doors of the sanctuary. And, in more recent times, the people's responses have been taken away from them by cantors or choirs, who often stand not among the congregation but at some distance away, in a choir loft. The laity have thus become an audience watching a performance put on by the clergy and the singers. The adoption of pews by Orthodox in America makes our churches resemble theatres and further enhances the perception of the laity that they are a passive audience attending a show. This notion of liturgy as a spectator sport is further encouraged by the symbolic interpretations of the liturgy which abound and which explain it as a pictorial demonstration of the life of Christ. All these developments serve to minimize the laity's role in the liturgy, except as passive spectators. And, because the laity are not engaged in the liturgy, it has little transformational effect on their lives.

What is needed, therefore, is a concerted effort to restore their proper role to the laity. Some steps are already being taken. Frequent communion has become more common, in fact has become the rule in many parishes. The recitation aloud of the so-called "secret prayers" is beginning to gain acceptance. But much remains to be done. There needs to be a broad discussion among our hierarchs, clergy and laity about their respective roles in the liturgy, and in the life of the church in general. The clericalism which abounds needs to be overcome. Ways need to be found to involve the laity more directly in the liturgy: why, for example, is it necessary to have a choir or cantor sing "Amen" or "Lord, have mercy"? Could not at least some parts of the service be sung congregationally? Antiphonal psalmody, with the people singing refrains, could also easily be restored without altering the structure of our services. Knowledge of liturgical history is particularly helpful in this regard, since it allows us to see how liturgically impoverished we have become, as well as offer some models, particularly from the ancient cathedral rite, which we might find useful in the present situation.

All this will come to nothing, however, until we all – hierarchs, clergy and faithful – come to understand the priestly identity of all Christians acquired by virtue of our baptism into Christ. When we are baptized we are incorporated into Christ and his Church; we assume our proper function as kings, priests and prophets. Through baptism we are adopted into sonship and become co-heirs of the Kingdom, "a chosen race, a royal priesthood, God's own people" (1 Pet 2:9). Yet baptism is virtually absent from the liturgical life of our churches. Most of the time, it is a private affair conducted at some convenient time with only family and friends in attendance. For many of the laity, it has little if any significance, except as the occasion for a party, and its ecclesial dimension is simply lost. Few people are even aware how central baptism was in the life of the early Church, how the structures and services of Lent, Holy Week and Easter were centered on the preparation of candidates for baptism, which was carried out as the highlight of the paschal vigil and culminated in the Eucharist, at which the neophytes partook of the eucharistic banquet.[15] How far removed we are from this today!

Indeed, it would be fair to say that baptism has largely slipped from the memory of the Church. The modern emphasis, in both East and West, on the Eucharist and eucharistic ecclesiology, while certainly appropriate, is deficient if it is not balanced by an equally strong emphasis on baptism and on *baptismal* ecclesiology. Just as baptismal liturgical practice has slipped from the realm of the Church's public liturgy by becoming privatized and marginalized, so too the Church's baptismal theology. While much ink has been spilled in composing books on the Eucharist, relatively few serious works on baptism have seem the light of day. Many contemporary issues both within Orthodoxy and on the ecumenical scene could be addressed, were we to develop a sound baptismal theology and ecclesiology.

A first step, which can easily be implemented at the parish level, is to restore baptism as a liturgical activity of the entire parish. This would mean, first of all, performing baptisms in the presence of the entire community, and not just selected family and friends. Ideally, this would also mean celebrating baptisms in the context of a eucharistic liturgy, in order that all may see that baptism is incorporation into a local, eucharistic community, rather than a private event. The baptismal service can easily be incorporated into the regular Sunday eucharistic liturgy. In the case of adult baptisms or chrismations, these can be integrated into the lenten and paschal cycle, with a catechumenate during Lent and baptism and chrismation at the liturgy of Holy Saturday.[16] In this way, the faithful will be regularly reminded of their own baptism and its implications, as well as of their responsibility to nurture their own faith and that of others.

Daily prayer

Rejoice always, *pray constantly*, give thanks in all circumstances; for this is the will of God in Christ Jesus for you. (1 Thes 5:16-18)

Christianity developed out of a Jewish tradition that knew the discipline of daily prayer. The pious Jew, and Jesus among them, prayed at least two or three times a day. The *Didache*, the earliest book on "church order," dating to the early second century, instructs Christians to recite the Lord's Prayer three times a day. By the end of the second century, the times of prayer are generally fixed, typically at morning, noon, evening and midnight. At first performed in private by each Christian, in the fourth century daily prayer moved into the public arena with the development of the cathedral and monastic offices. Through the centuries, the Church has maintained the practice of daily prayer in numerous ways, adapting the daily cycle to the exigencies of each age.[17] Evidently, being Christian did not begin or end with attending the eucharistic liturgy on Sunday morning.

Undoubtedly the chief casualty in the process of transplanting Orthodoxy to the New World has been the tradition of daily prayer. Not only the daily office, but even Saturday evening vespers and Sunday morning matins,[18] are on the verge of extinction. Indeed, it would not be an exaggeration to say that the most significant liturgical reform of the twentieth century has been the virtual abandonment of the office.

The reasons for this development are numerous: increased secularization; the fact that people do not live close to their parish church; the absence of monasticism, which has always maintained the ideal of constant prayer; imitation of western, Protestant patterns of worship; competition from television, sports and other forms of entertainment... Whatever the causes, the results are worrisome. Not only have we abandoned a discipline of prayer, which always has been central to Christian life, but in the process we have also abandoned the rich body of Byzantine hymnography, which has formed and educated countless generations of Orthodox Christians.

Orthodoxy cannot survive as a Sunday-only church. We must recover the practice of daily prayer, both private and liturgical. Being a member of the Church implies that we have a living, ongoing relationship with God and with the members of Christ's Body, the Church. This is not a relationship that we can simply turn on and off, once a week. Should we not at least begin discussing how we might go about restoring this essential dimension of Christian life? The tradition of the Church provides us with numerous models: there is much variety in times of prayer, in the types of celebrations, both communal and private, cathedral and monastic. Drawing on this rich heritage, we need to develop resources that might be used by families, by small groups, as well as by our parishes. But what is needed first of all, of course, is a conversion among ourselves and our faithful, a realization that Christianity is a way of life, and not simply the fulfilling of a "Sunday obligation."

The lectionary

The reading of Scripture and the sermon have always formed an integral part of Christian worship. It is not possible here to go into a detailed analysis of the development of the Orthodox lectionary,[19] but it would not be unfair to say that scriptural literacy has all but disappeared. Our only exposure to Scripture is through the brief selections from the epistle and the gospel read on Sunday, as well as through the sermon (assuming that the homily has any connection to the readings, which is not always the case). The vast corpus of Byzantine hymns and prayers, largely inspired by Scripture, has, *de facto*, become inaccessible to the faithful, because the Sunday liturgy, the only service the great majority ever attend, contains almost no variable hymnography. And even when the faithful do attend vespers or matins, the hymnography is often performed in a language or musical style that renders it virtually incomprehensible. As for the prayers, including the anaphora, these are still read silently in a majority of parishes.

We are left, therefore, only with the reading of the epistle and gospel on Sunday morning. These two brief selections now must bear virtually the entire weight of transmitting our scriptural heritage. The Old Testament reading, once an integral part of the Liturgy of the Word, has long since disappeared.[20] And the selections from the New Testament are very limited in scope. Key texts, such as the Sermon on the Mount or St. Paul's eloquent passage on Christian love (1 Cor 13) are *never* read on any Sunday, while some passages, such as the account of the Gerasene demoniac, are repeated several times! The image of Christ that emerges from our Sunday lectionary is that of a miracle worker, a magician, more than that of a teacher. And pastors do eventually run out of ideas preaching about pigs jumping into the sea.

The faithful must be provided with access to Scripture. The Bible must be read in church, and it must be preached about. It is not sufficient to hand out copies of the Bible to our parishioners and tell them to read it at home. Nor are Bible studies adequate. To understand Scripture, one must have "the mind of the Church," and this can only be achieved within an ecclesial, liturgical context. Private interpretation is, for the Orthodox, never sufficient.

In order to make the Bible live again within our liturgy, we must begin by broadening our Sunday lectionary, at least for the period between Pentecost and the beginning of the pre-Lenten cycle. The present Byzantine lectionary spreads the reading throughout the week, with the result that the selections appointed for Monday through Saturday are never heard: the Eucharist is celebrated daily only in monasteries. What would be desirable, then, is some provision for a sequential reading on Sundays alone, which would mean the creation of a two- or three-year cycle. This would make it possible a course reading of entire books and allow preachers to deal with texts in sequence and in their proper context. This is precisely what we find, for examples, in the sermons of great preachers like John Chrysostom, who obviously had the freedom to work his way through one book at a time. The faithful would in this way have the opportunity to hear far more of the Scriptures, and pastors would have a richer lode of material to draw upon.

Conclusion

The crisis about which Fr. Schmemann wrote nearly forty years ago has only deepened. The canonical problem has not been resolved. The spiritual problem is as acute as ever. The liturgical problem is still with us, despite many positive developments in recent years. Yet the challenge of the Church today is no different than it was nearly two millennia ago in Palestine, or two centuries ago in Alaska. The Church's primary task, now as then, is to bring humanity face to face with the person of Christ, to restore communion between God and humanity. Everything that the Church does, all its structures, all its programs and activities, are never ends in themselves, but must be directed toward this goal and judged for their effectiveness in bringing this communion about. This applies particularly to the Church's liturgy, because the liturgy, the Eucharist in particular, is the privileged locus of this divine–human encounter. And for most people, the Sunday liturgy is their *only* encounter with the Church. This implies a constant reevaluation, as well as sensitivity to the times and to the society in which the Church is called to exercise its ministry. It implies as well an openness to change – and in this regard the Byzantine liturgical tradition has undergone more changes, has been more adaptable, than any other liturgical tradition!

We can simply do nothing and complain that we are losing our "traditions," not to mention our people. Or, at the dawn of the twenty-first century, we can put on the "mind of the fathers" and respond, faithfully, creatively, and boldly, to the challenges of a new age.

NOTES

[1] "Problems of Orthodoxy in America, I: The Canonical Problem," *St. Vladimir's Seminary Quarterly* 8 (1964), pp. 67-85; "II: The Liturgical Problem," *ibid.*, 8 (1964), pp. 164-185; "III: The Spiritual Problem," *ibid.*, 9 (1965), pp. 171-193.

[2] *Ibid.*, p. 165. Emphasis in original.

[3] *Ibid.*, p. 166. Emphasis in original.

[4] *Ibid.*, pp. 166-68.

[5] See the introductions to their liturgical books, which typically include an introduction stating their views on the question: e.g., *A Book of Prayers* (Cambridge, NY: New Skete, 1988), pp. xvii-xlv; *Sighs of the Spirit* (Cambridge, NY: New Skete, 1997), pp. xvii-xxxix.

[6] See M. Arranz, "Les grandes étapes de la liturgie byzantine: Palestine-Byzance-Russie. Essai d'aperçu historique," in *Liturgie de l'église particulière, liturgie de l'église universelle* (Bibliotheca *Ephemerides Liturgicae* Subsidia, 7) (Rome, 1976), pp. 43-72. For a more popular survey in English, see R. Taft, *The Byzantine Rite: A Short History* (Collegeville: Liturgical Press, 1992). The so-called "Typikon of the Great Church," used by most Greek and Arabic churches, is but a late nineteenth-century adaptation of the Typikon of St. Sabas. It has nothing in common with the original Typikon of the Great Church, which regulated the cathedral rite of Hagia Sophia up to the early thirteenth century before being replaced by a monastic Typikon after the sack of Constantinople by the Crusaders in 1204.

[7] The renowned Russian liturgical scholar, M. Skaballanovich, describes an experiment at the Kievan Theological Academy in the early twentieth century to celebrate a complete vigil: it took months to prepare, cost several thousand rubles to find and print the necessary texts, and lasted from 6 p.m. to 1:50 a.m. He reported that the project generated much enthusiasm, but was not repeated. See his *Tolkovyi Tipikon*, vyp. 2 (Kiev, 1913), pp. 330-336.

[8] The survey responses are published in three volumes, *Otzyvy eparkhial'nykh arkhiereev po voprosam o tserkovnoi reforme* (St. Petersburg, 1906). For an analysis, see J. Cunningham, *A Vanquished Hope: The Movement for Church Renewal in Russia, 1905-1906* (Crestwood, NY: St. Vladimir's Seminary Press, 1981). See also the unpublished M.Div. thesis at St. Vladimir's Seminary by John Shimchik, "The Responses of the Russian Episcopate Concerning Worship – 1905 and the Liturgical Situation in America" (1980).

[9] *Otzyvy* I, p. 537.

[10] "The Problems of Orthodoxy in America: I," pp. 172-74.

[11] This is what is known as "eucharistic ecclesiology." See, for example, the writings of Metropolitan John Zizioulas, esp. his *Being as Communion* (Crestwood, NY: St. Vladimir's Seminary Press, 1985).

[12] See my article, "The Liturgical Path of Orthodoxy in America," *St. Vladimir's Theological Quarterly* 40 (1996), pp. 43-64.

[13] English translation from *The Divine Liturgy of Our Father Among the Saints John Chrysostom* (Oxford University Press, 1995), p. 32.

[14] Not until the fourth century is the term "priest" applied to ordained clergy. The best discussion on this can be found in R.E. Brown, *Priest and Bishop: Biblical Reflections* (New York: Paulist Press, 1970). See also my article cited in note 12 above, pp. 55-7.

[15] For a popular presentation on this subject, see A. Schmemann's seminal work, *Of Water and the Spirit* (Crestwood, NY: St. Vladimir's Seminary Press, 1974).

[16] The Holy Saturday liturgy is the original paschal, baptismal vigil.

[17] On the early Christian period, see P. Bradshaw, *Daily Prayer in the Early Church* (New York: Oxford, 1982). On the development of the office, see R. Taft, *The Liturgy of the Hours in East and West* (Collegeville, MN: Liturgical Press, 1986).

[18] In Slavic and Athonite practice, according to the "Typikon of St. Sabas," Sunday matins is celebrated on Saturday evening after vespers, and not on Sunday morning.

[19] But see the useful survey of this topic in D. Petras, "The Gospel Lectionary of the Byzantine Church," *St. Vladimir's Theological Quarterly* 41 (1997), pp. 113-140.

[20] This probably happened as early as the seventh century, though Old Testament readings did survive in Lenten vespers, as well as on the eves of feasts. Cf. Juan Mateos, *La célébration de la parole dans la liturgie byzantine* (=Orientalia Christiana Analecta, 191) (Rome: Pontificium Institutum Studiorum Orientalium, 1971), pp. 130-33.

LITURGICAL ADAPTATION: THREE ILLUSTRATIONS

JOHN KLENTOS

It is very difficult to address a topic that is also being treated by the two established experts in the American field, Fr. Alkiviadis Calivas and Prof. Paul Meyendorff. I am truly thankful for this opportunity, and have chosen to reflect on practical liturgical adaptation as response to concrete parish needs here and now. Some initial theological background and a brief statement of our current position will preface three practical illustrations.

I. THEORETICAL BACKGROUND

Our discussion properly begins with the term itself: the English word *liturgy* comes from the Greek *leitourgeia*. Derived from *leitos* (of the people) and *ergon* (work*)*, the word means simply *work of the people*. In this sense, *liturgy* can refer to any sort of act by, for, or on behalf of the public. A specifically Christian understanding of *liturgy* is based upon the biblical use of words relating to *leitourgeia*, found in well over 150 verses in the Septuagint and Greek New Testament, and can be summarized as ritual worship of God and proclamation of the Gospel.

Liturgy is focused on salvation

If liturgy is the work of the people, we are faced with the question: What is the aim of this action? Why *do* liturgy? Whenever I ask this, people usually maintain that we do liturgy because God requires it. Such an answer, however, misses the mark. The prophet Isaiah's words are enough to make any liturgist quake:

"What to me is the multitude of your sacrifices?" says the Lord; "I have had enough of burnt offerings of rams and the fat of fed beasts; I do not delight in the blood of bulls, or of lambs, or of goats. When you come to appear before me, who asked this from your hand? Trample my courts no more; bringing offerings is futile; incense is an abomination to me. Your new moons and your appointed festivals my soul hates; they have become a burden to me, I am weary of bearing them." (Is 1:11-14)

Alexander Schmemann has explained that we do liturgy not because God needs it, but because it is the condition of our Christian life.[1]

Liturgy is fundamentally related to our divine mission and quest for union with God. As St. Luke put it: "Jesus called the twelve together and gave them power and authority over all demons and to cure diseases, and he sent them out *to proclaim the kingdom of God and to heal*" (Lk 9:1f). In the Epistle to the Ephesians, we discover that our destiny as Christians is that "we might live for the praise of [Christ's] glory" (1:12).

Beyond proclaiming the Gospel and praising Christ, the liturgy offers union with God, as explained by St. Nicholas Cabasilas: "By [the sacred Mysteries] we are begotten and formed and wondrously united to the Savior, for they are the means by which, as Paul says, 'in Him we live, and move, and have our being'."[2]

We celebrate liturgy: to *proclaim* the present and coming Kingdom of God; to *offer* the divine, gratuitous gift of salvation; and to *respond* to all this with commemoration, thanksgiving, and praise.

Liturgy is ecclesial action

People are often tempted to treat liturgy as a static thing which can be dissected, analyzed and replicated. This approach, however, is an abstraction and a reduction. Christian liturgy is the dynamic *action* of the people – their celebration of and participation in the mystery of salvation.[3] Kenan Osborne articulates this existential dimension of liturgy using the language of postmodern theology:

Theologians and church officials speak freely of baptism and eucharist. Baptism, they say, is this or that. Eucharist, they say, is this or that. However, baptism is not a replication, a verbal phrase emphasizing a thing. Each baptism is not a duplication of a rote activity, nor is each baptism the enfleshing of a duplicative reality. Rather, each baptism is an existential event, an existential action, an existential *Ereignis*. Each baptism is an individualized, historically discrete, temporally unrepeatable moment in the life of an individual, of a particular community of Christians, and of the temporal-historical presence of an active God. Each baptism is a unique event; each eucharist is equally a unique event. To use a Scotistic term, there is an *Haecceitas* – a "thisness" – about each sacramental celebration. The reality of baptism can only be found in the singularized happenings of these existential baptisms and eucharists. Outside of these actualized and singularized baptismal and eucharistic events, the very terms baptism and euchairst have at best some generic, nonrealistic, linguistically conventional meaning.[4]

Liturgy is action and event. It is *not* about ink on paper. God's saving power dwells not in the written text, but in the activity of the women and men who have gathered as the Church of God and Body of Christ. Liturgical books are nothing more than records and guidelines concerning how a particular community worshiped God at a particular time and place; they become liturgy only when enacted by the local Church.[5]

The intimate connection between local Church (i.e., concrete worshiping community, following Zizioulas) and liturgy results in an interesting paradox. Because liturgy belongs to the Church, it does not belong to *me*. Since liturgy belongs to the Church and I am a part of the Church, liturgy is *mine*. It is precisely because of this tension that the whole question of liturgical revision is so explosive.

Liturgy has changed over time

Liturgy – especially Byzantine liturgy – has always been richly diverse.[6] One need only glance at the tenth-century *Typikon of the Great Church* to observe how different that liturgy was from the liturgy prescribed by the current *Typikon of the Great Church* edited by George Biolakis. In the course of 1000 years Orthodox liturgy has evolved from very little poetic hymnody to a sometimes overwhelming amount of non-biblical chants. Then the crowds of people sang very brief refrains over and over again; today a single chanter or small choir might chant several lengthy troparia without involving the laity at all. Not only has our liturgy developed and changed over time, even during the same period, liturgy has varied from place to place. In the eleventh century, Nikon of the Black Mountain observed great liturgical diversity even in his own, limited environment. He writes: "I came upon and collected different typika, of Stoudios, of Jerusalem, and one did not agree with the other, neither Studite with another Studite one, nor Jerusalem ones with Jerusalem ones."[7]

But this multiformity comes as no surprise to those who have studied the history of liturgy.[8] Anton Baumstark said it well over half a century ago: "Liturgical forms are so intimately bound up with the external history of the world and of the Church and with the development of the religious sentiment, itself conditioned by historical happenings, that they are constantly being subjected to very great modifications."[9]

Since liturgy is so intimately connected to time and place, it is only natural that as the context changes, so must liturgy. When a group of Palestinian monks established themselves in Constantinople's Stoudios Monastery, the combination of their liturgical traditions with those of the locals resulted in a creative explosion.

Orthodox liturgical practices shifted from diversity to uniformity only with the printing press. It is somehow fitting that just as fifteenth-century technology ushered in 500 years of liturgical rigidity, late-twentieth-century technology has enabled our generation to rediscover liturgical pluralism.[10]

II. Our Task At Hand

Whether we want to admit it or not, parishes throughout the country are engaged in some degree of liturgical adjustment. It may be as generally accepted as men and women sitting together in church, as common as omitting parts of the Midnight Office or canon at Orthros, as pastoral as re-reworking the Kiss of Peace, or as radical as introducing Advent Wreath rituals into the liturgies of Christmas Lent. The methods are anything but new – in Byzantium "Monastic legislators, compilers and copyists sifted through the sources from a plethora of related usages, picking and choosing what suited them, not haphazardly but within the parameters of basic fidelity to a tradition that was in their blood."[11]

Exactly the same thing is happening today, with two major differences. First, today's sources may or may not be entirely trustworthy. Modern publishing and information technologies make available a wealth of non-Orthodox liturgical material – much of it is putrid, some is good, but very little is compatible with our Orthodox liturgical tradition. Second, liturgical changes are often being made by people who lack the proper background and training to do a good job. I sometimes joke that we're more concerned about having well-trained people cut our hair than we are about who cuts the Orthros. To shift analogies: Before even considering operating on a liturgical service, we should be totally familiar with its structure and workings, lest we inadvertently amputate a vital element and endanger the well-being of the entire service.

As one illustration of improper liturgical change, allow me to share experiences I have had with two priests, both contemporaries of mine at Holy Cross. Neither one celebrates the Sacrament of Baptism in its entirety, yet neither will admit that he modifies the service in any way. One reads the first seven lines of each prayer before skipping to the final doxology. The other begins each prayer more than halfway through, omitting all references to God's saving action in history and beginning with our requests to God. So we know *what* we're asking God to do, but we have no sense of *why* we're asking it. Completely lost is the firm hope that God will hear our voice and save us because he has heard and answered our ancestors.

Acknowledging that liturgical adjustment is a perfectly natural reality that is not inherently evil, it is imperative for us to direct this evolution in such a way that succeeding generations will inherit a tradition of proclaiming and celebrating God's salvation in ways consistent with our *ethos*, *ephos* and *phronema*. Denial of ongoing liturgical adjustments will allow mutations to arise and grow unchecked, resulting in a form of worship that is genetically flawed.

Orthodox parishes today have the essential and sometimes difficult task of preserving our faith tradition in sometimes inconvenient settings. This, of course, is nothing new. The local parish is the central locus of the evangelical and liturgical experience: it is precisely there where the majority of people hear the Gospel, learn the faith, and celebrate salvation. On the positive side, we are in a position to use the handrail of tradition to guide Orthodox Christian communities from the past into the future. On the negative side, however, we are one link in the historical chain and if we fail, all future generations may lose their connection and fall away from the Church. Either way one views the situation, our ultimate goal is to sanctify creation, reuniting it with God.

III. THREE PRACTICAL ILLUSTRATIONS

In the final part of this presentation, I would like to draw on a few examples of how certain liturgical issues are being addressed (or how they might be addressed more positively). Over the years, I have been associated with several Orthodox parishes and have seen much liturgical diversity and more than a few liturgical abominations. Although it is tempting to present a cavalcade of liturgical horror stories, here are three examples of what I think are responsible attempts to adapt our liturgical tradition to pressing parish needs. They are presented simply as springboards for thought and discussion. As a trustworthy presenter I must warn you: *Do not try these at home.* Liturgical revision can be a dangerous thing and should be done only under the close supervision of competent ecclesiastical authorities.

A. Streamlining an existing service

Every Tuesday evening, the Orthodox Christian Fellowship of the University of California, Berkeley, gathers to celebrate the Divine Liturgy. As Lent approached, those who coordinate the program were faced with a challenge: how can the Divine Liturgy of the Presanctified Gifts be celebrated in less than one hour, maintain its essential character in spite of the fact that we lack talented singers, and promote community participation? I would venture to guess that most parishes are concerned with a lack of necessary singers and parishioners pressed for time.

A very successful adaptation resulted from the following modifications:

1. Kathisma Eighteen of the Psalter has been omitted, following the practice of thirteenth-century Constantinopolitan monasteries which recited psalmody only when the Presanctified Liturgy was *not* celebrated in conjunction with Vespers.[12]

2. Instead of inserting ten troparia between the final verses of Psalm 140/141, the original response "Hear me, O Lord" is now chanted between the

psalm verses, replicating the responses chanted at Hagia Sophia and restoring the original priority of scriptural material over poetic hymnody.[13]

3. Repetitive Small Synaptes have been replaced by the priestly prayers they currently obscure. By proclaiming the prayers aloud, we are now in conformity with *Novella 137* promulgated by Emperor St. Justinian the Great, requiring all prayers related to Eucharist and Baptism to be said "in a voice that can be heard by the faithful people, that the minds of those who listen may be excited to greater compunction."

4. Prayers for Catechumens and those preparing for Baptism are now said only if such people are present. And since they are not expected to leave, the liturgical command to depart is omitted.

5. In order to expose the faithful to a wider variety of prayer texts, the standard Preparatory Prayers "I believe, O Lord, and I confess," "How shall I who am unworthy enter," "Merciful Master," and "Of your Supper, the mystical and sublime" were replaced by prayers attributed to St. Basil the Great, St. John Chrysostom and St. John of Damascus.

B. Adapting an existing service

Sometimes new contexts require received liturgical services to be adapted in order to restore them to a conspicuous place in the life of the parish. One of the most moving examples of this was when a beloved member of a parish was scheduled to undergo chemotherapy. As a way of highlighting the Church's sacrament of healing, the local priest (with the blessing of his bishop, of course) integrated Unction into the Divine Liturgy on the Sunday before treatment began.

At the end of Orthros, during the Trisagion of the Great Doxology, the sick man and his family came to the solea and were greeted by the priest. The service took the following shape:

1. Great Synapte with biddings for oil and the infirm
2. Prayer of the Oil – "O Lord, who in your mercy and bounties..."
3. Prokeimenon and Epistle – James 5:10-16
4. Alleluia and Gospel – Luke 10:25-37
5. Ektene and Prayer – "O Lord, who are without beginning, eternal..."
6. Prayer and Anointing – "Holy Father, Physician of our souls and bodies..."
7. Prayer of Forgiveness – "Holy King, compassionate and most merciful..."

The entire family stayed at the front of the church and were the first to receive Holy Communion.

Celebrating the sacrament of Holy Unction at the conclusion of Orthros and the family's visible presence throughout the Divine Liturgy was a very powerful expression of the parish's concern and love. Liturgy was truly a medium through which God's merciful and healing presence was mediated.

C. Creating a new service

This past September, I was present at a rather unusual liturgical event, the consolidation of two small parishes, one of which (because of demographic shifts) was no longer able to be self-sufficient. On the one hand it was joyful because Greek Orthodox faithful who lived in the same geographic area were able to gather around one altar table to celebrate the mystery of Christ's Body and Blood. On the other hand, it was profoundly sad because it was the last time that the members of the St. Dionysios parish were worshiping God in the church building that had been sanctified and inhabited by their parents, grandparents and great-grandparents. We do not have to look far beyond the year 2000 to predict that such consolidation of parishes within and between Orthodox jurisdictions will become more and more common.

Earlier in the process of consolidation I was at the Diocese Offices when the local Hierarch was discussing this bittersweet event. He was well aware of the anxiety felt by members of the smaller parish and their justifiable resistance to the planned consolidation. In a typically American response to this situation, one of the people present suggested that a lawyer draw up a "Memorandum of Understanding" formalizing the property arrangements, which could be signed by the Board Members.

On the appointed day, His Eminence presided at the Divine Liturgy, which was celebrated as usual, with a special request before the Great Entrance to remember the founders and beloved members of the parish while the Metropolitan completed the commemorations at the *proskomide*. After the Liturgy and before the distribution of antidoron, the deacon formally read the legal document and the melancholy members of the St. Dionysios Board literally signed their church building away. One woman rushed out, overcome by emotion, exclaiming "I guess we're nothing more than a piece of property now." At the luncheon, however, the mood improved when any and all were invited to share their memories of the past and hopes for the future.

A few days after the event, the priest of the newly unified parish of St. Demetrios and I had breakfast and discussed the situation. Being somewhat obsessed with liturgy, I had reflected on what the rites themselves communicated and realized that it could have been handled in a different, perhaps more positive, way. The dominant model was legal rather than sacramental: a ritual signing of a quasi-contractual agreement had sealed the deal. This community constituted by sacramental celebration had been drastically reconfigured by a thoroughly secular document. No doubt similar consolidations will take place in the future; how might they better reflect our Orthodox Christian worldview? Here understand that I am simply suggesting one possible model that Church leadership might consider, since only they are empowered to introduce such liturgical rites.

While legal considerations are important in this type of situation, it seems that we would be well served to turn to the Sacrament of Marriage for a paradigm.[14] At its core, parish consolidation is not unlike this holy rite where "a man leaves his father and his mother and clings to his wife, and they become one flesh" (Gen 2:24. cf., Mt 19:5). Of course, such an important event would require the presence and blessing of the local hierarch who is theologically father, shepherd and symbol of unity. As the people chant the final troparion of the Ainoi, "Today salvation comes to all the world," the clergy process to the narthex where representatives of both parishes come together to "plight their troth." Besides simply Parish Council members, it would be beneficial to imitate the tradition at church consecrations of including the oldest and youngest members of the parish as well as representatives of the various parish organizations. In the narthex – which is sometimes said to signify the world – the solemn reading and signing of the legal document would take place. As the people sing the Doxology, the clergy and representatives of both parishes would process to the front of the church where special seats would be prepared. Following the ancient practice of the Church, whereby hierarchs can appoint special scriptural readings appropriate to the time and place (cf., *Typikon of Evergetis* and *Egeria*), the prokeimenon might be taken from Ps. 132/133 "How very good and pleasant it is when kindred live together in unity!" with the Epistle reading taken from St. Paul's First Epistle to the Corinthians (1:10-17) which speaks of agreement and unity, and which asks the powerful question "Has Christ been divided?" An appropriate Gospel passage may be taken from John 17, Jesus's prayer that the Church may be one as the Father and Son are one. Following the Scripture readings and homily, a special Prayer of the Faithful would invoke God's blessing on the union of this newly reconstituted parish. The spiritual union would be accomplished sacramentally when the two formerly distinct parishes come together at the altar and chalice. Continuing the marriage metaphor, the union would be celebrated at a communal meal following and extending the Eucharistic banquet.

This is only a preliminary attempt to give a liturgical shape to a very practical situation. But I offer it as an example of how we might analyze a specific parish situation, formulate and articulate a theological perspective, and fashion an appropriate liturgical celebration. We Orthodox have come too far to lose sight of the fact that everything we do should, in some way, be an expression of God's salvation of his holy people. Every event should be accomplished and sanctified within the context of the Liturgy - when the Church is most authentically Church.[15]

CONCLUSION

In this brief presentation I have hoped to highlight the importance of liturgy in the ongoing life of Orthodox parishes. We would do well to remember that ours is not the only time when radically changing contexts have required a reinterpretation of our ancient and venerable liturgical traditions. The Orthodox Church in the United States needs to face its particular context with confidence. The Holy Spirit which was poured out upon us at Pentecost is still active today; just as it empowered the early Church to face its evolving role in the world, it will enable us to address our own unique situations. We should not feel constrained by historical practices, but should use tradition as a living and dynamic guide toward our eschatological goal. In some cases we may be able to turn to that tradition for clues about how our ancestors adapted in order to recover semi-forgotten practices that will enable us better to proclaim the gospel of salvation and to minister to the needs of God's chosen and holy people. Other cases will compel us to create from the treasury of history new yet completely traditional liturgies invoking God's protection, assistance and merciful blessing on our ongoing quest to "make disciples of all nations, baptizing them in the name of the Father and of the Son and of the Holy Spirit" teaching them to obey everything that [Jesus has] commanded" (Mt 28:19f).

NOTES

[1]Alexander Schmemann, "The Liturgical Revival and the Orthodox Church" in Thomas Fisch (ed.), *Liturgy and Tradition: Theological Reflections of Alexander Schmemann* (Crestwood, NY: St. Vladimir's Seminary Press, 1990), p. 109.

[2]Nicholas Cabasilas, *The Life in Christ*, trans. by Carmino J. deCatanzaro (Crestwood, NY: St. Vladimir's Seminary Press, 1974), p. 49.

[3]Constantin Andronikof, *Le sens de la liturgie: La relation entre Dieu et l'homme* (Paris, 1988), p. 22ff.

[4]Kenan B. Osborne, *Christian Sacraments in a Postmodern World: A Theology for the Third Millennium* (New York, 1999), p. 58f.

[5]Alexander Schmemann, *Introduction to Liturgical Theology* (Crestwood, NY: St. Vladimir's Seminary Press, 1986), p. 34f. See also John D. Zizioulas, "The Local Church In a Perspective of Communion" in John D. Zizioulas, *Being as Communion: Studies in Personhood and the Church* (Crestwood, NY: St. Vladimir's Seminary Press, 1985), pp. 247-260.

[6]Paul Bradshaw discusses liturgical plurality in the Early Church in *The Search for the Origins of Christian Worship: Sources and Methods for the Study of Early Liturgy* (New York: Oxford University Press, 1992).

[7] Robert F. Taft, "Mt. Athos: A Late Chapter in the History of the 'Byzantine Rite'," *Dumbarton Oaks Papers* 42 (1988), p. 179.

[8]Useful studies of the evolution of Byzantine liturgy include: Amfilohije Radovic, "Reformes liturgiques dans l'Èglise de Grece" in *Liturgie de l'Èglise particuliére, liturgie de l'Èglise universelle* (Bibliotheca Ephemerides liturgicae: Subsidia 7. Rome: Edizioni liturgiche, 1976), pp. 261-271. Paul Meyendorff, *Russia, Ritual and Reform: The Liturgical Reforms of Nikon in the 17th Century* (Crestwood, NY: St. Vladimir's Seminary Press, 1991). Peter Galadza, "Restoring the Icon: Reflections on the Reform of Byzantine Worship" *Worship* 65 (1991), pp. 238-255. Robert F. Taft, *The Byzantine Rite: A Short History* (Collegeville, MN: The Liturgical Press, 1992). Ibid, "Holy Week in the Byzantine Tradition" in Antony George Kollamparampil (ed.), *Hebdomadae sanctae celebratio: Conspectus historicus comparativus.* (Rome: C.L.V. Edizioni liturgiche, 1997), pp. 67-91. Thomas Pott, *La rèforme liturgique byzantine: Étude du phènoméne de l'èvolution non-spontanèe de la liturgie byzantine* (Rome: C.L.V. Edizioni liturgiche, 2000).

[9]*Comparative Liturgy*, p. 1.

[10]See Susan J. White, *Christian Worship and Technological Change* (Nashville: Abingdon Press, 1994).

[11]Taft, "Mt. Athos," p. 179.

[12]Juan Mateos, "La psalmodie variable dans l'office byzantin" in *Acta Philosophica et Theologia Dacoromana,* vol 2 (Rome, 1964), p. 334.

[13]Oliver Strunk, "The Byzantine Office at Hagia Sophia" *Dumbarton Oaks Papers* 9-10 (1955-56), p. 185.

[14]I am grateful to Patrick Viscuso who offered valuable insights into connections between Orthodox marriage and my hypothetical rite. See his book *A Byzantine Theology of Marriage: The* Syntagma kata stoicheion *of Matthew Blastares* (Ann Arbor MI: UMI Dissertation Services, 1989).

[15]John Zizioulas, "Eucharist and Catholicity" in *Being and Communion*, p. 154.

This morning I would like to introduce you to a friend whom I have known and loved for a little more than forty-five years. In the process of those years, now more than four decades, I have grown closer to my friend and have felt the support only this friend could bring.

In the passing of time there have been increasingly greater difficulties brought against my friend. Irresponsible and thoughtless remarks, caustic comments, and even, on occasion, unfounded stories. I wondered if those stories would ultimately smear my friend's character. My commitment to my friend at this time has grown, not lessened, and my respect has remained as it has always been. My friend is the *holy priesthood and the ministry it represents*.

The ministry and I became acquainted in the 1950s. At a very young age, I assumed the responsibilities of this high calling and through the years have remained in awe that I could join the ranks of the great saints of the Church and such dynamic personalities I have come to know and highly respect. Following six years of studies at our beloved *Schole* in Brookline, I was ordained in August of 1955 as Deacon and Priest on the day of remembrance of the first and Great Martyr of our Church, St. Stephanos.

These years have been a learning experience for my family and me. When I was first called to the holy priesthood, it was a respected profession. People who were ordained priests and moved into a community were considered an asset and reviewed with respect and dignity. The office was upheld in the minds of individuals as the highest of callings. There was no suspicion, rather a growing appreciation for a priest and his family. But times have changed. It grieves me and grieves all who love the Lord to think about how those times have changed. Understand that no one in the holy priesthood deserves it, and no one is qualified to do it without flaw, without sin, without failure. We come from diverse backgrounds that are known to God, Who in His mysterious and wondrous way continues to love and shed His mercy upon us. With great trepidation and hope, I responded to the call and entered the holy priesthood.

I find encouragement when I come to a passage like the one my Bible is open to in 1 Timothy, Chapter 1. For the Apostle says in verse one, "I thank Christ Jesus our Lord who has enabled me, because He counted me faithful, putting me into the ministry." I am so grateful that I am so honored. He considered me perfect? No. He put me into service because He considered me faithful. Here is the disclaimer of Paul whom we love: "I was formerly a blasphemer, a persecutor and an insolent man; but I obtained mercy because I did it ignorantly in unbelief. And the grace of our Lord was exceedingly abundant, with faith and love which are in Christ Jesus."

St. Paul was so careful with his life and lifestyle. He sinned, he periodically failed, I am sure at times gave poor counsel, he misjudged people, he had critics who questioned his motives and looked disparagingly on his authority and told him so and often behind his back. But when the final chapter had been written and the book had ended, he had withstood the test of scrutiny and no one could rightly prove that he had brought disgrace to Christ or to the ministry.

It's with a sigh that I now go into my ministry to share with you my views on the shaping of the parish through worship, preaching and teaching.

I have completed forty-one years of ministry at the church I presently serve, The Twelve Holy Apostles. And in that period of time, I have felt the hand of God in all the parish activities and I acknowledge that all that has been accomplished has been done for God's glory and honor. Whatever I share with you today, I do so not for the purpose of pride but to express my profound thanks and gratitude to the Church and especially Archbishop Ezekiel (Tsoukalas) of blessed memory, who ordained me, and His Eminence Archbishop Iakovos, who had the courage to send me to disciple and to serve the newly established church of Westchester, Illinois, in July of 1959.

I had no previous experience in organizing a parish. I had pastored a small flock at St. George in the Berkshires (western Massachusetts). Where does one begin? An assignment of this magnitude required courage to make the decisions for Christ and His Church. I recalled the words of my spiritual father and teacher, Archbishop Ezekiel, who said, "You are now filled with the Holy Spirit, go forth with humility and obedience and serve the God who loves you."

Gifts and virtues cannot remain hidden in one's heart. A godly priest radiates, manifests through all he says, does and lives, the treasure residing within him, namely the Holy Trinity. St. Basil clearly stresses the responsibility of sharing these gifts with others: "It happens that the Spirit-bearing souls, those illuminated by the Spirit, are called and known as spiritual, and thus communicate the grace to others as well."

Everyone creates an image according to his own views, which certainly produces other confusion and frustration. If we ask the man on the street how he would like his priest to be, we get a plethora of answers. Some want him to be more sociable, more active, more involved in the current issues, without, of course, restricting them in any way. Some want him to minister more to the poor, the lonely, the unprotected and abandoned; in short, they want the priest to be more in the world and less at the altar, to be ever-present in struggles for justice, freedom, human rights, etc., and less hieratical; to be simple and easily approachable, to be a gentleman.

Others oppose the priest's traditionalist style with its inherent authority, preferring him not to dictate or speak *ex cathedra* about evil, hell, or the Last Judgment. They want him to be a friend of the little people rather than of the ruling classes, fully committed, eager to reform and change, following the trends of the day, contemporary, in dialogue with the world, a man of compromise, full of charity. This is not all. Because an ascetic once said, "I have two ears, one to listen to what people say to me, and another to listen to what they do not say!"

As I have learned in these years, human imperfection includes people in the priesthood. God called individuals into His vineyard. Not one of us is a paradigm of perfection. We have embarrassing or impatient moments. We make snap judgments that are wrong. We arrive at decisions that are questioned and corrected. We need at all time to be accountable to God, others and ourselves in our ministry. We need to conduct ourselves in a responsible manner so that it will sustain the trust, not only granted by the living God, but by our flock. We owe our Lord an integrity that we must sustain.

A priest is essentially a pastor, a shepherd, who should know, love, care and constantly pray for those committed to his charge. A man with no genuine interest in people, without any real care, concern, or compassion, may well doubt his calling to the ministry. Even more important is the work of prayer, the real foundation of his ministry. At his ordination, each priest promises to be diligent in prayer with which is coupled the proclamation of the truth and the Faith. What I have learned in these years is that I had to make my own opportunities for prayer, even though the pressures and the distractions are many. The temptation to say, "I have no time" is always present. Amid the competing demands of his earthly ministry, Christ spent whole nights in prayer where there was no time to pray during the day.

St. Basil asks, "From where did Moses get his extraordinary grace?" Certainly not from his studies in Egypt's learned schools. They were unable, with the wisdom of this world, to offer such heavenly insights and divine aspirations. It was rather the Spirit of God. This was the source of his leadership during forty wandering years in the desert. The study of the divine words needs a whole life, as is seen in the example of Moses. The first part of his life was spent in the land of Egypt. The second forty years were dedicated to pastoring. He was left in the solitude in the desert where he contemplated the origins and happenings of beings and nature. Privileged in seeing God through God's love, he was then transferred to the caring of men. Even then he did not remain constantly in the function of looking after the people, but often returned to contemplative life.

The study of these lives of the Saints of the Church continues to be a source of inspiration and learning for me.

Shaping through worship

There are so many facets to the priesthood. I firmly believe the possibility of the new challenges that come with each day help to stimulate all the emotions to help make the priesthood exciting and fulfilling. As a priest, you may not punch a clock, but every day you live before the eyes of a Holy God who has called you to represent Him. There are so many privileges that go along with the priesthood that it is difficult for me to delve into various categories saying that one is more important than another. All are necessary, all complement one another, and all make an indivisible unity.

When the Holy Apostles Church was established and chartered in 1959, one of the first steps taken was to determine what phase of the building program was to be first. The membership cast a unanimous vote to make the erecting of a sanctuary the priority. This was a clear indication of the values and importance of parish life. I firmly believe that choosing to build the sanctuary first with an area for teaching brought about God's incredible blessings upon this infant church. We honored the name of God and acknowledged the significance of worship in our lives.

The Divine Liturgy, therefore, became a preeminent qualification for the parish. We were compelled to worship Him, to praise Him and to thank Him. We learned that we cannot rightly serve our fellow man until we first serve and worship our God.

It is obvious that if the early Church had not looked upon assembling for worship as a primary duty, the Church would very quickly have gone to pieces and nothing more would have been heard of it. The Book of Acts (2:46-47) reminds us of the early days of the Church "continuing daily with one accord in the temple, and breaking bread from house to house, they ate their food with gladness and simplicity of heart praising God and having favor with all the people. And the Lord added to the church daily those who were being saved."

Worship in the early days of our parish was not conducted in an elaborate environment. Weekly, with patience and humility, the altar was set in a gymnasium. It was within this atmosphere the Spirit of God became real to us. Worship gave us a sense of belonging and underscored the unity with Christ and one another. Soon we came to know that divine service is primarily a sacrifice of praise and an instrument of edification.

The era of new meanings was conveyed. A one-size candle replaced the multiple sizes with different prices for each. Donors were taught it was God's command that anonymity be practiced. These practices continue today.

The gathering at the weekly coffee hour following the Liturgy, along with the receptions following weddings, baptisms and funerals, were looked upon as opportunities to reach out to the flock. The numbers were small at the beginning, allowing opportunities for the members to grow in grace and love together.

Awaken to God

Ministries are like houses. On the outside, they may appear well-built and sturdy, but once you move in, it doesn't take long to discover the hidden flaws. And so I walked through the worship routine and put a few of the features to test. When you turn on a faucet, does a clear stream of biblical truth flow out, or have some worldly contaminants polluted the water? Do the doors to the hearers' lives swing open freely, or are they stuck shut? If your "house" needs remodeling, maybe the reason is that it was built using faulty construction methods. In the early years of development when setting the foundation was essential for the future of the church, I was committed to do the best I could. The words from Hebrews flashed in my mind, "For every house is built by someone, but He who built all things is God" (Heb 3.4). I examined my heart and prayed for guidance.

Holy Apostles was a community established on the concept of stewardship. The only message predicated on the premise that churches should be built and sustained by the gifts of the people came from my knowledge of Scripture. In the Sixties, I admired the work of Fr. Nicholas Triantafilou for leading the Archdiocese Stewardship Task Force. Like Johnny Appleseed, he traveled throughout cities and towns spreading seeds on stewardship. I volunteered to join his efforts and offered my humble service so that together and with the cooperation of the parish, we could establish the base of giving in our churches.

In the mid-Eighties, I suggested to the Parish Council that we dedicate the following year to the theme "Love is Risky." The plan was to give every parishioner $10 and charge them with the responsibility of good Christian stewardship. As you would imagine, the congregation was amazed and even confused. The church asks for money but seldom gives it away. Soon people began to respond in their own inimitable ways. One person purchased $10 of seed and planted a garden on a plot of land he owned. At harvest time, he sold the produce and donated the profit to the church. Others simply multiplied the amount and invested. Most responded like the faithful servants in Scripture. Few were like the one servant who chose to bury the treasure. The community learned the importance of stewardship as a way of worship and adoration for God.

In the fall of 1966, I introduced the segment known to this day as "Awaken to God." It was a teaching session between Orthros and the Liturgy. This fifteen minute bite-size introduction is open to everyone, adults and children. From this truth, we can draw one primary principle of ministry: we must be willing to leave the familiar methods without disturbing the essential message. If we aren't willing to change, we risk having a cold, lifeless dust settle on our ministries as time moves by us. Awaken to God soon became a regular part of Sunday worship and an integral part of the edification of the saints. The program was enthusiastically received and the results were rewarding, as the number of attendees at Orthros increased and by the time the Liturgy began, the church was filled. Worship took on a new meaning.

Preaching

Some wonderful things have occurred over the years with regard to preaching. Early in our development and with the perfecting of our teaching efforts in "Awaken to God," we were allowed to place the sermon immediately following the Gospel reading.

We do injustice to the priority of preaching when we make it appear as thought it is not part and parcel of the Liturgy. St. Irenaios said, "The glory of God is man become fully alive, and the life of man is the vision of God." It is the preacher's task to hold up before us the vision of God that brings life.

Preaching has remained for me a sacred moment. I have permanently placed on the pulpit this inscription, "Thus saith the Lord." Every other form of speech is horizontal by nature; man speaking to man. In preaching the horizontal is derived from the perpendicular.

Preaching is not a throne of eloquence, but an opportunity to grapple with human lives. St. Basil compares the messengers of the gospel and their words to arrows sharpened through the power of the Holy Spirit: "The arrows, falling in the hearts of those who were at some time enemies of the King, draw them to a love of truth, draw them to the Lord, so that those who were enemies to God are reconciled to him through its teachings." The purpose of the sermon was to form Christ-like images and the mind of Christ. Preaching is not the giving of good advice, but the sharing of good news. It is not the giving of an editorial, but the proclamation of God's truth in Christ. It is like an icon: it is a reflection of celestial glory.

For the preacher, the moment a parishioner quotes a text you preached in the past is richly rewarding. Recently a grandfather approached me in the coffee hour and said, "Father, you should receive comfort to know that your words are not wasted on Sunday morning. Last week our five-year-old grandson was listening to a conversation and someone said, "I wish my eyesight would improve." The little boy said, "If you had been with us in church last week, you could have heard how Jesus helped a blind man see by just placing some mud over his eyes." The best compliment that can be paid to any sermon is a changed life. This is clearly something we cannot accomplish alone but with God. We sow the seed, but only God can give growth.

Moments such as these are rewarding because sermons come alive. Harry Fosdick in his fine work "The Living of These Days" declares, "Preaching is not merely to discuss repentance, but to persuade people to repent; not merely to debate the meaning and possibility of Christian faith, but to produce Christian faith in the lives of listeners; not merely to talk about the available power of God to bring victory over trouble and temptation, but to send people out from their worship on Sunday with victory in their possession. A preacher's task is to create in his congregation the thing he is talking about."

In 1984, one of our young adults suggested taping the Sunday sermon to mail to shut-ins, college students, and anyone who wished to subscribe to it. After some cajoling on his part and discussion with the Reach-out Committee, it was agreed that a small recorder be purchased to begin this phase of ministry. In a short period of time, we were reaching out to those who were not able to worship on Sunday and to those persons who traveled extensively. Some confessed that I became a regular companion on their business trips. Perhaps one of the most rewarding experiences was when I began to receive letters from inmates in prisons scattered across the country. On one occasion, a young man who had been serving a life sentence shared the weekly tapes with two other cellmates. In time the two became interested in the Orthodox Faith and they requested literature and any information we could provide. I contacted the Greek Orthodox priest in the area and requested a pastoral visit to the prison and begin catechetical instruction to the interested persons. In six months, both men were baptized and received in the Greek Orthodox Faith. The Holy Spirit had been at work and opened new opportunities for us. Without ever being present in prison, the voice of Orthodoxy was proclaimed and continues to go forth weekly to 354 subscribers.

St. Basil says that those who proclaim the gospel are the lips and the eyes of the body of Christ. As lips they lend their voices to the Holy Spirit in order that he may write "the word of eternal life in the hearts of the faithful;" as eyes their function is to "discern between good and evil and guide the members of Christ toward that which benefits each."

St. Basil further writes that those who preach lend their voices to the Holy Spirit so that he may write words of eternal life in the hearts of the faithful. He calls them fathers and nurses since they beget new members for the Church. Those who preach, continues Saint Basil, lead the disciples of Christ "to blooming and fragrant nourishment of spiritual assistance of the Holy Spirit, raise them up and nourish them until they produce fruit; then they guide them to rest and safety from those who lay snares to them."

In the three priestly roles of worship, teaching and preaching, it should be the priest's task to maintain as well as he can and strive for excellence. The Letter to the Philippians (Ch. 3) shows several ways in which the apostle Paul pursued excellence. We have seen that he was able to establish his priorities and was motivated by a strong desire to know Christ more fully. In verses 13 and 14, we see a third element in Paul's pursuit of excellence. He says, "Brethren, I count not myself to have apprehended: but this one thing I do, forgetting those things which are behind, and reaching forth unto those things which are before, I press toward the mark for the prize of the high calling of God in Christ Jesus. I leave the past behind, and with hands outstretched for whatever lies ahead, I go straight for my goal, my reward, the honor of the high calling of God, in Christ Jesus." Paul is not saying, "I know exactly where I am going." I'm not suggesting he doesn't have a goal; he does. But while he knows where he's going to end up, he doesn't know how long it will take him to get there or where the path will lead him before he gets there. He's on the way to glory, but before he gets to glory, he says, "I must pursue my goal."

Now each of us must have a goal. You know the old story – if you never aim at anything, you will hit it every time. That's true. I think it's important to have yearly goals and daily goals. And it is important to write those things down. One reason we do not accomplish things we want to accomplish is that we have not verbalized what it is we want to do. St. Paul was very different from that. He had something to aim at. He pursued his goal of seeing the Philippian church come into full maturity in the Lord. Have you ever observed how the icon of the Platytera is placed in position? The iconographer labors many hours to position the head in just the right angle so that the eyes follow the beholder wherever he may be in the church nave. So must the sermon reach out to the hearts of the listeners. Jesus traveled from village to village. He taught in synagogues; he preached in the open air. On one occasion a boat was his pulpit. Later the disciples brought the message of Christ to the people. No worker for Christ waited for crowds to come to him. Thus in addition to preaching and teaching at all liturgical gatherings, baptisms, weddings, funerals, parish council meetings and the like, a monthly prayer-breakfast is held at the church. A young man who has assisted in the altar for thirty-five years prepares a complete meal, which is followed by a meditation. Also an early Liturgy – 5:00 am – is celebrated during Christmas and Easter. Approximately eighty-five are in attendance. Often the attendees are not regular worshipers on Sunday morning, nor at the mid-week Bible Study. The spirit of reaching out to believers where they are is an important principle to which we have adhered.

In Matthew 28:19-20 is recorded the great commission: "Go therefore and make disciples of all the nations, baptizing them in the name of the Father, and of the Son, and of the Holy Spirit, teaching them to observe all the things that I have commanded you." Someone has called this the Christian's marching orders for the generation in which he lives; another the believers' major objective in every generation.

In 1983, acutely aware of this Christian mandate, we introduced The Celebration of Books, a form of festival of books. We assemble all the books in our Resource Center (in excess of 2000 Orthodox texts) and exhibit them in our social hall for one week. Since its inception, we have been graced with numerous renowned scholars and Orthodox theologians, many of whom authored books in the exhibit. They came to enlighten and thrill the hearts of large crowds and offer spiritual nourishment for hungry and thirsty souls. Their presence and participation has affirmed the commitment to teach.

Knowledge apart from application falls short of God's desire for His children. He wants us to apply what we learn so that we will change and grow. The Celebration of Books has been prepared with these goals in mind.

There's an old legend that takes us back and recounts the time when Jesus Christ returned to His Father in heaven after he had died on the cross and had been raised from the dead. Before He was seated at the Father's right hand, He was met by the angel Gabriel, says the legend.

Gabriel frowned as he saw the marks and the scars during the tortuous years on earth, especially those from the scars from His crucifixion. Gabriel asked: "Master, you suffered terribly for those earthlings down there, didn't you?"

"Yes, I did," was the reply from Jesus.

Gabriel continued, "And now they know about your love and forgiveness? Have they all heard about your death and resurrection?"

"No," said Jesus. "Right now only a handful knows. Only a handful of people know about my death and resurrection."

Gabriel looked perplexed. Then he asked, "How will everyone find out about your wonderful life and your sacrificial death and your triumphant resurrection?"

Jesus responded, "I have asked Peter, James, John, and a handful of my friends and followers to tell other people about it. And when other people hear and believe, they in turn will tell still others. And Gabriel, by and by, the planet will hear the message."

Still frowning the angel responded, "But, um, you know how people are on earth. What if Peter, James and John get tired? What if they tell the story and then the next generation gets all involved in their pursuit? What if way down by the eighteenth or twentieth century people just aren't committed any longer to your commission? Have you made other plans?"

The Lamb of God looked directly at the angel of God and He said, "I have not made any other plans. I am counting on them."

These words resonate with deep meaning in my heart. There are no other plans. We must do our very best where God has planted us.

THE GOSPEL IN THE PARISH:
DISCOVERING THE ORTHODOX EVANGELICAL ETHOS

THEODORE STYLIANOPOULOS

About twenty years ago Bishop Anastasios Yannoulatos, now Archbishop of the autocephalous Church of Albania, published an article with the striking title "Discovering the Orthodox Missionary Ethos."[1] The thrust of the article was to underscore what he saw, during the Sixties and Seventies, as "a rekindling of missionary interest" in the Orthodox Church. Highlighting Orthodox missionary activities particularly in Africa, where he himself was a pioneer, the Archbishop emphasized that "the awakening of the Orthodox missionary conscience" was "no innovation but a rediscovery" of an essential dimension of the Church.[2] Today, thanks to the work of His Beatitude and others, both clergy and laity, many more Orthodox have not only been awakened to but are now strongly supportive of missionary work in distant lands, what we usually think of as "external mission." The Orthodox Christian Mission Center in Florida, a vital and growing pan-orthodox ministry, is the administrative and inspirational center through which Orthodox clergy and laity of America channel their sense of missionary resurgence.

The thesis of the present essay is that, as the new millennium beckons us forward, a parallel rekindling and rediscovery of another closely-related ministry of the Orthodox Church is needed, having to do with the "internal mission" of the Church, namely, the evangelization of rank-and-file Orthodox Christians at the level of each parish. The crux of the matter is the ministry of evangelism to the baptized. We are talking about not only the proclamation but also the actualization of the Gospel in the parish. At stake is the discovery of the inner evangelical spirit of the Orthodox Church by which the Church may be empowered to continue to fulfill its mission in North America. It may be rather startling to suggest that, after twenty centuries of Church history, Orthodox clergy and laity need to reawaken to the Gospel of Christ, the core message of salvation. And yet it is precisely true in the sense of Archbishop Anastasios' words: it is a matter not of

175

"innovation" but of "rediscovery" – the rediscovery of a precious and dynamic treasure already enshrined in the Holy Scriptures, the Divine Liturgy, the hymnology, the theology and tradition of the Church. But the treasure in the treasure box is not adequately appreciated, nor sufficiently effective, unless it is brought out into full view so that its beauty and power may be released by God's grace.

In our generation a significant number of formerly evangelical Protestant Christians joined in mass the Orthodox Church in the United States and now constitute one of the fastest-growing parts of the worldwide family of the Orthodox.[3] Over the last decade they have stirred things up in American Orthodoxy, bringing with them a fervent personal faith, a zeal for the Scriptures and the Gospel, and a high level of Christian commitment sometimes discomfiting to Orthodox Christians born into the faith. At the same time, they have earnestly sought to live and express the gifts they have brought with them in terms of an authentic liturgical and doctrinal Orthodox mindset (*phronema*). We so-called 'cradle' Orthodox have been learning from them and they have been learning from us, sometimes in creative tension. Whatever our reciprocal lessons and perceptions, whatever our mutual gifts and tensions, the substantive task is clear and decisive for all: What is the direction and shape of the Orthodox Church in America that we should strive for as bishops, priests and laity? What is the enduring message of Orthodoxy according to its own authentic identity as the One, Holy, Catholic and Apostolic Church? What is the dynamic spirit by which to build up the spiritual character of our parishes and to help them become local missionary centers across America? Certainly, one of the major tasks that lie ahead is that of the evangelism of the baptized membership. The future growth of the parishes, the spiritual vigor of the whole Church, as well as the mutual reinforcement of the internal and external mission of the Church, will significantly depend on the effective proclamation, as well as the actualization of the Gospel in the parish. At issue is nothing less than the evangelical nature of the Orthodox Church and the rediscovery of the Orthodox evangelical ethos.

The urgency of the task

The twenty-first century is bound to be a century of continuing globalization, multi-culturalism and pluralism – all powerful currents undermining the sociological soil of the Christian faith and thereby people's linkage to their local parishes. Dramatic changes have already occurred and will continue to occur in the way huge numbers of people in our society live, feel, think and act. We face the cultural phenomena of what have been called modernism and postmodernism – massive technological, social, economic, and intellectual forces in both conflict and interaction powerfully shaping our shrinking world. Some of the key factors which define the character our culture may be quickly mentioned: the growth of big cities; the astonishing scientific and technological progress; the movement and mixture of peoples; the meeting of religions and subcultures in the neighborhood, school and place of work; the drive for individual freedom and acquisition of material goods; the pursuit of pleasure and entertainment; the explosion of communications through the printed and electronic media; the pernicious effects of war, economic disparity and ecological neglect; the failure of systems of government, education, law and even religion; and the consequent loss of clear boundaries of community, identity, value, meaning, purpose and direction.

The upshot of all the above is an enormous sociological dynamic which, though it does not impact everyone equally, influences all members of our society, including our fellow parishioners, in both conscious and unconscious ways. A Christian author described the tectonic cultural changes of recent generations by saying: "The world has moved, but it neglected to send a change of address card."[4] He meant an address card to the Churches, since many Christians, both leaders and ordinary faithful, seem to be either unaware of or unmoved by the radical changes in our times. Nevertheless, we are all passengers on the same ship, the impact being greatest on the young. It is our youth who unavoidably breathe the air of the postmodern popular philosophy: all religious faiths and values are relative, there is no certainty of truth, do your own thing, be tolerant of the choices and lifestyles of others, and have fun enjoying the ride into an uncertain future. The following words of a man interviewed in the streets of Boston may well express a diffused aspect of the postmodern consciousness often floating across the hearts and minds of people in our own parishes, especially the youth: "I don't know what I believe in. And if I believe, I believe there's some Higher Power, I think. But I don't know. But I'm open to everything. So I like to believe in everything, because I don't know what it is I truly believe in."[5]

This cultural crisis of faith is not something new. Church leaders and theologians have been talking about it for years. Among the Orthodox, the late Alexander Schmemann, Dean of St. Vladimir's Theological Seminary, sounded a clarion call some forty years ago when he warned about the institutions of marriage, family, education and work being understood in secular terms even by Orthodox Christians. He critiqued the inundation of worldly values into the membership of the Church, for example, reliance on success, ambition, affluence, status, profit, prestige and the like.[6] He wrote: "It is this American secularism which an overwhelming majority of Orthodox wrongly and naively identify with *the* American way of life that is, in my opinion, the root of the deep spiritual crisis of Orthodoxy in America."[7] Unfortunately, his call was a voice in the wilderness, bearing little impact against the influence of modern culture crashing upon us like a mighty tidal wave.

Archbishop Iakovos, former head of the Greek Orthodox Archdiocese of North and South America, issued a similar call for renewal in 1986[8] and soon established a theological commission to develop a comprehensive working agenda for the Church. The commission's final report in 1989 engaged issues of parish life, the changing composition of membership, the weakening of ethnic ties, as well as the cultural crisis of faith exemplified by the fact that our young people are more deeply influenced by society than the local parish.[9] Let it be noted that the crisis of faith is not a personal crisis, that is, a crisis of conscience in people who have grown up with a meaningful Christian commitment and come to question it. Rather, it is precisely a cultural crisis, that is, an absorption of a sociological loss of Christian commitment in a secular society where Christian faith is one of many options, an individual and personal choice often not seriously considered at all. The predictable results are drifting membership and perfunctory participation in the sacraments as, for example, in the case of couples that come to be married in the Church, even though they have been blissfully cohabiting for years, and then seem to be surprised by the Church's disapproval. To draw such couples into the life of the parish, speaking to them the truth with love and compassion, rather than with sternness and rejection, is a typical pastoral problem today of no small magnitude for the persons involved and for the parish itself.

In view of the crisis of faith in our culture, the above theological commission emphasized the crucial responsibility of the entire Church in stemming the tide of drifting membership and religious nominalism by means of planned and consistent action. The ecclesial and spiritual bonds of parishioners, if not supported and enhanced by purposeful and concerted efforts, will continue to diminish, especially in view of the overwhelming percentage of interfaith marriages and the progressive weakening of ethnic ties. To quote the commission: "In this free, pluralistic society *the Orthodox Church must take upon itself the prime responsibility for maintaining and strengthening the Orthodox identity among its members both as an intrinsic goal as well as a presupposition for effective mission in the world.*"[10] The significant implication is that the parish cannot be isolated from the larger Church and its institutions. To achieve its role and potential, the parish must be given the appropriate spiritual leadership, the basic presuppositions for effective ministries, and vigilant supervision and direction. The whole body of the Church, both leaders and faithful, need to work together as we confront the enormous tasks created by the influence of modernity and postmodernity on our people.

The most potent answer to the cultural crisis of faith, according to the theological commission, is nurturing a sense of living faith in the parish. The commission called for challenging and guiding our people beyond external formalism to an "internalization" of Orthodox truths and values, that is, an inward appropriation of the Orthodox way of life. In our parishes, we have the liturgical context of beautiful services, especially the treasure of the Divine Liturgy, which itself cries out for greater actualization among all the faithful. Our sacred tradition possesses the truths and practices to fortify the Church's identity as the Body of Christ. We have a rich spirituality to inspire the administrative structures and formational programs of the Church. Efforts are being made to enhance the socially supportive environment of the community as a parish family – social activities, conferences, camps, study groups, and philanthropic ministries.

The critical question is what will be the electrical spark which gives birth to personal faith in Christ, strengthens faith, energizes people spiritually, motivates them to action, and ties together all the aspects of parish life enhancing their particular functions. The commission pointed to prayer, clear teaching and the Gospel. According to the commission, living faith occurs in a parish context of "personal faith inspired by prayer, enlivened by a mystical sense of communion with the risen Christ, and communicated with an evangelical spirit as a heralding of the good news."[11] These words sum up the essential ethos of Orthodoxy: the experience of union with Christ, nurtured by prayer and worship, and communicated with an evangelical spirit as good news of grace. All these key components, which are integrated and mutually supportive, are definitive and indispensable to the Orthodox way of life. Prayer and worship constitute long and rich traditions. But evangelism must receive far greater prominence as a way of reawakening the faithful to the treasures of prayer and worship themselves. Evangelism is preaching and teaching with conviction and the living voice, focusing on the centrality of Christ, and connecting all that we do in the parish with Christ, His saving work, and the blessings that flow from it. It is through evangelism that souls are particularly stirred, faith is awakened, commitment is strengthened, and an evangelical ethos is nurtured in an Orthodox context – an ethos centered on Christ, filled with prayer, and penetrating all parish activities in a vital and unifying way. To quote the theological commission once again: "A true evangelical spirit keeps alive the horizon of living faith by which we apprehend that the risen Christ is present in the Church, guiding us in our education, spiritual formation, liturgical life, moral and social concerns, youth programs, administration and finances."[12]

The power of the Gospel

One of the most remarkable phenomena in history was the spread of Christianity in the Greco-Roman world. Propelled by a transforming experience of the presence and power of God, the Christian movement triumphed in a society much like our own – a world of many gods and religions, of constant wars and migration of peoples, of diverse philosophies and lifestyles, of the breakdown of local boundaries and structures of meaning, and of a profound longing for personal security and protection from seen and unseen evil. Within a few decades, the early Christians founded communities in virtually all the major centers of the Roman Empire, even Rome itself. In just over three centuries the Church established itself as the dominant religion of the Roman Empire, claiming the emperor himself as its most powerful convert and supporter.

Historians have long reflected on the reasons behind the amazing success of Christianity in the ancient world, reasons that are totally instructive for our own cultural situation. One factor was the cohesiveness of community and family life among Christians, transcending racial, social, economic and generational boundaries. Despite conflicts and disagreements in the ancient Church, Christians possessed a strong sense of unity in Christ, bound by love for Him and for each other as brothers and sisters. Christians nurtured a consciousness of being an alternative society, distinct from and countercultural to ancient paganism, a distinction enhanced by the experience of persecution. Another factor was their observable renewal of life. The Christian presence and witness touched and changed ordinary people. In contrast to pagan society, where anything was possible and everything permissible, the Christians had the disarming ability to point to their own way of life as concrete proof of what they proclaimed – God's love and forgiveness, holiness of conduct, honest business dealings, and unselfish service to others. Even pagan writers and opponents of Christianity, such as Lucian, publicly acknowledged that the Christians helped not only themselves but also pagans in need.

However, the greatest factor behind the astonishing triumph of early Christianity was its evangelical spirit: living, preaching and teaching the good news. For the early Christians the proclamation of the Gospel was neither a matter of grand, abstract theology nor an issue of triumphant claims about the past. It was the announcement of a new way of life in Christ backed up by the transforming experience of the presence and power of God in the community. It was the sharing of the joyous conviction that Christ was alive, that the Holy Spirit energized the community of believers, that God was truly at work in their midst. Early Christianity was a spiritual movement, an explosion of spiritual dynamism, with an invincible sense of mission based on the assurance that Christians knew the true way of life to be shared with all. This powerful evangelical spirit can be seen not only among the Apostles but also among the Church Fathers such as St. Justin Martyr, St. Irenaeus, St. Athanasius, St. John Chrysostom and many others. For example, in his work *On the Incarnation of the Word*, St. Athanasius likens the spread of the Gospel to a sunrise that is the work of the risen Christ Himself. He writes: "The Savior is working mightily among people; every day He is invisibly persuading numbers of people all over the world. Can anyone, in face of this, still doubt that He has risen and lives, or rather that He is Himself the Life?"[13]

But has not the Church preached and taught all these things for centuries? Do we not find all the above ideals not only in Holy Scripture but also in the writings of the Church Fathers? Does not the theology of the Church continue to expound and defend the essential truths of the Gospel interpreting the mystery of the Trinity, the sacraments and Orthodox doctrine? Above all, does not our worship and hymnology gloriously celebrate the whole Gospel – the majesty and power of the Holy Trinity, the saving events of the life of Christ, and all the blessings flows from the good news of salvation? Certainly, all these questions should be answered in the affirmative. The fullness of the Gospel is enshrined in the total life of the Church, especially its rich tradition of worship.

And yet there is something seriously amiss. The deficiency is not in the treasure box itself; not in the richness of liturgical services, not in the lack of theological treatises expounding Orthodox doctrine, not in the lack of catechetical material, not in the lack of books on spirituality. Rather, *the lack lies in the focus, the perception, the orientation, the living of the evangelical ethos*. It is widely evident that, for many, the liturgical services are not celebrated with joy but endured as a burden. Most theological treatises are incomprehensibly abstract for the average person. The catechetical material and programs often bear too heavy a classroom orientation. The books and instructions on spirituality require motivated hearts to be of lasting benefit. Although individuals may be inspired and benefit by reason of their own initiatives, the parish as a whole seems to be rather unconscious and unmoved by the inherited treasures. All the received gifts of the Church, precious in themselves, are not adequately seen, communicated, heard, lived, and celebrated as good news by the majority of the faithful. The Gospel is enshrined in the total tradition but it is not adequately communicated with the living voice. In other words, the Gospel is not proclaimed and taught with sufficient focus and clarity as Gospel, and with ample faith and conviction, to create an atmosphere of purposeful awakening and a responsive stirring in which parish worship, teaching and pastoral practice can come fully alive by the grace of God.

Indeed, if the Gospel resounded in the parish as in the case of the early Christians, similar results would follow. No Christian can say that God loved the ancient world more than He now loves us in the postmodern era. No Christian can assert that the gift of Christ, in terms of its beauty and truth, is less needed or potentially less effective today. No Christian can allege that the power of the Holy Spirit has diminished over the centuries. No Christian can rightly suggest that the good news of salvation has lost either its relevance or potency in modern times. On the contrary, countless men and women today yearn for an authentic message of love and forgiveness in Christ. They long to be part of a caring and supportive community. They are ready to commit themselves to a way of life that is purposeful and beneficial to others. If we see parishes faltering, their spiritual focus waning, their identity unclear, their worship feeble, their service orientation minimal, and their witness impotent to attract and hold their own baptized membership, then we know that something is out of kilter at the level of priorities and basic orientation. What is more, we do not have the luxury of escapism. We cannot blame the world, its pride and disobedience, its lust and moral decadence, its 'lostness' and despair, since these were the very traits of the ancient pagan world in which Christianity originally triumphed.

Are we then to resort to self-criticism alone, blaming ourselves and our own people for lack of faith and commitment, for squandering our sacred treasures and surrendering to the allurements of a world ruled by Satan? No, a response of this kind will not do either, because there is a better way. The better way is to center on Christ, to refocus on the good news, to start with the message with which Christ started, to repent and embrace the good news, and thus to recover the evangelical ethos of Christian life – all in the context of the treasures that we already possess and celebrate as Orthodox Christians.

Discovering the Orthodox evangelical ethos

Jesus began His ministry with the announcement of the good news of God's kingdom, saying: "The time is fulfilled, and the kingdom of God is at hand; repent, and believe in the Gospel" (Mk 1:14-15). A formidable challenge that Jesus faced was how to break through "a wall of casual familiarity and complacency" in order to stir people's heart and minds, and thus convey His message in a personal and living way.[14] He lived among a religious people with a long tradition of worship and sacrifice, a people deeply aware of a rich heritage centered on the Mosaic Law and the Prophets, a people familiar with religious language and proud of the privileged status among all the nations allotted to them by God. The problem was that, as far as Jesus could see, it did not make much difference in their daily lives. It was as if the religious forms and ceremonies, the institution of religion, had taken the place of the living God. Jesus' answer was to confront them with the presence and power of God. He assured them that He "did not come to abolish but to fulfill the Law and the Prophets" (Mt 5:17). His own focus was on the immediacy of God's presence as the source of renewal of human hearts and the inherited religion. That is what He meant by kingdom which He himself made real through His presence, deeds and words.

The Orthodox preacher and teacher today confront a similar reality in the parish. Orthodox Christians have a general familiarity with the form and language of the liturgical services. They have listened to the Bible, and particularly the Psalms, recited many times. They have heard the frequent doxologies to the Holy Trinity and have chanted the triple *Kyrie Eleisons*. Parishioners know that Christ is God and Savior according to the Creed. He is the Leader of the Church, whose lordship is symbolized by the Pantokrator icon in the dome of our churches. They are aware and proud of the long and rich tradition of the Orthodox Church. But somehow the spiritual beauty and power of the banquet set before them do not penetrate very deeply into their hearts and minds. For the majority, religious life is a familiar routine partaken of selectively, with little effect on daily life, while the burden of individual cares and the pull of modern culture seem overwhelming.

The most timely and effective answer to this reality of religious familiarity and complacency is evangelization conceived as internal mission by means of evangelization – preaching and teaching the Gospel. The following basic elements or aspects of preaching and teaching may serve as examples of how evangelization can be conducted in the parish in order to reawaken an evangelical spirit and nurture a broader evangelical ethos embracing the whole life of the community.[15]

The first and most important element is focus on the central message of salvation – the conviction that the Church has a message to proclaim, a *kerygma*, a heralding of good news. This message derives from its Holy Scriptures, its worship and theology, and the depths of its historical experience of God. Jesus began with the heralding of God's kingdom as a present reality. The Apostles began with the announcement that Jesus Himself was the agent of the kingdom, the risen Lord and Savior, the victor over death and corruption, the giver of light and life (Acts 2:22-36). The Church has the same apostolic message to proclaim about Christ and the kingdom today – a message of truth and grace, of love and forgiveness, of healing and reconciliation, of hope and joy – which must resound within the parish and beam out to the world as from a radio station which never goes off the air.

To be agents of evangelization, priests, teachers and other parish leaders must have first embraced the good news of Christ and the kingdom for themselves in word and deed. They must see themselves as heralds proclaiming the message with the conviction that it is ultimately dependent not on their wisdom and skill but on God's authority and power. It is a message that comes from God, it announces the work of God in Christ, it tells about God's blessings and demands, and it leads to God.

What must be emphasized in a particular way is that the evangelical quality of preaching and teaching arises from the conviction that the Gospel mediates God's presence and power here and now. The Gospel is not simply an abstract theological truth or an important event in the past, but an announcement which carries with it the active presence of the Holy Spirit. When St. Paul wrote to the Romans that "the Gospel is the power of God for everyone who believes" (Rom 1:17), he meant it for the ongoing present. Day by day as he conducted his ministry the great apostle was aflame with the evangelical spirit by which, as in the case of Jesus, he could announce the transformative grace of God breaking into people's lives: "Behold, now is the acceptable time; behold, now is the day of salvation" (2 Cor 6:2)! Orthodox preachers and teachers must be convinced of the Gospel's spiritual power and convey the confidence that the faithful announcement of the good news ushers the same blessings today as in the days of the first Christians. When the name of Christ is mentioned and praised, when His gracious work of love and forgiveness is proclaimed and taught in various ways, when His offer of new life and joy is celebrated, the same gifts that are announced become realities in the present. In other words, evangelical preaching and teaching is a spiritual event; it is not merely the transmission of information or elucidation of it, but the imparting here and now of the same new reality which is being preached, an ephiphany of God's grace transforming simultaneously the lives of preachers and listeners.[16]

In practical terms, preachers and teachers do not have to be biblical scholars or great theologians, as if great learning would justify or prove the validity of the Gospel. Such a mentality is counterproductive because it does not perceive, nor therefore allow, the living God do His work through the faithful proclamation of the good news. They do not have to be eloquent speakers, although they must be willing to put serious effort behind their work. Nor do they have to raise their voices to high decibels, or thump on the pulpit, in order to add value or potency to the message. But they must be faithful to the message and receptive of God's grace. They must love Christ, love the Scriptures, love the congregation, love to proclaim the good news, and seek to connect it with every aspect of the parish.

Is there a meeting of the Parish Council or the Ladies' Society tonight? Is there a pastoral visitation at a home or in the hospital tomorrow? Is there a confession to be heard or a counseling meeting scheduled the next day? Is there a meeting with the youth or an adult recreational group on Saturday? Do not lose an opportunity to read or recite with conviction a carefully chosen passage from Scripture, presenting it as good news – affirming, re-phrasing, celebrating and applying the passage to present circumstances. Let the whole range of the imagery and language of the Gospel – the good news, the message of salvation, the word of God, the word of the Cross, the heralding of the new creation, the announcement of grace, God's gift of love and forgiveness – resound again and again in the life of the parish. Talk about Christ's encounter with Zacchaeus, or the blind man, or the Samaritan woman, or the thief on the cross as encounters which bear good news for today's listeners. In many and various ways, not only in worship, but also in meetings, educational sessions, recreational events, seek this one thing: to bring God into the lives of people and the people into the presence of God. By unceasing focus on the message, as well as by loving pastoral nurture, raise people's awareness that we are God's coworkers and witnesses, that we are doing God's work, and that we are doing it with God's guidance and power. And let God do the rest. The result will be an awakening of the evangelical spirit, a God-centeredness, and a growing evangelical ethos in the parish.

A second important element in evangelization is an emphasis on the good news as a gift. The Gospel is that "God so loved the world that He *gave* His only Son, that whoever believes in Him should not perish but have eternal life" (Jn 3:16). When Jesus met the Samaritan woman, He said to her: "If you knew the *gift* of God, and who it is that is saying to you, 'Give me a drink,' you would have asked Him, and he would have *given* you living water" (Jn 4:10). In the Epistle to the Romans, St. Paul asks: "He who did not spare His own Son but *gave* Him up for us all, will He not also *give* us all things with Him?" (Rom 9:32)? And again in Ephesians: "For by grace you have been saved through faith; and this is not you own doing, it is the *gift* of God" (Eph 2:8). At the most sacred moment of the Divine Liturgy, when the priest offers the Eucharistic Gifts, he chants: "We offer to You these *gifts* from Your own *gifts* in all and for all." Orthodox theology teaches that Christ, the Gospel, the Church, the Holy Spirit, our families, our children, the life of each human being, all are gifts of God.

And yet the popular perception of Christian life and the Church itself is not in the perspective of a gift but that of an obligation. We often hear about fulfilling our religious duties and meeting our parish obligations. Christian life is often seen in moralistic categories. The prevailing view is that, to gain salvation and somehow obtain a ticket to heaven, one must accomplish so many good works and fulfill so many religious obligations, although these may be neither enjoyable nor very inspiring. Not infrequently and with all good intentions, priests and parish leaders reinforce this view of 'obligatory Christianity' by harping on parishioners to come to Church more often, to give more of their time and money, and to be far better Christians than they are with little or no attention to the very essence of Christianity is a gift, above all the gift of Christ Himself through whom we share the life of God the Father by the power of the Holy Spirit.

To be sure, the Gospel is both a gift and a task. It entails both blessings and demands. We need but to remember Christ's words about the straight and narrow; and to review with our mind's eye the Sermon on the Mount. The way of Christ is the way of the Cross. But the Gospel as gift comes first. It forms the foundation from which we seek to fulfill our Christian duties. Before Christ delivered the demands of the Sermon on the Mount, He began with the Beatitudes: "Blessed are the humble... blessed are the meek... blessed are the merciful... blessed are the pure in heart... blessed are the peacemakers" (Mt 5:3-9). This blessing was a present blessing. It was not intended only for the afterlife, but for the daily lives of those who heard and welcomed His message of the kingdom. Indeed, unless we first receive and are transformed by the gift and power of the kingdom, unless we are truly blessed by God's grace, the fulfillment of the kingdom's righteousness would be an exercise in futility. The gifts and graces of God always come first.

Preaching and teaching must reverse popular notions of 'obligation Christianity' and develop an awareness of Christian life as a gift, a privilege, a joy. Preachers must avoid dwelling on what have been called "try-harder sermons," thus crushing the conscience of worshipers who are already burdened with a myriad of personal, family and work obligations. The One who said, "Take up your cross and follow me" (Mt 16:24), first said: "Come to me and I will give you rest" (Mt 11:28). The blessings of Christ, His love and mercy, His forgiveness and healing, His strength and comfort, must receive primary attention because His demands can only be accomplished on the basis of His blessings. An essential aspect of evangelization is proclaiming the good news as a gift, creating a sense of gratitude and appreciation for God's blessings, and thus inspiring and empowering Christians to live a life worthy of the Gospel.

A third element of evangelization is leading the hearers to a positive response to the Gospel. The very nature of the Gospel as a gift requires a response. The ministry of Jesus is marked by such questions as: "Do you believe?" "Do you want to be well?" "Do you want to enter into life?" Jesus taught that we must ask in order to receive and we must actively seek in order to find (Mt. 7:7-11). Christ came to the world and shed His precious blood on the Cross, not merely to be observed and admired, but to be received and acknowledged as Redeemer and Lord.

The wall of routine in the parish can gradually be broken by drawing attention to this element of response through appropriate, loving words. The response is the essence of the personal act of faith on the basis of free will. The response is not simply to this program or to that worship service, but to Christ Himself and life with Him. Responding is like turning on the lights spiritually. Not all would want to turn on the switch of personal Christian commitment, but all should at least hear and know that that marks the serious beginning of the life in Christ.

While we do not have altar calls in the Orthodox Church, our worship services, the readings from the Bible, as well as the teachings and examples of the Saints, offer numerous lessons and opportunities to underscore the necessity of response to the Gospel – not only once but again and again. The response is essentially none other than that of faith, repentance and obedience as an expression of authentic Christian life. Faith is the affirmation that Christ is true and reliable, both deserving and requiring our ultimate commitment. Repentance, a consequence of faith, is less a regret for past sins and more a matter of a new orientation, a changed world view, and a new way of life based on the Gospel. Obedience is primarily obedience to Christ Himself evidenced by a stable Christian life in service to Him and our neighbor. When the Gospel is preached and taught as both inviting and requiring a response, its power is released in the hearts of listeners by the grace of the Holy Spirit. It becomes evident in a sense of conversion and renewal in the hearts of individual believers. When the response reaches a certain critical mass, the atmosphere and character of the parish itself takes on an evangelical spirit and ethos.

A fourth element in evangelization is attention to the process of spiritual growth by means of prayer and holiness of conduct. The Gospel looks to create a sense of permanent relationship, an abiding sense of communion with Christ, the risen and living Lord, who is constantly with us and guides us in our daily walk. In the Gospel of John, Christ compares His relationship with His followers to that of a vine and its branches: "I am the vine, you are the branches. Whoever abides in me, and I in him, he it is who bears much fruit" (Jn 15:4-5). Jesus taught the disciples not only to abide in His love and in His word, but truly in Him by means of a mutual indwelling, a mystical union: "If anyone loves me, he will keep my word, and my Father will love him, and we will come to him and make our home with him" (Jn 14:23). The same sense of mystical union with Christ is found in St. Paul who wrote: "For me to live is Christ" (Phil 1:21). And again: "I have been crucified with Christ; it is no longer I who live, but Christ who lives in me; and the life I now live in the flesh I live by faith in the Son of God, who loved me and gave Himself for me" (Gal 2:20). This consciousness of personal connection and communion with Christ can arise only from a disciplined life of prayer and a sense of Christian integrity in all our daily affairs. The deepest aspects of Orthodox spirituality, theology and worship – the whole understanding of salvation as participation in the life of God (*theosis*) – are anchored on this evangelical teaching of the mystical union with Christ, the source of the greatest spiritual power and renewal in the parish.

Such biblical passages and spiritual principles must be attended to and be taught to our people, especially the principle of Christ-centeredness. The treasure is not tapped if preaching and teaching concentrate on explaining Christian virtues in the abstract and giving practical advice without connecting the discourse specifically with Christ. Often one hears valuable sermons on love, humility, sacrifice, forgiveness and generosity in which the name of Christ is hardly mentioned. Little is heard about Christ Himself – His own love, humility, sacrifice, forgiveness and generosity as exemplified in His ministry. And yet it is an easy matter to lift up an event or teaching from the Gospels expressing these qualities. In fact it makes the task of preaching more concrete, clear and effective. In similar fashion, teaching sessions in the classroom or church hall offer valuable instruction on fasting, icons, the lives of Saints, traditional customs and important events in Church history. The opportunity need not be lost to connect these treasures with Christ, to remind participants of the centrality of Christ, and to celebrate the gift of His holy presence in our midst. Evangelical preaching and teaching, while affirming all the treasures of the Orthodox tradition, seeks to bring Christ into the center of things where He truly belongs and thus to create the conscious awareness that the Christ of the Pantokrator icon in the dome of our sanctuaries is truly the Lord of the parish and the Lord of our personal lives as well.

A final element in evangelization is witness. Jesus used the metaphors of salt and light to describe the disciples' role of witness and mission in the world. When Christ dwells in the hearts of believers, when the local parish is Christ-centered in its mindset and activities, then all who bear the name Christian will spontaneously function as salt and light wherever the may be in the world. In the early chapters of 2 Corinthians, St. Paul uses other striking imagery to describe his missionary work, which he connects with the proclamation of the Gospel, as well as the light of the new creation that the Gospel imparts to receptive hearts. St. Paul speaks of his apostolic ministry as "the fragrance of the knowledge of God" and "the aroma of Christ to God" being spread among believers and unbelievers (2 Cor 2:14-15). This aromatic fragrance of Christian witness, according to St. Paul, is not some external additive but an intrinsic quality arising out of "the light of the Gospel of the glory of Christ" shining in the hearts of those who gladly hear and receive the good news. The Apostle uses the imagery of the act of creation to describe the mystery of how God Himself lights up the light of His grace by means of the Gospel: "For what we preach is not ourselves but Jesus Christ as Lord, with ourselves as your servants for Jesus' sake. For it is the God who said, 'Let light shine out of darkness,' who has shone in our hearts to give the light of the knowledge of the glory of God in the face of Christ" (2 Cor 4:5-6). St. Paul goes on to say that this act of creation in the soul, which is the source of witness and mission, is also "the treasure in earthen vessels," the transcendent power of God in us which upholds us in times of suffering so that, afflicted we are not crushed, perplexed we are not driven to despair, struck down we are not destroyed, so that the life of Jesus may be manifest in our mortal humanity (2 Cor 4:7-10).

Evangelization, the preaching of the Gospel, is not the only ministry in the Church. There is also worship, catechesis, pastoral guidance, philanthropy and mission. However, all ministries of the Church, to function properly and in full power, must be penetrated with an evangelical spirit – the love of Christ, the zeal to proclaim the good news, the joy to see people coming to Christ and growing in Christ, the commitment to pray and work for the cause of the kingdom and its righteousness. The evangelical spirit is none other than the burning faith that the risen Christ in His great love and mercy is in our midst doing His gracious work in us and through us. In this perspective of living faith, all believers have the possibility of becoming the "aroma of Christ," "the fragrance of the knowledge of God" wherever God has placed us. When a sufficient number of believers shine with the light of Christ, then the local parish itself, by the grace of God, becomes a burning bush of God's presence for all to see and respond.

NOTES

[1] Bishop Anastasios Yannoulatos, "Discovering the Orthodox Missionary Ethos," *Martyria/Mission: The Witness of the Orthodox Churches Today*, ed. by Ion Bria (Geneva: World Council of Churches, 1980), pp. 20-29.

[2] Yannoulatos, p. 20.

[3] Peter E. Gillquist, *Becoming Orthodox: A Journey to the Ancient Christian Faith* (Ben Lomond: Conciliar Press, 1992) and the abundance of literature published by Conciliar Press. A similar evangelical stirring through incoming coverts is occurring in England. See Michael Harper, *A Faith Fulfilled: Why Are Christians Across Great Britain Embracing Orthodoxy?* (Ben Lomond: Conciliar Press, 1999).

[4] David W. Henderson, *Culture Shift: Communicating God's Truth to Our Changing World* (Grand Rapids, MI: Baker Books, 1998), p. 16. See also Stanley J. Grenz, *A Primer on Postmodernism* (Grand Rapids, MI: Eerdmans, 1996) and Nancey Murphy, *Anglo-American Postmodernity: Philosophical Perspectives on Science, Religion, and Ethics* (Boulder, CO: Westview Press, 1997).

[5] Henderson, p. 183.

[6] Alexander Schmemann, "Problems of Orthodoxy in America: The Spiritual Problem," *St. Vladimir's Theological Quarterly* 9:4 (1965), pp. 171-193.

[7] Schmemann, p. 174.

[8] In his keynote address to the Clergy-Laity Congress in Dallas, Texas, entitled "Rekindling an Orthodox Awareness." See the address in *The Collected Works of Archbishop Iakovos, Vol. 1, Visions and Expectations for a Living Church*, ed. Demetrios J. Constantelos (Brookline, MA: Holy Cross Orthodox Press, 1998).

[9] Commission on the Archdiocesan Theological Agenda, "Report to His Eminence Archbishop Iakovos," *The Greek Orthodox Theological Review* 34 (1989) pp. 283-306. This report, dealing with issues of faith, leadership, the parish, and social realities facing the Church, and including a modern Greek translation, was republished in a separate small volume and distributed to all the delegates of the Clergy-Laity Congress in Washington, D.C. (1990) under the title: *Report to His Eminence Archbishop Iakovos Concerning the Future Theological Agenda of the Greek Orthodox Archdiocese* (Brookline, MA: Holy Cross Orthodox Press, 1990). It is still highly instructive today.

[10] Commission on the Archdiocesan Theological Agenda, "Report to His Eminence Archbishop Iakovos," *The Greek Orthodox Theological Review* 34 (1989), p. 287 (emphasis in the original).

[11] Report to Iakovos, p. 288.

[12] Report to Iakovos, p. 288.

[13] St. Athanasius, *On the Incarnation of the Word*, trans. and ed. by a Religious of C.S.M.V. with an Introduction by C. S. Lewis (London: Mowbray, 1953), p. 61. The citation occurs in chapter 30 of St. Athanasius' work.

[14] This idea and language is taken from W. A. Elwell and R. W. Yarbrough, *Encountering the New Testament* (Grand Rapids, MI: Baker Books, 1998), p. 138.

[15] See further Theodore Stylianopoulos, *The Good News of Christ: Essays on the Gospel, Sacraments and Spirit* (Brookline, MA: Holy Cross Orthodox Press, 1991), pp. 1-29.

[16] Anthony Coniaris, *Preaching the Word of God* (Brookline, MA: Holy Cross Orthodox Press, 1983), pp. 8-9.

A Systematic Conceptualization of Intermarriages in the Greek Orthodox Archdiocese of America

Charles Joanides

Approximately sixty-seven percent of all marriages conducted in the Greek Orthodox Archdiocese of America (Archdiocese) are designated interChristian. [1] When marriages taking place outside the Archdiocese are also considered, it is estimated that seventy-five to eighty percent of all marriageable adult members are intermarrying. As a result of these trends, the Archdiocese commissioned the Interfaith Research Project (IRP) in an effort to (a) develop a clearer understanding of this population's unique challenges, and (b) seek to minister more effectively to this growing group of faithful. One outcome from this research has been the emergence of an Orthodox developmental ecological grounded theory of interfaith marriages in the Archdiocese. This paper will seek to outline the methodology employed to generate this theory. Two illustrations will also be offered describing its utility. Additional discussion of this theory's usefulness for clergy and lay workers will also be presented.

Introduction

Statistics kept by the Archdiocese suggest that the intermarriage challenge is not only real, but is deserving of more careful attention. A cursory look at a few figures kept by the archdiocesan Department of Registry suggest that over the past twenty-two years the percentage of interChristian marriages conducted in the Archdiocese has steadily increased from forty-six to sixty-four percent. [2] In addition, statistics also suggest that nearly two of every three marriages are now designated interChristian. It should also be noted here that Archdiocesan statistics only reflect those weddings performed in the Archdiocese, and do not account for those persons who identify themselves as Greek Orthodox, but have chosen to marry outside of the church. When efforts have been made to factor these faithful into the statistics kept by the Archdiocese, some scholars have speculated that intermarriage rates exceed Archdiocesan statistics, while others have been

191

more specific and estimated that intermarried rates are currently "over eighty percent."[3] Irrespective of exact percentages, what is very clear is that even the most conservative figures indicate that nearly sixty-seven percent of all marriages conducted in the Archdiocese are interChristian, intercultural, and in some instances, interracial in composition.[4]

In addition, since there is no evidence to suggest that these trends will change in the foreseeable future, it has been maintained that if interfaith marriages are not currently the norm in the Archdiocese's parishes, they will likely be in the near future.[5] One can also convincingly argue – as many respected scholars have – that indifference to these trends could negatively impact the Archdiocese's efforts to enter into the twenty-first century as a viable, healthy, religious, and spiritual presence.[6]

Responding to these statistics and trends

Because of the large numbers of interChristian marriages conducted in the Archdiocese, an Intermarriage Research Project[7] (IRP) was commissioned in 1998 to examine these marriages. While it is impossible to discuss all the results that emerged from the IRP, this paper will seek to summarize a central component of this work. To be more specific, this paper will describe and outline a grounded theory that emerged, entitled *An Orthodox, ecological, developmental grounded theory of interfaith marriages in the Archdiocese.* Furthermore, like all theories, it is anticipated that this theory will assist the reader in developing a clearer, more sophisticated understanding of a very complex challenge that faces the Archdiocese, to God's glory and the salvation of the marriages and families discussed in this paper.

METHODOLOGY

A qualitative approach

A qualitative research methodology was chosen. Some of the salient reasons prompting this decision follow. First, social scientists have utilized qualitative research approaches to help them study and understand the human condition for decades. Second, qualitative research is emergent and discovery-oriented, and has been deemed well-suited to study complex human phenomena that are typically not well understood. Specifically, qualitative research permits the examination of large amounts of diverse, seemingly contradictory information. This means that new interpretations and connections are discovered between the various disparate pieces of information that emerge during the research process. Third, consumers of qualitative research vicariously participate in respondents' lived experiences. Fourth, qualitative research tends to be heuristic in character. The range of possible solutions to a problem, or the number of possible answers to a question, are thus reduced through a qualitative investigation.[8]

A qualitative grounded theory approach

There are a number of methodological approaches available to qualitative researchers, and each approach is uniquely suited to the research question being considered.[9] Since one of the objectives of this research was to generate a thick, rich, systematic description and theoretical conceptualization of the challenges that interChristian couples face, a qualitative research methodology was selected and utilized as the method of choice for the IRP.[10] This approach allowed a conceptually rich, systematic theory to emerge that was grounded on 376 respondent's observations and descriptions.

Description of the sampling technique

After receiving permission from each Diocesan bishop, priests were contacted in each Diocese in an initial effort to recruit couples for this study. In total, thirty-eight Greek Orthodox priests assisted me in my efforts to identify potential informant couples for the IRP.

Participating clergy in each Diocese submitted the names of couples to me, and a pool of potential couples was assembled. I subsequently contacted couples by phone in an effort to form focus groups. During the selection process, I was particularly interested to include participant couples who could provide a rich description of their lived experiences as interChristian couples and parents. As such, a purposive sampling approach was employed.[11]

Description of collection method

Because of the potentially large numbers of respondents involved in this study, a decision was made to conduct focus groups. Focus groups have proven to be an efficient and effective way to gather information from large numbers of respondents.[12]

The researcher also attempted to form groups with participants who have as much in common as possible. This technique made it less likely that participants would be debating each other, and more likely that a recursive, reciprocal dialogic process would develop that would allow participants to build upon one another's observations and descriptions.[13] In most instances, two different types of focus groups were conducted in each Diocese. However, there were two exceptions: the Chicago Diocese and the Archdiocesan District, where there were three groups conducted. One type of focus group was comprised of "Generation X"(ages 20-34) couples, and a second type of focus group was comprised of "Baby Boomers" (ages 35-50). This decision was made in an effort to isolate any idiosyncratic cohort differences. Each group met for a two-hour block of time. In total, twenty focus groups were conducted.

I also sought to include as many different perspectives as possible in these conversations. Spouses with high, moderate and low levels of religious and/or ethnic attachments were recruited. As such, immigrants, first-, second-, third-, fourth-, and fifth-generation participants, as well as converts, were represented in this study. This approach was taken to ensure that the emerging information would be reflective of a wide range of voices and perspectives.

In addition to the focus groups, twenty individual one-hour follow-up debriefing telephone interviews were conducted with selected focus group participants. These interviews took place after the researcher had analyzed the transcripts from each focus group. The researcher simply read his analysis to focus group participants and requested feedback. These debriefing interviews functioned to strengthen the trustworthiness of the data collection process.[14]

Description of respondents

A total of two hundred and two participants took part in one of twenty focus groups that were conducted from April 1998 to December 1999. One hundred and twelve Baby Boomers who were married an average of thirteen years, and had 2.1 children, and ninety "X"ers who were married an average of four years and had 0.9 children participated. Each participant couple was comprised of one Greek Orthodox Christian and one non-Greek Orthodox Christian. Fifty percent were Orthodox or Greek Orthodox, thirty-two percent were Roman Catholic, sixteen percent identified themselves with a Protestant Church, and two percent failed to declare a religious affiliation. Many couples (twenty-eight percent) identified themselves as interChristian, and in most cases, interChristian and intercultural (sixty-five percent). Some identified themselves as interChristian, intercultural and interracial (five percent). Respondents were from twenty-nine different cities, with varying levels of affiliation with one of twenty-four different Greek Orthodox parishes.

In addition to focus group participants, one hundred and seventy-four individuals reviewed the emerging results that were posted on the Interfaith Marriage Web Site, and offered feedback on either an interfaith couples feedback form or stakeholders feedback form.[15] These participants examined the results that were periodically posted, and offered observations and descriptions on feedback forms. The inclusion of these remarks served to reinforce the credibility of the information that was emerging and infused

additional richness into the emerging results. When focus group participants, together with those who filled out feedback forms on the Interfaith
Marriage Web Site are considered, results from the IRP reflect 376 respondents' observations and descriptions.

Types of questions utilized[16]

Before each focus group was conducted, each individual was asked to
complete a twenty-four item questionnaire[17] that was designed to (a) gather
demographic information, (b) identify factors contributing to their decision to intermarry, and (c) gather attitudinal information about interfaith
and intercultural marriage. Prior to conducting each focus group, couples
were reminded that they were not simply sharing information with the
moderator/researcher, but would indirectly be speaking to the clergy and
lay leaders of the Archdiocese. I also sought to cultivate respect and candor
for all perspectives. Confidentiality was assured to each respondent. Respondents were assured that their comments would not be identified with
them in any future reports and publications.

Open-ended questions were utilized to generate conversation. Examples
of the type of questions utilized follow: What has it been like being involved in an interfaith marriage? What have been some of your surprises,
blessings, challenges and difficulties?

Open-ended questions also tended to change as the research process un-
folded. When I determined that I was reaching a point of saturation (a
point when redundant information was essentially emerging) new questions were constructed and new areas of inquiry were probed and introduced
into the research process. This approach ensured that a broad, systematic
description of interfaith spouses and couples' personal experiences would
emerge.

Techniques used to ensure trustworthiness

Code notes were used to assist me in generating conceptual labels, categories, properties and dimensions. These notes would ultimately function to
form the essential features of the grounded theory described in this paper[18].
Theoretical notes were employed to assist me in my efforts to begin conceptualizing and formulating relevant subcategories, their properties and
dimensions. Theoretical notes would also help clarify the given relationships
that existed between the subcategories, properties and dimensions, as well as
help to discover some of the essential features of the grounded theory that
would ultimately emerge. Operational notes were comprised of memos that
would provide me with direction regarding sampling, questions, and the possible comparisons that I should follow as the research process continued.[19]

In order to ensure that credibility, transferability, dependability and confirmability issues were considered and satisfied, the following techniques were also employed. The use of member checks, peer debriefing, persistent observation, and the establishment of referential adequacy served to ensure that credibility issues were considered. [20] The use of purposive sampling and my efforts to generate a thick, rich, systematic description of respondent's perceptions would serve to satisfy transferability issues. The use of an audit trail would serve to meet dependability issues. The use of an external auditor and my efforts to practice reflexivity would serve to meet confirmability issues.[21]

Analysis

The analysis proceeded in three stages.[22] In the first stage, typically termed "open coding," I attempted to open the data up in an effort to begin building a conceptual framework. This process also allowed me to tentatively begin grouping concepts together and collapsing them under cover terms that are called categories and subcategories. This process also assisted me in tentatively identifying different attributes and characteristics properties of each category – called properties – and allowed me to begin dimensionalizing each given property. The second stage in the analysis process, termed "axial coding," allowed me to piece together the data that had been taken apart during the first stage of analysis. Axial coding also served to assist me in my efforts to begin putting respondent's descriptions and interpretations of their religious and spiritual lived experiences back together in a systematic form. The third stage in this analysis process is termed "selective coding."[23] During this stage I typically sought to explicate and identify a story line that was conceptually and systematically dense, and was derived from the collected data. Thirteen subcategories emerged from this process, which served to form the basis of the grounded theory that emerged.

An Orthodox developmental ecological grounded theory of interChristian couples in the Archdiocese

In the simplest of terms, a theory "is a set of related concepts and constructs that exist in meaningful relationship to one another. Each concept or construct has no meaning in its own right. The relationship is one of complementarity and meaningfulness in context and only in context."[24] Family scholars and researchers utilize many theories to help them understand and explicate individual, marital and family behavior. In addition to my Orthodox perspective, two theories seemed especially useful in my efforts to interpret and organize the volumes of emergent information during the collection and analysis stage – social ecological theory[25] and family de-

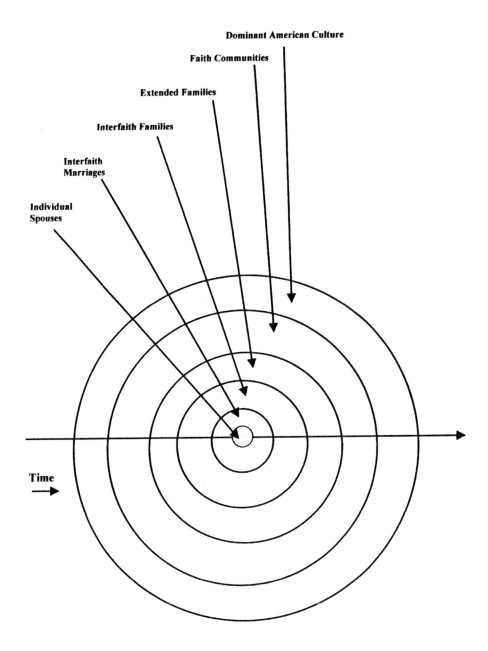

An Orthodox Developmental Ecological Grounded
Theory of Interfaith Marriages in the GOA

velopment theory.[26] A succinct description of their usefulness will briefly be discussed below.

An examination of the ecological dimension

As results from the IRP emerged, participants' observations and descriptions repeatedly alluded to a distinct social ecology that impacted individual, couple and family religious and spiritual well-being. This social ecology also influenced couples' efforts to incorporate ethnic traditions into their marriages and families. The above diagram describes this social ecology. Specifically, this diagram provides a visual picture of the main human ecological subsystems that affect interChristian couples who worship in one of the Archdiocese's parishes. The smallest circle at the center suggests that interfaith spouses are part of an interfaith marriage. This schematic diagram indicates that interfaith marriages are part of an interfaith family, and interfaith families are part of at least two extended family systems.[27] This diagram also illustrates how interfaith spouses, their marriages and families, as well as their extended families, are generally couched within two faith communities. These faith communities are also embedded in our dominant American culture.

What is not as evident from an examination of this diagram is another prevailing observation that typically characterized respondents' remarks. Specifically, participants repeatedly observed that interfaith spouses have certain needs, as do interfaith marriages, interfaith families, extended families, and the faith communities to which they belong. Moreover, in a perfect world where everything lines up and fits together, all these disparate needs fit together perfectly. In an imperfect world like the one that we all live in, these needs do not always fit together perfectly, but conflict with each other. Consequently, interChristian spouses and couples repeatedly described numerous challenges they faced in their efforts to strike a balance between these conflicting subsystem needs.

Respondents also stated that if they were successful in striking a balance between conflicting subsystem needs, their religious and cultural differences were generally perceived from a positive, enriching perspective. Furthermore, they maintained that their religious and cultural differences seemed to have a generally positive impact on individual, couple and family stability and well-being. Conversely, if participants were unable to strike this balance, spouses' religious and cultural differences were construed from a deficit perspective. In these instances, participants viewed their religious and cultural differences as potential threats to individual, marital and family satisfaction and stability. They also observed that their religious and cultural differences had a negative impact on individual, couple and family stability and well-being.

A closer look at the developmental dimension

As we mature, we pass through a life cycle, encountering qualitatively different challenges from one stage of the life cycle to the next. For example, while teens are busy differentiating from their parents, young adults might be trying to acquire financial independence, middle-aged adults might be busy raising families and cultivating careers, and older adults may be preoccupied in reviewing their lives and finding positive closure. Just as the individual encounters different developmental challenges as he or she matures and ages, social scientists have also posited that marriages and families pass through a life cycle that challenges them with specific tasks that must be negotiated and resolved.[28]

With regard to the IRP, respondents' comments repeatedly alluded to how individual, couple and family maturation tends to influence subsystem needs and challenges. Specifically, they observed that the challenges newlyweds will encounter and negotiate will be different from the challenges that couples with young children will face, or the challenges that couples with adolescents will face, or the challenges that couples who have launched their children may face. Respondent's observations and descriptions clearly indicated that individual, couple and family maturation can have a profound impact on the types of needs and challenges intermarried spouses, couples and their families will have and encounter.

Two examples

Listing and discussing all the potential needs and challenges that participants described is impossible in a short article. Nevertheless, the following two examples, together with related commentary, should suffice in helping the reader begin to understand both the value and utility of this theory. As the reader considers the information that follows, he or she might observe how this theory functions to organize and make more understandable an otherwise complex area of interest. The reader might also contemplate the utility of this theory for (a) intermarried couples and their families, and (b) clergy and lay leaders who seek to minister to this population of faithful.

Balancing individual and couple needs

Martha (31) and Gus (33) have been married for about six years. Martha is Mexican Catholic and Gus is Greek Orthodox. Gus considers himself nominally religious, but is firmly connected to his ethnic background.

Martha has higher levels of religious commitment and an equally high level of connection to her ethnic background. Moreover, almost from the beginning of their marriage, this couple admits that they have both constantly and unsuccessfully argued about their religious and cultural differences. Issues such as where they should worship, their future children's names, where they should baptize, and which ethnic and religious traditions they should include in their family life have remained unresolved.

As a result, out of frustration, Gus unilaterally decides that the couple should belong and pledge to the Greek Orthodox Church, and submits a pledge. When Martha hears about this, she becomes angry and resentful because she views herself as "the religious one." She confronts Gus, and demands an explanation. In response, Gus retorts, "I'm Greek, and I can't deny that about myself any longer," but refuses to engage in further conversation. Martha becomes angrier and makes some insulting remarks. Gus leaves the house, and does not return for several hours. By then, Martha's interest in arguing wanes, but her resentment lingers. Gus is somewhat relieved because he does not have to hear Martha yell, but he remains discouraged with the religious and cultural differences in his marriage.

Martha continues to celebrate most religious feast days alone. Both spouses also celebrate ethnic holidays alone. Their decision to start a family is also postponed.

Some observations

Participants from the IRP frequently stated that their religious and ethnic connections fulfilled numerous spiritual, moral, psychological and social needs at a personal level. Moreover, these individual needs were often described as being compelling and important enough to cause them to find ways of fulfilling these needs.

Respondents also stated that if they desired marital stability and satisfaction, they could not simply consider their own personal religious and cultural needs to the exclusion of their partner's needs in their efforts to cultivate a healthy, functional marriage. Furthermore, to the extent that participants were successful in striking a balance between their personal and marital needs, couples were able to meet their personal religious and cultural needs, as well as achieve marital stability and satisfaction. When spouses either ignored their own needs, their partner's needs, or their relationship's needs, then one or both spouses would generally experience some internal conflict which often translated into some external marital and family instability and dissatisfaction.

Given these first two observations, the following can be stated about the challenges that Gus and Martha appear to be encountering. First, both spouses appear to have certain definite religious and/or ethnic needs. Second, the strategy they have employed to meet their personal needs has had a toxic effect on (a) individual well-being, (b) couple stability and satisfaction, and (c) their future plans to start a family. Third, this couple appears to be caught in an unresolved stalemate. Moreover, the longer they remain stuck, the greater the likelihood more damage will be inflicted on their individual, marital and family well-being. Fourth, this couple's individual distress and marital conflict will negatively impact their religious and spiritual development. Fifth, if this couple could be helped to see what is occurring between them, there might be a possibility that individual and couple satisfaction could be improved. Specifically, if they could be helped to see that in their efforts to meet their personal religious and cultural needs, they have ignored their needs as a couple, this could give them a different perspective of the impasse in which they are ensnared. In addition, if this couple can be convinced to strike a balance between their needs as individuals and a couple, chances are good that the stalemate will loosen and disappear.

Balancing nuclear family needs with extended family needs

Balancing nuclear family needs and extended family needs is a skill that couples must also master. When couples are unsuccessful in accomplishing this task, individual, couple, nuclear family and extended family well-being can suffer. The following example illustrates how this can happen.

John and Mary

John (27) and Mary (25) have been married for about one year. John is a first-generation Greek Orthodox Christian, and Mary is a non-practicing Roman Catholic from a mixed ethnic background. This couple is happily married, but also admits to encountering some serious challenges. Some of the reasons to account for this last statement are chronicled below.

When John and Mary began dating, John's parents were quick to point out that "it was fine that you date a non-Greek for fun and games' sake, but you should only permit yourself to become serious with a Greek girl, since marriages with non-Greeks do not work out." John politely listened to his parents, but because of his increasing affection for Mary, he quickly found that he could not live up to this advice and continued to date her. John also determined to hide his parent's dissatisfaction from Mary, fearing that if he shared this information, it would somehow compromise their relationship. Even though John hid his parents' displeasure, Mary sensed his parents' disapproval, and remained mildly concerned.

Several months passed, and John and Mary became very serious, until one day when John proposed marriage, and Mary accepted. The next day, John shared this news with his parents privately, because he was unable to predict how they might react, and did not want his fiancée to hear any negative remarks regarding their decision to wed.

Predictably, John's parents did not take this news well. They began to issue threats and ultimatums like, "If you marry this girl, we will disown you."

After a few days, as they began to notice that John was pulling away from them, their tone softened, and they began to state that they would tolerate his decision, but would also "not be surprised if this marriage did not survive."

Since John knew that Mary was a non-practicing Catholic, he asked her if she would agree to get married in the Greek Orthodox Church, stating that "this would please his parents." He did not, however, share the full extent of his parents' reservations and disappointment with their decision to wed. Mary also failed to ask any questions, even though she continued to be concerned about John's parents' feelings about their decision.

Wishing to improve her rather distant and cold relationship with John's parents, Mary consented to this suggestion, and the couple was married in the Greek Orthodox Church. Unfortunately, to Mary's chagrin, after the marriage, her in-laws continued to remain distant, but cordial toward her.

About six months after the marriage, John's parents would approach him, strongly urging him to ask Mary to join the Greek Orthodox Church. They also told him that he "should convince Mary to convert, since this would be good for their children and family." As a result of these and other similar remarks, John went home that night and awkwardly began making the following proposal, "I think we should have a family church – the Greek Church. It would also be nice if you thought about converting. I think this would be good for our future children."

Dumbfounded and surprised at these suggestions, Mary responded, "Where in the world has this come from, John? You've never suggested to me that religion was important to you before this day. I don't know; that's a lot to think about."

Not wishing to disclose who prompted him to make this statement, John defensively responded, "So what's wrong with having a family church and being the same religion? And what's to think about? It's no big deal. We go once in a while and everyone's happy."

Upon hearing this last statement, Mary then states, "Now I get it. It's your parents who put you up to this. And now you're siding with them. Aren't you?"

"And what if it's true?" stated John more defensively.

"Do you know how that makes me feel when you talk to them about things that concern us, before you talk to me? It makes me feel betrayed, John. And another thing, how can I trust you, if I think you're withholding information or siding with them?"

That night was a long and emotional evening for both John and Mary. Fortunately, John would finally tell Mary the truth about his parents' feelings for them. He would also ask for Mary's forgiveness, and promise never to withhold information from her again. The couple would also formulate some new boundaries of the type that would not allow John's parents to divide the couple again.

Some observations

Participants' comments from the IRP clearly stated that members from both partners' extended families have needs – particularly parents. For example, parents have a need to see their adult married children and future grandchildren actively practicing their religious and ethnic traditions. In an effort to meet this need, parents may apply overt or covert pressure on intermarried couples and families. As such, balancing nuclear family needs and extended family needs is a talent that couples must master.

Participants also repeatedly stated that it was necessary for them to learn how to draw healthy boundaries between themselves and their extended families to protect their nuclear families from unwanted extended intrusions. As couples learned how to love and honor their parents, while also drawing clear boundaries between themselves and their parents, this approach made things easier for everyone concerned.

Participants also observed that when intermarried couples were unsuccessful in drawing clear boundaries between themselves and their extended family, some respondents were forced to subordinate and/or ignore their nuclear family needs in an effort to meet extended families' expectations and needs. Furthermore, this tended to have a negative impact on marital satisfaction and nuclear family religious well-being.

In light of these observations, what can be stated about John and Mary? First, in John's desire to honor and attend to his parent's needs, he lost sight of (a) Mary's needs, and (b) his developing relationship's needs. These omissions distressed Mary, and created marital conflict. Second, while Mary's contributions are not as clear, a strong case could be made that she also made similar mistakes. Even though Mary sensed that John's parents were displeased, she did not request any clarification from John. All of which suggests that Mary's silence also inhibited this couple from meeting their individual and couple needs. Third, only after some serious discussion is this couple able to make the necessary adjustments, and strike a balance between their individual needs, their needs as a couple, and John's parents' needs. Until then, these needs remain unattended and serve to negatively impact both spouses.

Some implications of this theory's usefulness
- As a result of intermarried couples' religious, cultural and, in some instances, racial differences, they encounter challenges that differ from the challenges that homogamous couples experience. Pastoral approaches that seek to attend to these unique challenges will likely be more successful than pastoral approaches that ignore them. This theory allows pastors and lay workers this latitude, since it is inherently concerned with how these spousal differences can impact individual, marital and family stability and well-being.
- As the two above examples clearly suggest, interfaith couples' social environment can create some unique challenges for them. The many conflicting layers of subsystem needs can function to negatively impact individual, marital and family stability and well-being. Moreover, diminished marital satisfaction and family stability can inhibit religious and spiritual development. By acquiring a working knowledge of this theory, clergy and lay workers can develop a more sophisticated understanding of these challenges. This knowledge should also function to positively impact the manner in which they minister to this population of faithful.
- A working knowledge of this theory can assist intermarried spouses and couples in their efforts to understand the social ecological challenges they face. This knowledge can assist couples in their efforts to prayerfully resolve the conflicting subsystem challenges they encounter.
- Results from the IRP also suggest that intermarried couples' challenges change as they pass through the individual, marital and family life cycle. As such, this theory can assist clergy and lay leaders to account for developmental life cycle changes, and encourage them to consider how these changes may be impacting individual, marital and family stability and religious and spiritual well-being.
- This theory can also provide intermarried couples with a clearer understanding of how maturation impacts individual, marital and family stability. A familiarity with the developmental challenges they will face can positively impact individual, marital and family well-being.
- Interfaith couples can also differ from one partner to the next and from one couple to the next with regard to their level of religious commitment. In some instances, some couples may have equal amounts of religious commitment, while in other instances spouses may have unequal levels of religious commitment. Since this theory considers individual needs, spouses'

religious differences are indirectly considered, as well as how these differences might have an impact upon marital and family stability and well-being.

- Interfaith spouses can differ from one partner to the next and from one couple to the next with regards to their level of attachment to the dominant American culture. In some instances, spouses may have equally high or low levels of attachment to the dominant American culture and weak attachments to their ethnic backgrounds. In other instances, one partner may have a stronger attachment to his or her ethnic background, while their partner may have a high connection to the American culture, and relatively few connections to an ethnic background. This theory allows pastors and lay workers to account for these differences. It also allows clergy and lay workers to examine how conflicting dominant American cultural attachments and ethnic attachments may be adversely impacting these marriages and families.

- One of the challenges facing the Orthodox Church in America is to discern how it can minister to the growing numbers of intermarried couples without compromising its theological integrity. Since this theory is grounded on intermarried couples' observations, it is maintained that an understanding of the developmental and ecological challenges that these couples face can facilitate the Church's efforts in ministering to this population of faithful. Specifically, this theory can assist the church in developing a higher level of understanding of the effects (both negative and positive) that its current pastoral approaches are having on intermarried spouses, couples and their families. And where possible, it can assist the Church in making adjustments. These adjustments will require the prayerful collaboration of the Church's best and brightest.

- Participants from the IRP repeatedly stated that pastoral approaches that were more respectful and collaborative were preferred to those that were directive and judgmental. It is thus asserted, that as priests and lay workers utilize this theory in their work with intermarried spouses, couples and their families, they will acquire a more respectful appreciation of the challenges that these faithful encounter. Moreover, this understanding can facilitate a pastoral approach that is more respectful and collaborative in nature and, by extension, more effectual.

- Participants from the IRP constantly observed that their attendance, commitment and participation in the Orthodox Church were directly connected to how welcome they felt. When they felt as if the congregation welcomed them and was sensitive to their needs, this positively affected attendance, commitment and participation. Given this observation, it is maintained that when clergy and lay leaders understand this theory, this will assist them in their efforts to help their congregations become more sensitive to intermarried couples' unique needs. Moreover, this should have a direct, positive influence on this population's attendance, commitment and participation.

Conclusion

In our efforts to address ourselves to the interfaith marriage challenge, we should remember that "God desires all men to be saved and come to the knowledge of the truth" (1 Tim 2:4), and that the Church's message is inherently inclusive and evangelical in nature. Furthermore, numerous examples of the inclusive, evangelical nature of the church's ministry can be given. For example, from its inception at Pentecost (Acts 2), up until our present-day efforts to deal with the interfaith marriage challenge, the church continues to be inclusive and evangelical.

We might also take heart in our Lord's promise that "all things are possible to him who believes" (Mk 9:23). Viewed from this blessed perspective, the interfaith marriage challenge simply requires us to do our part and be faithful.

The information presented in this paper has been inspired by these Divine dictates. This paper has sought to introduce the reader to a theory that can assist the Church at all levels in its efforts to prayerfully address itself to the interfaith marriage challenge. This paper has maintained that an understanding of this theory can assist clergy and lay leaders – at all levels of the church's structure – to reach out more effectively to the interfaith couples who choose to worship in one of the churches in the Archdiocese, to God's glory.

NOTES

[1] The population of marriages that this paper will concern itself with is rich and diverse. As a result, the following three descriptors have been selected, and will be utilized in this paper: interChristian marriages, interfaith marriages and intermarriages. Inter Christian marriages will refer to marriages that have taken place in the Archdiocese between a Greek Orthodox Christian and a non-Orthodox Christian. Interfaith marriages will refer to marriages that are interChristian or interreligious. These types of couples may or may not have been married in the Archdiocese. These marriages can also be intercultural and interracial. The term intermarriages is the most inclusive term. This descriptor will utilized to refer to interChristian, inter religious, intercultural, interracial marriages, as well as marriages that take place between a Greek Orthodox Christian and a non-religious person.

[2] *Yearbook 2000: Greek Orthodox Archdiocese of America* (New York: Greek Orthodox Archdiocese of America, 2000).

[3] See for example, the work of J.S. Counelis, "Greek Orthodox Church Statistics

of the United States, 1949-1989: Some ecclesial and social patterns," *Journal of the Hellenic Diaspora*, 16 (1989), pp. 129-159; C. Moskos, "Faith, language and culture." In S. J. Sfekas, & G. E. Matsoukas (Eds.) *Project for Orthodox Renewal* (Minneapolis, MN: Light and Life Publishing Co., 1993); and S. Lorant and G. Wingenbach, *Proceedings from 33rd Clergy-Laity Congress: Report of the Committee on Interchurch and Interfaith Marriages* (New York, Greek Orthodox Archdiocese, 1996).

4 C. Joanides, *The interfaith marriage challenge: A manual for clergy and lay leaders* (forthcoming).

5 S. Harakas, S. "Emerging ecumenical families." In A. C. Vrame (ed.) *InterMarriage: Orthodox Perspectives* (Brookline, MA: Holy Cross Orthodox Press, 1997). See also Counelis, "Greek Orthodox statistics" and C. Moskos, *Greek Americans: Struggle and success* (New Brunswick: Transaction Publishers, 1990).

6 See the articles by Constantelos, Harakas, Krommydas and Patsavos in Vrame, *InterMarriage*. See also C. Moskos, "Faith, language and culture" and C. Moskos, *Greek Americans*.

7 While much of the information included in this article may have some application to all types of intermarried couples, it should be noted that the primary focus of the IRP was to investigate interChristian couples. That being the case, the reader should be aware that many of the challenges facing other types of intermarried couples will not be considered in this paper. For additional information about the IRP, write Rev. Fr. Charles Joanides, Ph.D., LMFT at 8-10 East 79th Street, New York, NY 10021 or e-mail Fr. Charles at Joanidesch@aol.com.

8 N. K. Denzin and Y. S. Lincoln, *Handbook of Qualitative Research* (Thousand Oaks, CA: Sage Publications, 1994).

9 J. W. Creswell, *Research Design: Qualitative and Quantitative Approaches* (Thousand Oaks: Sage Publications, 1994). See also Denzin and Lincoln, *Handbook of Qualitative Research*.

10 B. G. Glazer and A. L. Strauss, *The discovery of grounded theory: Strategies for qualitative research* (New York: Aldine Publishing Co., 1965). See also A. Strauss and J. Corbin, *Basics of qualitative research: Grounded theory procedures and techniques* (Newbury Park, CA: Sage, 1990); A. Strauss and J. Corbin, "Grounded theory methodology: An overview." In N. K. Denzin & Y. S. Lincoln, eds., *Handbook of Qualitative Research*, 273-285 (Thousand Oaks, CA: Sage Publications, 1994);. A. Strauss and J. Corbin, *Grounded Theory in Practice* (Thousand Oaks, CA: Sage Publilcations, 1997).

11 Y. Lincoln and E. G. Guba, *Naturalistic Inquiry* (Beverly Hills, CA: Sage Publications, 1985).

12 R. A. Krueger, *Analyzing and reporting focus group results: Focus group kit 6* (Thousand Oaks, CA: Sage Publications, 1998). See also F. P. Piercy and V. Nickerson, "Focus groups in family therapy research." In D. H. Sprenkle & S. M. Moon, Eds., *Research Methods in Family Therapy*, (New York: Guilford Press, 1996), pp. 173–190.

13 D. L. Morgan, *Planning focus groups: Focus group kit 2* (Thousand Oaks, CA: Sage Publications, 1998). See also Piercy and Nickerson, "Focus groups in family therapy research."

[14] C. J. Joanides, L. Brigham, and H. Joanning, "Co-creating a more cooperative client-therapist relationship through a debriefing process," *The American Journal of Family Therapy* 25 (1997) 139-150.

[15] This site served to strengthen the credibility of this research, and can be accessed through the following address at www.interfaith.Archdioceserch.org. Additionally, stakeholders were identified as people who had a vested interest in this subject such as clergy, social scientists, parents, divorced persons.

[16] A copy of the open-ended questions utilized during this study can be obtained by contacting Fr. Charles Joanides.

[17] A copy of this questionnaire can be obtained by contacting Fr. Charles Joanides.

[18] Strauss and Corbin, *Basics of qualitative research*. Strauss and Corbin, "Grounded theory methodology;" Strauss and Corbin, *Grounded Theory in Practice*.

[19] Strauss and Corbin, *Basics of qualitative research*.

[20] Y. Lincoln and E. Guba, *Naturalistic inquiry* (Beverly Hills, CA: Sage Publications 1985). See also S. E. Rafuls and S. M. Moon, "Grounded theory methodology in family therapy." In D. H. Sprenkle and S. M. Moon, eds., *Research Methods in Family Therapy* (New York: Guilford Press, 1996) 64 – 82.

[21] Lincoln and Guba, *Naturalistic inquiry*.

[22] Strauss and Corbin, *Basics of qualitative research*; Rafuls and Moon, "Grounded theory methodology in family therapy."

[23] Strauss and Corbin, *Basics of qualitative research*.

[24] D. S. Becvar and R. J. Becvar, *Family therapy: A systemic integration* (Needham, MA: Allyn & Bacon, 1996) 356 – 357.

[25] U. Bronfrenbrenner, *The ecology of human development* (Cambridge, MA: Harvard University Press, 1979). M. M. Bubolz and S. Sontag, "Human ecology theory." In P. G. Boss, W. J. Doherty, R. LaRossa, W.R. Schumm, and S. K. Steinmetz, Eds., *Sourcebook of Family Theories and Methods: A Contextual Approach*, pp. 419 – 447 (New York: Plenum Press, 1993).

[26] B. Carter and M. McGoldrick *The changing family life cycle* (Boston: Allyn & Bacon, 1989). R. H. Rogers and J. M. White, "Family development theory." In Boss, Doherty, et al, *Sourcebook of Family Theories and Methods*, pp. 225 – 254.

[27] If spouses have been previously married, then the children may be part of the divorced partner's extended family. In these cases, one or more extended families can potentially influence interfaith families.

[28] Carter and McGoldrick, *The changing family life cycle*. See Rogers and White, "Family development theory."

MUSIC IN THE PARISH: "THE SINGING PARISH"

STEVEN KARIDOYANES

Introduction

When designing this two-hour discussion and workshop on the broad topic of "Music in the Parish," I felt it was necessary to focus on one goal. That goal was to leave every participant with ideas for available action-steps to better support and facilitate their parish's music ministry. Areas of discussion would include, but were not limited to, improving their congregational singing, their choir, or their Sunday school music curriculum. Achieving this goal depended on the interaction, the participation and the group dynamic of the session attendees.

Our gathering included parish council members, church musicians and interested lay-people from around the country, as well as several seminarians and one young priest. Resource material was both displayed and distributed. To tailor the ultimate content of our discussion to the specific needs of the parishes represented, I believed, a vital exchange of ideas, concerns, perspectives and passions was necessary. The following article is a summation of this session.

Misconceptions versus the current reality of music in the parish

A lively and passionate discussion ensued during this conference session. Each participant was invited to share his or her perspective on music in the parish. What became clear during this discussion is that there is a tremendous chasm between what is the current reality of the music ministry in the parishes of the Greek Orthodox Archdiocese in America and an uninformed perception of this music ministry.

Several in attendance revealed both their point of view and personal disdain for what they perceived to be the current state of music in the parishes. Comments made reflected a lack of exposure to the rich musical legacy of the parishes and the spirit in which these music ministries are offered.

Here is a partial list of concerns shared by participants, which have been paraphrased. These concerns are followed with a point-by-point response:

209

Misconception 1:

The reason there is so much influence of Western-styled and harmonized music in the Greek Orthodox Church of America is because, around 1900, our immigrant forefathers experienced cultural pressures to fit in. The incorporation of Catholic and Protestant musical idioms in our service music was a direct response to their perceived need to "Americanize" Greek Orthodox worship in this country.

The Athenian psalti, John Theophrastos Sakellarides (c.1853-1938), published his Byzantine notation transcriptions of the Divine Liturgy and other hymns in Greece early in the twentieth century. Not only did Sakellarides publish these melodies, he published them harmonized in what we would consider "Western" harmony. The Sakellarides publications became the primary source material for how worship music was to be rendered in the Greek Orthodox Archdiocese of America for nearly a century. Most notably, the hymnal by George Anastasiou, first published in this country in the mid-1940s, became the widely distributed, widely available liturgical source, strongly influenced by the Sakellarides Byzantine notation transcriptions.

Misconception 2:

Many Byzantine melodies currently in use and serving as the basis of our church music were transcribed incorrectly. Therefore, they must be changed. To knowingly continue using these incorrect melodies amounts to being "un-Orthodox" and shows a questionable sincerity as to why church musicians participate in the Divine Liturgy.

There is no argument Byzantine melodies have been transcribed incorrectly. But these melodies, flaws and all, have become the aural fabric of the Orthodox Church in this country for nearly a century. This is the history of the Greek Orthodox Archdiocese in America. To deny this fact and couple it with the judgment of insincerity is harmful. This sentiment will alienate a large percentage of a congregation who associate the hymns they have learned with their devotion to the Church.

Misconception 3:

Although Russian in its origin, the music of the Orthodox Church in America (OCA) is truer to the Byzantine tradition, both in terms of chromatic use and emphasis of melody over harmony, than the current musical practice of Greek Orthodox parishes in America. This includes the four-part harmonizations currently in use by the Greek Orthodox parishes in this country.

The OCA/Slavonic melodies and pitch (chromatic) choices are, in actuality, very different from Byzantine chant. The Slavonic tradition evolved into a harmonic tradition, not, exclusively, a melodic one. Regarding four-part harmonization, consider this brief overview. First, the tradition of Slavonic chant evolved first from a single melody, then to two voices harmonized in parallel, finally with the addition of a pedal tone (an *ison*). This made the music a three-part texture. To then add (compose) another, fourth, vocal part wasn't too far a stretch. Second, the Byzantine chanting tradition currently taught also evolved from a harmonized melody and an *ison*. It isn't a tradition as handed down through the ages but rather an eighteenth-century practice. Third, the majority of the music as presented in the Greek Orthodox Church of America evolved from the melodies as transcribed by Sakellarides, harmonized with parallel vocal parts with an added *ison*. Formal harmonizations were subsequently composed based on Sakellarides' efforts.

From this, the following point must be made clear: Music for worship *evolves* due to matters of culture and other influences.

Misconception 4:
Those responsible for making musical decisions choose to do things incorrectly. All people involved should care enough to read Byzantine notation and to "do it right," for our faith lies in our Byzantine music.

The current reality of Greek Orthodox parishes in America includes people who do not read Greek, nor Byzantine notation, nor "Western" musical notation. They sincerely do the best they can with the limitations they possess. These individuals believe singing to the glory of God is its own reward. In most parishes, those who sing in the choir are also active volunteers in other aspects of their church's life. This is especially true for parishes which, by choice or necessity, practice congregational singing.

Communication between parish priest and music leader
Some worshipers come to know their faith as they read the printed word and some through hearing it. The message and content of the Orthodox faith is further enhanced when the medium of its delivery, in this case the sung word, is strategically considered. Certain practical measures, properly addressed, will magnify the message.

Addressing these matters requires a clear channel of communication between the parish priest and the music leader. Whether the music leader is the choir director, the psalti or the person who leads the congregation in congregational singing, the ultimate goal is to create an environment conducive to prayer. Strategically considered choices can heighten the worship experience. Here are some considerations:

1. *The choice of music.* Regardless of whether sung by a choir, congregation, or both:
- Does the music itself cause a distraction?
- Is the music too difficult to sing?
- Does the music make congregational participation, whether audibly or inaudibly, difficult?
- Are the sung responses configured in such a way that the celebrant has difficulty finding the appropriate intoning pitch?
 -Is the music written in such a way that the text is difficult to understand?
- In the case of choral music: Does the music reasonably reflect the ability and limitations of the choir?

As the entire worship service is sung, the parish priest and parish music leader must continually consider and evaluate the music selected by the parish to optimize a prayerful environment.

2. *Rehearsal.* Choirs understand the necessity of rehearsal. However, few music leaders have experienced the benefit and comfort of rehearsing the responsorial portions of a worship service with their parish priest. This type of communication can be truly enlightening. If there is a church choir to consider, the priest and music leader should first practice alone, then with the choir. It is also most beneficial to practice in the acoustical environment of the church sanctuary. An intoning pitch emanating from a pitch pipe or organ is not necessarily perceived the same way by the priest standing behind an icon screen in the sanctuary. Distance and volume of space *will* change how a pitch is heard. This phenomenon is *real* and its negative affect must not be underestimated.

3. *Agreeing on the pitch.* In an ecclesiastical tradition where everything is sung, agreeing on which intoning pitch serves the worship best is vitally important. This need not be a sensitive issue. In most every case, extremes need to be avoided. And throughout a worship service, the agreed-upon intoning pitch needs to be reconfirmed, adjusted, or changed altogether, depending on the needs of the service.

Sounding an agreed-upon, yet unobtrusive, intoning pitch by pitch pipe, organ or vocalized hum ensures a less distracting and more beautifully flowing worship service. Here are some suggested places within a Divine Liturgy where establishing the best possible intoning pitch might be very helpful:
- Before "Blessed is the kingdom…" at the beginning of the Divine Liturgy;
- Before "Let us pray to the Lord/Lord, have mercy" which precedes the *Trisagion Hymn*;

- Immediately following the *Cherubic Hymn*;
- Immediately following the *Creed*;
- Immediately following the *Megalinárion*;

These are only suggestions. Through respectful communication the parish priest and music leader can make decisions which best serve the worship for their community.

The use of English

The use of English in a parish is an individual matter. But, just as great care must be given to the choice of music, the same care must be given in considering English settings of Orthodox worship music.

- Is the English translation doctrinally correct?
- Does the English text fall naturally on the ear?
- Does it flow easily when spoken or sung?
- Is the English set in such a way that the text is easily understood?
- In its musical setting, does the English make sense and is it grammatically correct?

This last consideration is neglected all too often. Those who are considering the Orthodox faith for themselves, or those who are non-Orthodox and experiencing Orthodox worship for the first time, will be attentive listeners. They shouldn't have to go through an unnecessary process to understand Orthodox worship – let alone be left with an unflattering impression.

The singing parish: What does this mean?

Although the churches of the Greek Orthodox Archdiocese of America are unified in faith, those who worship in these Orthodox parishes do not share the same aural experiences. How worship services are musically rendered varies greatly throughout the country. When rendered honestly and with the appropriate degree of humility, all variations are proper. Music, however, can benefit a parish outside the formal context of a Divine Liturgy. "The Singing Parish" refers to an integrated church experience, both within the setting of a worship service and without.

How church communities ultimately come to offer the hymns and responses of a worship service may be a matter of choice, resource, or both. There are parishes that wish they had a choir and those that choose not to have one. There are choirs led by music professionals and choirs led by caring volunteers who answered a call to fulfill a parish need. Hymns and responses in some parishes are sung by a psalti, either novice or experienced, or by the congregation, either led by someone or left on their own. There are situations where the musical experience encompasses a combination of the variables listed above. The choice and percentage of which language is sung is also a major variable. Regardless of the variables, the act of singing is inextricably linked to Orthodox worship.

Outside the confines of the worship service, however, singing is still a vital way of remaining connected to the Orthodox faith. The "sound of Orthodoxy" can be reinforced whenever the faithful gather. Religious music education needn't be limited to the activities of a Youth or Junior Choir. Much can be revealed to a Sunday school class or an adult education program by the study and singing of appropriately chosen Orthodox hymns. Retreats, camps and other spiritual or social gatherings are brought into focus in a meaningful way when the communal singing of hymns is included.

The resource material

Materials for display and distribution during this conference session were made available by the National Forum of Greek Orthodox Church Musicians, the musical ministry of the Greek Orthodox Archdiocese of America. Their efforts include:

- Liturgical Music Education: teaching young people the beauty of the Holy Orthodox Church through her hymns;

- Supporting Church music programs: as a service organization for choir directors, choir members, organists and psalti;

- Perpetuating the knowledge, use and appreciation of Byzantine chant.

For a more detailed introduction into the activities of this musical ministry, including a listing of available publications and resource material, contact the National Forum of Greek Orthodox Church Musicians directly. Their Internet website may be accessed through the website of the Archdiocese (www.goarch.org/goa/institutions/musicians). In closer proximity to each parish, almost every diocese in the country oversees a regional choir federation. These regional organizations also provide a wealth of information and support to your parish.

Conclusion

The Orthodox parish *is* a singing parish. To encourage singing in all aspects of parish life is to further nurture a parishioner's relationship with the Orthodox Church. It is necessary, however, for all the caretakers of the Greek Orthodox Church in America, both clergy and laypeople, to educate themselves in regards to a parish's music ministry. Greater vigilance is needed to evaluate how the facts, as well as *the truth*, are taught. When misconceptions are fostered because of a drought of information and understanding, a good shepherd is needed who, in a loving way, enlightens and edifies those who search for the current reality of music in the parish.

MISSION AND OUTREACH IN THE PARISH

JOHN CHAKOS

Introduction: Why do parish mission?
Developing, promoting and executing a viable and vital program of mission and outreach within the context of parish life would seem to be a goal that most Christ-loving people in the Orthodox Church would willingly embrace. This, in essence, is what my paper is about. Before getting into some specifics, though, it would seem useful, if not necessary, to establish some type of theological rationale before proceeding. What is the purpose of a local parish? This is a pivotal issue that must be settled before a parish can begin to understand the importance of mission and outreach, or even begin to take part in the process. From Abraham's call in Genesis 12 to be a blessing to the nations, right through John's vision in Revelation of representatives from every language and land, Holy Scripture reveals to us that God desires us to expand love's circle until it includes the whole world. The local parish, in order to achieve its calling to be a dynamic communion of Christian love, must not only serve as salt and light to its own people, it must make the kingdom of God manifest to the whole world.

Somewhere along the way it seems that the local church has lost sight of its purpose. Tom Sine, a missions strategist with World Concern, has said that "all too often, the typical local church in America is simply a cultural maintenance center, a place in which we can hold our weddings, funerals, social events, and raise our children."[1] Given this reality, we should not be surprised that the expectations for transforming the world at the local level are very low. In the words of Sine, "the absolutely last thing we ever expect is to see the world change because of our church's existence."[2] Added to this is the fact that in most Orthodox parishes there is so much internal activity, much of it very good and necessary, that one more program, especially one that seems to have little or no relevance to our world of narrow concerns, is more of a burden than a blessing. It's daunting enough, we say to ourselves, just to keep up with the demands of a very active parish, what with its busy sacramental, social, educational and cultural schedule. Besides

215

this, few in the parish really seem to care if we fail to reach out beyond the walls of our congregation. Why, then, should we make more work for ourselves, especially when it does not appear to be needed or even appreciated?

Such are the obstacles and temptations that confront all of us in parish life, especially the clergy. Why even begin to cultivate a missions-active church if it seems that we are bucking the current? If the local parish exists primarily as a vehicle to sustain its internal ministries then there really is no reason to try to make a difference on the outside world. Why try to connect with something that is foreign to us? Many of us still believe that we can still pursue God in our own private space, while separating ourselves from the problems of outsiders. We think that the external world is something that we can deal with or understand merely by reading a book, turning on a television set, or peering out a window, but such thinking is illusory. Whether we like it or not, however, the world is, according to Thomas Merton, "a complex of responsibilities and options made out of the loves, the hates, the fears, the joys, the hopes, the greed, the cruelty, the kindness, the trust, the suspicion of all."[3] The way to find the real world, the one that Christ came to save, is not merely to measure and observe what is outside of us, but to discover our own interior connection with it. Again, using Merton's words, the world "is a living and self-creating mystery of which I am a part, to which I am myself my own unique door. When I see my connection to this world, it is impossible to be alienated by it. Viewed in this way, the world cannot be a problem to me, something outside of myself. At one and the same time I see that Christ, the world, my neighbor, and my inmost being are interconnected."[4] Whether we like it or not, we are all a part of each other. In the words of John Donne, "no man is an island, entire of itself." I cannot separate the world out of my existence or the parish from its calling to reach out beyond itself.

This inner awareness of our connectedness to one another is taken to a new level in Christ. In the words of St. Paul, "so we, being men, are one body in Christ, and every one members of one another" (Rom 12:5). St. Cosmas Aitolos, understanding his responsibility for the world, left the comfortable confines of his Athonite monastery and risked all for the sake of his lost brethren. He describes this feeling of love for the world in this way: "My brethren, if it were possible for me to climb up into the sky, to be able to shout with a great voice, to preach to the entire world that only our Christ is the Son and Word of God, true God and the life of all, I would have done it. Because I can't do such a big thing, I do this small thing: I walk from place to place and teach my brethren as I can, not as a teacher but as a brother."[5] Possessed by a similar burning love for his neighbor,

Father Agathon could teach, "Love is to find a leper and gladly give him my body, and if it is possible, take his in return."[6] That same sense of solidarity with humanity also finds expression in the writings of Archimandrite Sophrony Sakharov who felt that "each of us must, and can, comprise all mankind in our own personal being."[7] Reaching out in mission then is our answer to the lawyer's question in St. Luke's Gospel, "Who is my neighbor?" (Lk 10:29).

From the writings of such holy people it should be clear to us that behind every sincere mission and outreach program of the parish there must be a group of compassionate people leading the way. Jesus called us to participate in the lives of others, which literally means to take part in. We must be willing to step out of our comfortable and busy lives and step into the lives of others, bringing them the fruits of the kingdom. We must be willing to recognize that there is no healing without solidarity or salvation without participation. Whenever we have stooped to the point of caring only for ourselves – sacrificing even those we love most for own advantage – then we have ceased to be human beings. Conversely, we may say that once we have reached the stage of caring absolutely for another we have begun to partake of the likeness of God. Henri Nouwen sums up the matter in these words: "Compassion manifests itself first of all in the consciousness of being part of humanity, in the awareness of the oneness of the human race."[8]

Being a parish in mission, then, is really all about recovering our humanity and not merely disseminating information or distributing aid. As such, a parish mission can never be just another program, one more thing to do on a busy schedule. We reach out because love compels us. The true program of the parish is never about organization and structures; it's about people and their needs; it's about us and our response to the world. The saints, who are examples of a fully-realized humanity, show us the way, for they embrace the sufferings of others and make them their own. This kenotic ideal finds full expression in the life of St. Paul, who wrote: "But in all things we commend ourselves as ministers of God: in patience, in tribulations, in needs, in distresses, in stripes, in imprisonments, in labors, in sleeplessness, in fastings." (2 Cor 6:5). When a parish is living out this ideal through its members, it is on the way to fulfilling its true purpose.

Developing a vision for mission and outreach in the parish
Breaking out of our shell of self-interest and launching into the deep and uncharted waters of service to others requires some type of awakening. We need to have a strong sense of where we are going. In this process leadership is critical. Leaders set the agenda and others commit to following, but

there has to be a moment when each one of us feels this calling as something personal and compelling. Let us recall the precise moment when the
mission of Jesus began to take shape. St. Matthew tells us that when Jesus
saw the crowds, "He had compassion for them because they were harassed
and helpless, like sheep without a shepherd." It is at this painful moment
that Jesus chooses the Twelve, sending them out into the world to "heal the
sick, raise the dead, cleanse lepers, and cast out demons" (Matt. 9:36).

We notice that from the very outset Jesus sent his disciples into dangerous and unsavory situations, places normally shunned by the healthy, sane
and well-adjusted. The disciples, following the visionary leadership of the
Master, did not offer aid from a safe distance, detached and uninvolved, but
they spent their time with the sick and possessed, entering totally into their
condition. And if their prayers conveyed healing, it was because they made
their own the anguish of those for whom they prayed. It is clear from all of
this that Jesus did not attempt to cultivate a dependence on His person for
everything. From the very outset He was raising up followers who would
themselves be equipped to reach out to the world.

A term that has been used to describe such caring followers is "world
Christians."[9] They are people who see the church not as an ethnic social
club, nor a sacramental feeding station, nor a spiritual fellowship of like-
minded people, nor a safe haven from the world's problems, but the instrument of God's redemptive plan for the world. David Bryant describes them
as Christians "for whom Christ's global cause has become the integrating,
overriding priority for all that He is for them …their life directions have
been solidly transformed by a world vision. Having caught a vision, World
Christians want to keep that vision and obey it unhesitatingly…. They are
heaven's expatriates, camping where the Kingdom is best served."[10] To develop a cadre of "world Christians" at the local level, a number of concrete
steps need to be taken

Mission education is a necessary beginning point for the cultivation of a
mission-active parish. This can be accomplished through Bible studies and
sermons that focus on mission themes, parish-sponsored missions and evangelism workshops, lectures, retreats and conferences, exposure to visiting
missionaries, articles and photos in the parish bulletin, photos on bulletin
boards depicting life in the mission field, a parish missions library, a parish
subscription to the magazine of the Orthodox Christian Mission Center
(OCMC) in St. Augustine, Florida, sent to each home, and church school,
summer camp and vacation church school programs that feature a mission
lesson or component.

Knowledge of the biblical principles undergirding missions and of those laboring in the mission field often gives rise to a desire to become more involved. The local parish can build on this interest by promoting short-term mission opportunities (for example, Project Mexico, OCMC mission teams), encouraging mission walks, establishing a parish mission committee and mission fund, supporting a mission student or mission priest (for example, the "Support a Mission Priest" program of OCMC), adopting a mission project, becoming an Agape Canister Partner (an OCMC program), participating in the Lenten Mission Appeal through the Mission Center, or like the parish of the Annunciation in Lancaster, raising one million dollars for a Chair of Missiology at Holy Cross Seminary through the "Endowment Fund for Orthodox Missions" (EFOM).

In my own parish we have been blessed to send individuals or small groups out into the mission field almost every year since 1987 to places like Kenya, Russia, Uganda, Tanzania, Haiti, Mexico, Upper Galilee, Mexico and Guatemala. These participants, in addition to learning about the work of mission from firsthand experience, have themselves become teachers to others in the parish. One woman in our parish tells of rediscovering the joy of worship while in Africa. This so impressed her that since that time she has become very active in the liturgical life of the parish. Her husband, who has gone on a number of teams, shares his joy at being able to work for the Lord using His hands in various mission construction projects. The example and commitment of all the returning missionaries has inspired others to consider similar types of outreach, whether at home or abroad.

This brings us to the role of the parish priest in cultivating a missions-active church. His personal philosophy of the local church will set the agenda for his parishioners. If his parish is defined by the personal needs of his flock, he will place a high priority on ministries inside the church – counseling, youth groups, afternoon language school, parish council development, weekly sermons, Bible studies, Sunday School, hospital visitations, fundraising, building programs, all of which are essential to a vibrant parish.

A parish that has an effective program of mission and outreach, on the other hand, is led by a priest who has a broad vision for missions and evangelism. His parish is the world, and so he expects his parishioners to make an impact not only at home, but in the most remote places on the planet. Behind every "world Christian" is a "world priest." Nothing should limit his scope when it comes to the Gospel. Of course, such a parish priest does not deny the importance of the local parish ministries. Instead, he sees them not as ends in themselves, but as a means to cultivate a fully-realized humanity which expresses itself in service to the world, whether down the street or around the globe. More than taking care of his flock, the priest should be developing a center for taking the love of Jesus to the ends of the earth.

It is truly the vision of the parish priest that brings the mission field into the life of the parish. He must not only lead the missions program in his parish, he must keep it in the forefront as a major item on the agenda of the church. Sometimes this may mean going into the field as a short-term missionary and living and working among the very people that are to be helped. In other instances this vision may grow out of a close working relationship with someone who is already serving as a missionary in the field. It has been said that the best promoters of missions among the clergy are those who have prayerfully entertained the possibility of going themselves. Like Isaiah they are willing to say, "Here am I, send me" (Is 6:9). If a priest has never felt that God wanted him to serve in the mission field, it is unlikely that he will be motivated enough to inspire anything but token support for the Great Commission.

What, ideally, is the parish priest's role in the missions outreach of his parish? First of all, he should foster a mentality within his parish that shows a radical openness to the outsider, the foreigner, the one who would not appear to fit the parish's mold. The new person walking through our doors may not be one of us, but until we open our arms to him, he will forever remain a stranger to us. To limit the outreach of the local parish only to those who "fit in" is to limit the power of the Gospel. This radical openness carries over into the mission field abroad. When we see the Orthodox Church taking root in these mission lands and finding expression and new vigor in the local vernacular, we realize that the message of the Church cannot be contained by any one expression of it. While traveling through the peasant villages of the lake region of Tanzania, I saw a vitality in Orthodox worship that exceeded anything I had ever seen in America. The Africans had taken the ancient faith and made it their own, adding to it the dimension of joyful, dynamic worship. To reflect this openness in our parish, we routinely use many languages at any given worship service. We want our parishioners to hear the words of the Liturgy as though it were another Pentecost.

Besides encouraging an openness to others, particularly those of other cultures, the parish priest is the key to bringing the mission field into the parish. He is the one to invite those working in the lands of mission to tell their story. He must encourage his parishioners to sponsor a missionary in the field or give support to a project like the building of a catechetical school, clinic or church. He must research the needs of the mission field to see where icons, vestments, liturgical articles, clothing, medicines, books and financial support are to be sent. In all of these efforts the guidance and support of the Orthodox Christian Mission Center is indispensable.

That such support can be very fruitful and rewarding is proven by my own experience. In 1984, my parish of Holy Cross began a relationship with a young Indonesian student, Daniel Byantoro, with a dream of establishing the Orthodox faith in his native land. After an active correspondence with a few of his compatriots and the support of my parishioners and Bishop Maximos, we prepared for the arrival, housing, clothing, chrismation and English language training of more students from Indonesia, who would soon make their way to Holy Cross Greek Orthodox School of Theology. They would later serve as the nucleus of the fledgling mission that the newly ordained Fr. Daniel would begin single-handedly in 1988. Today, the Indonesian Orthodox Church has eight priests, two deacons, and a few thousand adherents in a number of villages, cities and islands of this fourth-most populous nation in the world.

While supporting those in the mission field is a good start, sending short-term missionaries into the field is even better. Once again, the parish priest can play a crucial leadership role in this process. Each prospective missionary will need both the financial support and encouragement of the priest. His knowledge of the church's program of mission coupled with a genuine love for this outreach will inspire many to consider going. Without the priest leading the way, and in many instances clearing the way, the prospective lay missionary may lose heart. In many parishes there is a perception that money spent on missions diminishes the finances of the local parish. The experience of mission-supporting and mission-sending parishes is quite the opposite. Such outreach enriches the local parish in untold ways.

Since 1987, when the Greek Orthodox Board of Missions sent its first short-term mission team to Africa to build a church, opportunities for mission outreach have increased considerably. Now the Mission Center routinely sends teams all over the world to assist the hosting church. Mission teams of two to six weeks in duration are building and restoring churches, erecting and staffing medical clinics, constructing catechetical schools and church centers, teaching the faith and other needed skills in Third World countries. The long-term effect of such outreach in the local community is hard to gauge, but the positive effect on the lives of the visiting missionaries is dramatic. The Gospel comes alive for them as never before. When they return to their home parishes they become the best ambassadors for missions. Their enthusiasm is unbounded and contagious. Encouraged by their parish priest, they can form the nucleus of mission outreach within the parish.

While most returning short-term missionaries will settle into their home parishes transformed by their experience, a few may consider a longer commitment to the host country or region that they served in. It's very difficult to encounter a scene of human poverty and not be affected by it, especially when one considers that we in the American church have so much to offer a struggling mission church. The gap between the 'haves' and the 'have nots' begs for some type of a Christian response. It is in such settings that the claims of Christ on our love are most deeply felt. While not all can serve, each must ask the question, "What can I do?" Here again the parish priest as spiritual father must be prepared to offer guidance and support in such times of crisis. His vision for missions will help the prospective missionary work through such deep emotions, giving them credence and validation.

One who served as a short-term missionary in Tanzania described an event that later led him to serve in the mission field for two years. The American missionaries, sent by the Mission Center, were to arrive at the mission site on a given day to begin construction on a catechetical school. The parishioners of the Tanzanian Orthodox Church of St. Nicholas announced the upcoming project to the local inhabitants of the area. The long-awaited day came, but not the team members. Their arrival had been delayed by two days. The local people, many of whom had never seen a white man, began to openly doubt the veracity of the reports. The thought that a group of Americans would come to work in such a destitute and remote area seemed beyond belief. Finally, the construction team arrived in Kazikisi, eager to begin after the embarrassing delay. As they assembled to survey the work site, they lifted their eyes to the surrounding hills, only to behold an incredible scene. Coming to welcome them were over a thousand curious and incredulous onlookers. At that very moment, the future long-term missionary would say that through this mass movement of people he felt Christ calling him to serve. Stories like this abound in the mission field. They make the mission come alive for all of us.

Once again, it must be emphasized, the parish priest is the one who must challenge his parishioners to consider some type of service in the mission field. He is the key agent of change in their lives in this regard. Through his vision and teaching he can guide the parish into understanding the biblical mandate and priority of missions. He should also be prepared to lead the parish into proper financial support for those serving in the mission field. Without pastoral concern, interest in missions will falter. It is perhaps the single most important element to a missionary-supporting and -sending parish. The priest's commitment to missions impacts his philosophy of ministry, his understanding of the nature and purpose of the church, and the priority of missions in light of the whole purpose of God as revealed in the Scripture.

Prayer and the Orthodox missionary

As important as the priest's vision is to implementing a plan of missions in his parish, he must be accompanied by illumined laity who share this vision. A mission-minded parish is comprised of mission-minded parishioners. Unless they are truly inflamed by a love of the Gospel, nothing of substance will ever occur. This brings us to the spiritual life of those who would promote the cause of mission and outreach in the parish and beyond. Good intentions are not enough when it comes to this work. The Orthodox missionary, whether engaged in home or global missions, must above all be a person of deep faith and pure prayer.

Any serious consideration of missions and outreach must have as its models those who have already excelled in the field. Where better to begin than with the consummate man of prayer and action – St. Paul the Apostle. There can be no doubt that something was replicated in his life that continued the forward push of Jesus into the mission field. Although never knowing Jesus according to the flesh, Paul exhibited a progression in his spiritual growth that ultimately led him along the path that Jesus had pioneered for humanity. It is the leading thought of the New Testament, and it is the specially prominent thought in the writings of St. Paul, that the life of Jesus is to be repeated in the lives of His followers ("Be imitators of me, in so far as I in turn am an imitator of Christ" 1 Cor 11:1); that the stages of each Christian's experience are designed to be a reproduction of those stages by which the Son of Man passed from Bethlehem and Golgotha to the Resurrection and Upper Room.

The Church fathers, picking up on the theme of growth unto new life, developed a 'way' for us to follow, one which integrates the insights of the New Testament with the ascetical tradition of Orthodoxy. St. Symeon the New Theologian, for one, developed a four-step progression of the spiritual life which when applied to the life and letters of St. Paul shows this remaking of character in bold relief.[11]

In the first step proposed by Symeon we are to "curtail the passions, that is to say, guard the heart; for it is otherwise impossible to curtail the passions."[12] Using Paul's own words, we gain a picture of the great struggle needed to save the body from its baser impulses: "But I discipline my body and bring it into subjection, lest, when I have preached to others, I myself should become disqualified" (1Cor 9:27). This, then, is the struggle of all missionaries, to align their lives with the message they proclaim, to open a clear path for the Spirit of God to traverse. We must remember that Paul himself spent a considerable period of time in relative obscurity after his vision in Jerusalem at the Temple before going out to the ends of the earth.

After being blinded physically by the splendor of the Uncreated Light, he needed to retreat to Arabia, conferring not "with flesh and blood," but like Jesus retreating into the wilderness, enhancing his nascent spiritual faculties. He had to conquer a very strong individual and national consciousness to become the apostle to the Gentiles.

After such an extended period of curtailing his passions, he could with conviction say in Galatians 5:24: "Those who are Christ's have crucified the flesh with its passion and desires," and to those of Ephesus he could confidently affirm, "And you he has made alive, who were dead in trespasses and sins ...among whom also we all once conducted ourselves in the lusts of our flesh, fulfilling the desires of the flesh and of the mind" (Eph 2:1-3). He knew from personal experience that "to set the mind on the flesh is death"(Rom 8:6). It was only by the renewal of the *nous* that transformation could occur (Rom 12:2).

The mission field has proven the downfall of many missionaries. They began their lofty work with the best of intentions, only to be undone by their weaknesses in the flesh. Driven by a desire for personal glory, they have taken over Christ's work and made it their own. Although this can happen in the boardrooms of the parish as well as in the mission field, its consequences among those trying to embrace the faith are more catastrophic. Whole tribes in Africa have been known to depart from the faith because of ill-advised actions or scandalous behavior by those purporting to represent Christ. We cannot afford to enlist people in our parishes who are unfit for the work of missions. An absolute prerequisite is some modicum of control over our baser instincts and desires and a genuine love for the Gospel.

The second stage of our spiritual rebirth, according to St. Symeon, "is to devote oneself to psalmody; for when the passions have been curtailed and laid to rest through the heart's resistance against them, longing for intimate union with God inflames the *nous*. Strengthened by this longing the *nous* repulses all distractive thoughts that encircle the heart, attempting to get in, and it rebuffs them through attentiveness."[13]

St. Paul's own teaching in Ephesians on the importance of psalmody confirms the prescription of Symeon: "Do not be drunk with wine ... but be filled with the Spirit speaking to one another in psalms, hymns and spiritual songs, singing and making melody in your heart to the Lord" (Eph 5:18,19). This method of enhancing the presence of Christ is also encouraged in Colossians by "teaching and admonishing one another is psalms, hymns, and spiritual songs, singing with grace in your hearts to the Lord" (Col 3:16).

St. Theophan the Recluse's commentary on Ephesians 5:19 explains the purpose of Church hymns. While "the infusion of the Holy Spirit does not lie within our power, it comes as the Spirit Himself wishes. And when it comes, this infusion will so greatly animate the powers of our spirit that the song to God breaks out of itself."[14] These "spiritually-inspired outbursts of feelings towards God" render us more receptive to the grace of the Spirit, thus fulfilling their purpose, which "is to make the spark of grace that is hidden within us burn brighter and with greater warmth."[15] St. John Chrysostom's commentary, cited by Theophan, adds further clarity to what is meant by "those who sing in their heart to the Lord. It means: Undertake this work with attention, for those who are inattentive sing in vain, pronouncing only words, while their heart wanders elsewhere."[16]

Examples of souls moving toward God through psalmody abound in the mission field. In the poorer and more remote parts of the world the beauty of Orthodox worship finds expression in joyful hymns. This often proves to be the main attraction to the Orthodox faith and not the dogmatic teachings alone. In the humble setting of a children's orphanage, the Hogar Rafael Ayau in Guatemala City, for example, the music of the Divine Liturgy captivates the soul of the visitor by its sheer innocence and purity. We who go as missionaries are catechized by the simplicity of faith of the children. When they chant, they do so not only with their mouths but with their whole being, thus fulfilling the condition of the Apostle that songs must be sung not by the tongue only, but by the heart.

When we learn to focus our attention on the heart in prayer, we sometimes produce another effect, the "stirring up of evil spirits," as well as the "blasts of the passions" which violently assail the deep heart.[17] St. Symeon goes on to point out that the invocation of the Lord Jesus will utterly rout all such interior disturbances.[18] Although they have been driven out of the heart, the demons will continue to trouble the *nous* "through the senses."[19]

This brings us to the third stage of Symeon's prescription for rebirth, perseverance in prayer, making the spiritual transition from youth to adulthood.[20] As this is the stage of those who are advanced, this is "prayer that differs from psalmody just as the full-grown man differs from the youth and adolescent," according to the New Theologian.[21] While the demons still have the license to trouble the soul, they do so superficially, for the *nous* soon regains its serenity; nonetheless, it can never be completely free from attack.[22] Symeon reiterates: "Total freedom is found only among those who have attained to adulthood, who are totally detached from everything visible and who devote themselves unceasingly to the heart."[23]

That St. Paul had come to this stage of development in his own life cannot be doubted. In Ephesians he convincingly exhorts: "Put on the whole armor of God...praying with all prayer and supplication in the Spirit, being watchful to this end with all perseverance and supplication for all the saints" (Eph 6:10-18). He knew that "though we walk in the flesh, we do not war according to the flesh ... but mighty in God ... pulling down strongholds, casting down arguments and bringing every thought into captivity to the obedience of Christ" (2 Cor 10:3-5).

Clearly, Paul is a man who lives with a joyful sense of participation in the higher life of the Spirit, of adoption into the world of heavenly realities. Confident in his apostleship he can say without hesitation to those who challenge his authority: "If anyone is convinced in himself that he is Christ's, let him again consider this in himself, that just as he is Christ's, even so *we are Christ's*" (2 Cor 10:7). And to those troublesome Corinthians he could declare: "Am I not an apostle? Am I not free?" Also, he reminded them that the signs of an apostle were performed among them "in all patience, in signs and wonders and mighty deeds" (1 Cor 9:1 and 2 Cor 12:12).

Such statements make clear the remarkable transformation of this former persecutor of the way of which he is now the chief exponent. He now lives by "revelation" – deep and life-giving illuminations that sustain his apostolate – and the experience of the "pressure of the Spirit." He has attained to a state of maturity, or in the words of Evelyn Underhill, "a condition of interior harmony with, and joyful response to, the constant sense of a Divine Presence which accompanies it, floods the consciousness with a certainty of attainment, authority and power."[24] For Paul all of this derives from the glorified Christ, whose power can be "put on," a "Christ in me" which is the source of his confidence and inner resolve. He is a man who is "hard-pressed on every side, yet not crushed" (2 Cor 4:8,9), afflicted by a messenger of Satan, but upheld by the power of Christ, who draws His strength from Paul's weakness. He now possesses a superabundance of vitality against which external circumstance has no control. Both in terms of expanding the mission or fighting against the "powers and principalities," Paul feels invincible, or as he would say, "not I but Christ in me" (Gal 2:20).

This third stage of tenacious prayer that gives birth to hope must accompany the missionary in his work. Many are the obstacles – both interior and exterior – that can bring on despondency. If stage three of Paul's spiritual unfolding was that of full manhood, stage four gradually becomes, according to St. Symeon, "that of the old man with gray hairs," signifying "undeviating absorption in contemplation, which is the state of the perfect.[25] This last stage, Symeon continues, presupposes the other three, for we cannot put the roof on the house before laying the foundation.[26]

That the final breakup of his former life with its attendant external and internal upheavals is in process seems clear. As St. Paul explains to the Corinthians, "When we came to Macedonia, our bodies had no rest, but we were afflicted at every turn – fighting without and fear within" (2 Cor 7:5). Abandoned by friends, embittered by his failure to gain a foothold in Athens, impoverished, persecuted, in ill-health, together with the sharp and growing contrast between his exalted vision of the "third heaven" and its incomplete and tentative actualization in the Church; all this went step by step with his deep inner woes and turmoil. Paul's nature had returned to the crucible, to be remade on a spiritual plane, rearranged around those divine attributes of love and humility that take possession of a person in the last and highest stages of deification.[27]

The Epistle to the Romans, as Underhill suggests, seems to mark the last phase of Paul's transformation.[28] Chapters seven and eight see the birth pangs of his interior life coming to an end, the higher nature establishing itself over the lower nature. The painful awareness of sin and weakness intensifies as it clashes with the irrepressible thrust of the emerging noetic life: "For the good that I will to do, I do not, but the evil I will not to do, that I practice.… For I delight in the law of God according to the inward man. But I see another law in my members, warring against the law of my mind, and bringing me into captivity to the law of sin which is in my members. O wretched man that I am! Who will deliver me from this body of death?" (Rom 7:19-24).

What a graphic portrayal this is of the soul's agony experiencing its final catharsis. Here we stand with Paul at the cutting edge of new life, and with the opening verses of the next section of his letter, the transition is made: "For the law of the Spirit of life in Christ Jesus has made me free from the law of sin and death" (Rom 8:2).[29] A new infusion of life, which has been brought into time by Jesus, floods his nature, changing it to the condition of the "children of God" and citizens of the heavenly reality. In this moment of absorption in contemplation (*theoria*), Paul seems for the first time to penetrate to the very core of the mystery of the kingdom, applying it with joyful confidence to the collective consciousness of the Church: "You have received the spirit of adoption, by whom we cry out, 'Abba, Father.' The Spirit Himself bears witness with our spirit that we are children of God, and if children, then heir – heirs of God and joint heirs with Christ" (Rom 8:15-17).

Having achieved "the glorious liberty of the children of God" (Rom 8:21), Paul can now assert: "For I am persuaded that neither death nor life, nor angels nor principalities nor powers, nor things present nor things to come, nor height nor depth, nor any other created thing, shall be able to separate us from the love of God which is in Christ Jesus our Lord" (Rom 8:37,38). From this we see that Paul is no longer a servant but a son, not only a proficient but perfected and deified man, who in the captivity of his latter days and much anxiety can now exclaim: "I now rejoice in my sufferings for you, and fill up in my flesh what is lacking in the afflictions of Christ, for the sake of His body, which is the church" (Col 1:24). As a testament to his completed journey, let us add this verse as a fitting postscript to this consummate man of prayer and action: "Rejoice in the Lord always. Again I will say, rejoice!" (Phil 4:4).

The local parish as a mission center

That the spiritual life of the Orthodox missionary is crucial to the success of the Great Commission can never be overstated, but it must be remembered that he never works alone or for himself. The Orthodox Church has no special order of missionaries, nor does it leave the work of missions to select societies or representative agencies. Saving the unredeemed is the task of the whole Church. Therefore, if the Church is to be true to its calling, then missions must begin at home in the local eucharistic assembly. In the words of James Stamoolis, "To the extent the local congregations are involved is the extent to which mission will belong to the whole church."[30]

And where better than in the Liturgy itself do we find the motive for mission. Through the Tabor-like experience of eucharistic worship, the church members are transported to heaven for a privileged moment of communion with Christ, only to return again to the valley of life's challenges where the mission field is awaiting them. Through this transfiguring act of worship the Church is to be experienced both as fullness ("We have seen the true light") and as mission ("Let us depart in peace"). In this process something vital transpires – communion with the Holy Trinity – which gives impetus to our outreach in the world. The words of Jesus clearly articulate this mission dynamic: "Peace be with you. As My Father has sent Me, I also send you" (Jn 20:21). Thus the peace of Christ received through the Holy Eucharist becomes our reservoir of strength and the very motive for mission.

In light of the above, how is the local church to be known – by its organization and structure, or by its outreach to the world? If the local parish is the real presence of God's inaugurated Holy Kingdom upon the earth, its divine and sacred task is to embrace everyone in Christ's love. In the words of M. A. Siotis, cited by Stamoolis, "The essence and nature of the local church … are both divine and sacred: divine because every church constitutes the continuation on earth of the redemptive grace of Christ … sacred because every Church has as its mission the sanctification of its members, and through them, the sanctification of the world."[31] More than anything else, then, the Church is to be known by its communion with the living Christ, which activity "extends God's activity in the world."[32]

The responsibility for continuing the mission of the church, then, is that of every member and not just a select few. In the words of Siotis, "Those of the faithful who are being spiritually perfected in the Church, through their life in it in Christ, are also fulfilling their divine mission in the world."[33] According to this view, the principle of mission and outreach is to be found in each one of us individually and all of us corporately, for our personal sanctification takes place within the setting of the local parish, which results in "the extension of the Church's mission in the world."[34]

Conclusion: Christ's mission is for all

That Christ's mission is to be found in the very heart of parish life and every believer and not outside of it should be very clear. The local parish must come to see itself as the mission center par excellence of the Church, something that all of us take part in and give to. Seen in this light, our growth in Christ takes on cosmic proportions because it not only affects us but the whole of humanity. We can and must make a difference. Of course, not all of us are called to go to the ends of the earth. Nevertheless, we are not exempted from some type of involvement. We have a mission at home as well. Bishop Augustinos would have us take note of the fact that of the many who are baptized, few actually join themselves to the local parish. Then he challenges us to ask ourselves, "Am I perhaps responsible for this desolate church? Did I ever try to urge another to come to church? When the church bell rings on Sunday calling parishioners to worship, did I also sound an alarm, did I strongly urge everyone in my house to come with me to church? Unfortunately not…. We come alone and limit ourselves to fulfilling our ordinary duty in going to church. We do not lead others to Christ."[35]

Studies of active church membership consistently show that the vast majority of people who attend regularly come not because of the priest, some evangelistic crusade, a visitation, or some church program. Seventy-five percent to ninety percent come because a friend or relative encouraged them to do so.[36] It is estimated that the average person has this kind of decisive influence over twelve people, usually close family or friends.[37] Where an outsider cannot reach them, we can. The conclusion is obvious: The majority of us can trace our incorporation into the Body of Christ to a friend or relative. From this we see that each of us has a natural network within which to spread the faith. Are we using this persuasive influence to full advantage? Are we bringing the Good News to our own family and friends? If we don't, who will?

There is a famous story which tells how Jesus, after the Cross and the Resurrection, returned to His glory, still bearing the marks of His sufferings. One of the angels said to Him, "You must have suffered terribly for men down there." "I did," said Jesus. "Do they all know what you did for them? " asked the angel. "No," said Jesus, "not yet." Only a few know about it in Palestine so far." "And," said the angel, "what have you done that they should all know about it?" "Well," said Jesus, "I asked Peter and James and John to make it their business to tell others, and the others still others, until the farthest man of the widest circle has heard the story." The angel looked doubtful, for he knew well what poor creatures men were. "Yes," he said, "but what if Peter and James and John forget? What if they grow weary of the telling? What if, away down in the twenty-first century, men fail to tell the story of your love for them? What then? Haven't you made any other plans?" And back came the answer of Jesus, "I haven't made any other plans. *I'm counting on them.*"

That the work of mission is an unfinished task should be of concern to all of us. Christ is counting on us to be His emissaries, if not to the more remote regions of the world, certainly to our own family and friends. Our local parish must be the center for this divine and sacred task, both in terms of its liturgical worship, which is the fulfillment of the Kingdom in our midst, and of mission, which is the extension of the Kingdom in the world. A parish that understands its role is in living communion with Christ, and its members are the true expressions of His love for the world.

NOTES

[1] Tom Sine, *Cultivating a Missions-Active Church* (Peachtree, GA: ACMC, July 1998), p. 4.

[2] Sine, p. 4.

[3] Thomas Merton, *Contemplation in a World of Action* (Garden City, NY: Image Books, 1973), p. 161.

[4] Merton, p. 161.

[5] Nomikos M. Vaporis, *Father Kosmas The Apostle of the Poor* (Brookline, MA: Holy Cross Orthodox Press, 1977), p. 15.

[6] *Gerontikon* (Thessalonike: Ekdotikos Oikos: Vasileios Rigopoulou, 1969), p. 12.

[7] Archimandrite Sophrony Sakharov, *St. Silouan The Athonite*, (St. John the Baptist Monastery, Tolleshunt Knights by Maldon, Essex, England), p. 122.

[8] Henri J.M. Nouwen, " Compassion: Solidarity, Consolation and Comfort,"

America, 1976, p. 195.
⁹ Sine, p. 76.
¹⁰ Sine, p. 76.
¹¹ *The Philokalia*, Volume IV, Palmer, Sherrard and Ware, eds., (London: Faber and Faber, 1995), p. 73.
¹² *The Philokalia*, p. 73.
¹³ *The Philokalia*, p. 73.
¹⁴ *The Art of Prayer: An Orthodox Anthology*, compiled by Igumen Chariton (London: Faber and Faber, 1971), pp. 56-57.
¹⁵ *The Art of Prayer*, pp. 56-57.
¹⁶ *The Art of Prayer*, p. 58.
¹⁷ *The Philokalia*, p. 74.
¹⁸ *The Philokalia*, p. 74.
¹⁹ *The Philokalia*, p. 74.
²⁰ *The Philokalia*, p. 74.
²¹ *The Philokalia*, p. 74.
²² *The Philokalia*, p. 74.
²³ *The Philokalia*, p. 74.
²⁴ Evelyn Underhill, *The Mystic Way* (Atlanta: Ariel Press, 1992), p. 147.
²⁵ *The Philokalia*, p. 74.
²⁶ *The Philokalia*, p. 75.
²⁷ *The Mystic Way*, p. 154.
²⁸ *The Mystic Way*, p. 155.
²⁹ *The Mystic Way*, p. 155.
³⁰ James Stamoolis, *Eastern Orthodox Mission Theology Today* (Minneapolis: Light and Life Publishing, 1986), p. 122.
³¹ Stamoolis, p. 123.
³² Stamoolis, p. 123.
³³ Stamoolis, p. 123.
³⁴ Stamoolis, p. 124.
³⁵ Augoustinos N. Kantiotes, *Follow Me* (Belmont, MA: Institute for Byzantine and Modern Greek Studies, 1989), p. 65.
³⁶ Win and Charles Arn, *The Master's Plan for Making Disciples* (Monrovia, CA: Church Growth Press), p. 43.
³⁷ Arn, p. 52.

TEACHING PATRISTICS ON THE PARISH LEVEL

GEORGE S. BEBIS

Introduction

The question of how to teach Patristics has occupied me since the time I was a student at Holy Cross Greek Orthodox School of Theology, Harvard University and the University of Athens. An important discipline in theology, it was one of the most difficult, unpopular, uncreative, unproductive, and of course not very inspiring. Patristics was taught in a boring manner with the memorization of names, dates and nothing more. A glance at Orthodox patrologies of that era proves the fate that Patrology and Patristics could not attract the love and the interest of young theologians and seminarians.

However, two of my professors at Harvard University taught me to love the Fathers and to approach them with scholarly curiosity, but at the same time with respect, piety, love and faith to the Lord, which they emulated in their work. Those two professors were the late Fr. Georges Florovsky and the late Dr. George Williams. Fr. Florovsky had established well-constructed seminars always pinpointing the necessity of approaching and studying the original sources. Professor Williams introduced excellent seminars under the titles: "Problems of the Fourth Century" and "Problems of the Eleventh Century." Professor Williams also demanded rigorous study of the original sources, the writing of first-rate papers from his students, actively doing serious research in untouched original sources, and insisting on the knowledge of foreign languages.

Thus, when in 1957 the late Bishop of Elaia, Athenagoras Kokkinakis, then president of Holy Cross, asked me to teach Patrology, I decided to collect all the previous methods of teaching Patrology, even the methods of the late Professor Fr. George Tsoumas, who taught Patrology with much love for his students and faithfulness to the subject.

Immediately, I wanted to make the Fathers of the Church accessible to our students by eliminating secondary and unnecessary information and by focusing on the main aspects of the Fathers' lives, giving more emphasis on the writings of the Fathers, and by focusing on the important message they could offer to our times. It must be said here, that at that time, all the courses at Holy Cross were taught in Greek and bibliographies were scarce and hard to come by.

After two years of teaching Patrology at Holy Cross, I returned to Greece for my doctoral degree, at the command of Archbishop Iakovos. Once more, I had to sit in the chair of the student and be examined in Patrology. I had to memorize names, dates and nothing more. The writing of a thesis on Nestorius gave me the opportunity to take advantage of all my previous research and study of the Fathers. I took advantage of the excellent advice of the professors at the University of Athens, who assisted me with much affection to complete my thesis on time and was graded by the entire Theological faculty with *arista*.

In January of 1965 I was back at Holy Cross and once again teaching Patrology. Once more, I attempted to escape and liberate myself from the sterile and infertile method of teaching simply names and dates. I brought new bibliographies and introduced the study of ancient patristic texts from the first and second centuries, for instance, the *Didache* or *The Teaching of the Twelve Apostles to the Nations*, *The First Letter of Clement of Rome to the Corinthians*, *The Martyrdom of Polycarp*, and so on. Speaking about St. Athanasios, the Cappadocian Fathers, St. Cyril of Alexandria, the great ascetics like St. Anthony, St. John Climacus, and others, I presented the major events of their lives, their most important writings, the most important aspects of their theology, together with the practical application of their theological *phronema* (mindset) to an authentic patristic lifestyle.

In so doing, I continue to emphasize today that the course must have another ultimate goal: to prepare our students, the future priests, theologians, lay teachers to teach the Fathers of the Church in the parish and community. This is why I do believe that a proper and appropriate methodology of teaching the Fathers will enable our students to become successful teachers in transmitting the eternal and saving message of the Fathers of the Church to our parishioners. In other words a priest and a lay teacher well-versed in the Fathers would have and must have the spirit of the Fathers, and make it their own "property" so to speak, their own lifestyle, and their own theological beliefs. A priest and a layperson that is a good patrologist will be a good teacher in conveying the message of the Fathers to our lay people in our parishes.

Teaching the Fathers – the content
The first element and the prerequisite for a fertile teaching of the Fathers

to our people is to have the priest and the lay teacher love the Fathers, to know the Fathers, to have studied carefully the original sources, to know the bibliography, to be able to select the proper material for reading to their people, but above all to have been transformed themselves by the divine and illuminating light of Tabor, to have become real vessels of patristic wisdom and the patristic mystical experience.

The second point is that the priest and the teacher who initiates the teaching of the Fathers on a parish level must study carefully the size, the composition and the facilities of the parish and communities. What is the membership of the community? Are they children, adolescents, mature young people, adults, or the elderly? The teacher must look also into the people's level of education, their capacity to learn, and their educational and spiritual background. On the basis of this survey, the teacher must construct the qualitative and quantitative groups and then proceed to the formation of the groups to whom patristics are going to be taught. Needless to say, the use of contemporary technology, computers, videos, movies, and photographs will make the teaching more attractive. In this instance, the attraction and the invitation of adults from other faiths as a separate course will be a worthwhile effort. Vists to museums will also be encouraged. For instance, in October 2000 an exhibition on the ancient city of Antioch took place at the Worcester (Massachusetts) Art Museum. Antioch is a city where great Fathers of the Church were born and lived. A visit to such an exhibit would be most fruitful.

I come back to the issue of bibliography. Each group will require special books. For children, for instance, small books with drawings and photographs of the Fathers with small captions would be very helpful. For adolescents and young adults, reading and studying the book of St. Basil, *To the Young...* and readings from the book of St. John Chrysostom from the *Baptismal Catechesis* and *On the Education of Children...* would be good to introduce to them. To adults, without much education, letters from St. Basil would be read, readings from the *Didache*, a small book of the second century as well as the seven letters of St. Ignatius and the *Martyrdom of St. Polycarp*, as well readings from the *Gerondikon* should be encouraged.

There are many more possibilities for adults with a college education. For instance, the lives of the Apologists of the second century as well as the reading of the sixty-fifth and sixty-seventh chapters of the first apology of Justin the Martyr should be encouraged. Selections from the book of St. Athanasius *On the Incarnation of the Word of God* would be very interesting. Selections from St. Basil's book on Genesis, selections from his letters and especially his famous ninety-fourth letter to Patricia Ceasarea, as well as the reading of the twenty-seventh chapter from his book on the Holy Spirit should be read. As we all know the twenty-seventh chapter describes, in a most sufficient and successful way the teachings of the Church on the Holy Tradition. The 101ˢᵗ letter on St. Gregory the Theologian as well as his book *Against Julian the Apostate* should be read. Portions of the *Great Catechetical Oration of St. Gregory of Nyssa* and his famous book *On the Life of Moses* should be introduced. The famous book *The Ladder of Divine Ascent* of St. John Climacus should be studied with great attention and care. In connection with these readings, we should suggest 'thematic' books and readings, for instance, the books of St. Vladimir's Seminary Press *On Wealth and Poverty* and *On Marriage and Family* of St. John Chrysostom.

Because for Orthodox Christians the 'patristic era' has never really ended, I insist that people read the later Fathers of the Church. We have the *Philokalia*, St. John of Damascus, who summarized the Patristic tradition with his great book *On the Exact Definition of the Orthodox Faith*, Symeon the New Theologian, St. Gregory Palamas and St. Nicholas Cabasilas, St. Mark of Ephesus, St. Nicodemus of the Holy Mountain and St. Cosmas of Aitolos, and St. Nektarios. The Holy Spirit always produced Fathers, men of holiness, of Orthodox Doctrine, who have and still enjoy broad acceptance and recognition by the Church's *pleroma*.

Of course, for reasons of convenience, I stop in my introductory course at the eighth century, keeping in mind that after this century, I repeat, the Church continued to produce great Fathers. So the term and characteristic of 'antiquity' should be taken into consideration, when we teach the Fathers of the Church. For this reason, I have introduced some new courses at Holy Cross, namely "The Byzantine Fathers and Ecclesiastical Writers," as well as "The Post-Byzantine Fathers." Here I do not follow the venerable Demetrios Balanos, Professor of Patristics at the University of Athens who wrote a book with the title "The Byzantine Ecclesiastical Writers" but not the Fathers.

Certainly, when we teach Patristics on the parish level, we should acknowledge the distinctions between the Fathers of various eras. In my monograph on the "Tradition of the Fathers of the Church," I made all of these points very clear.[1] Nevertheless, I repeat that when teaching an introduction in Patrology, I stop at the eighth century. This is because of the following reasons. First, on Christmas Day, A.D. 800, we have the coronation of Charlemagne as the emperor of the western Holy Roman Empire. In reality, the empire has now been divided into two. For the Byzantines, there was only one empire, that of the Romans with Constantinople as the capital. Second, in the eighth century, we have the end of the great iconoclastic controversy, which divided the Byzantine Empire as well as the East and the West. There is also the completion of the so-called "Photian Schism," that is the great conflict of Patriarch Photius of Constantinople and Pope Nicholas I of Rome. It was the beginning of the end of relations and communion between the Eastern Church and the Roman Church. Thus, we may claim that the first patristic era ends at the eighth century. The Orthodox Church speaks, I repeat, of the Fathers of the Church who lived throughout the history of the Church, ancient, medieval, and most recent as well.

The Fathers and Scripture

One of the great problems, in conjunction with the teaching of the Fathers both on academic level as well as on parish level, is the relationship of the Fathers of the Church to the Bible. Unfortunately, Protestant theologians like Harnack, Barth, Brunner and others rejected the patristic tradition following, of course, the celebrated doctrine of Martin Luther, *Sola Scriptura*. According to the teaching of Martin Luther, which he cited in the heat of his controversy and fight against papal abuses, only the reading of the Scriptures is necessary for salvation. The correspondence on *Sola Scriptura* between the German Lutheran Reformers of the sixteenth century with the then Patriarch of Constantinople Jeremiah II is a very interesting exchange and still relevant.

Not too long ago, a book was circulated under the provocative title *The Orthodox Corruption of Scripture, The Effect of Early Christological Controversies in the Text of the New Testament.*[2] Ehram argues that the New Testament text, which we have in our hands today, has been "corrupted, so that it may fit with the Christological correctness of the Orthodox Fathers, as well as the Orthodox unknown and nameless scribes." The victory of Orthodoxy is for him the victory of the dominant group because he writes,

For it is a historical fact that, owing to a variety of reasons, one group within the early Christianity achieved social dominance and enforced its views on other groups that had supported divergent opinions. Looked at in socio-historical terms, orthodoxy and heresy are concerned as much with struggles over power as with debates over ideas.[3]

His "overarching thesis" appears to be as follows: "...proto-orthodox scribes of the second and third centuries occasionally modified their texts of Scripture in order make them to coincide more closely with the Christological view advocated by the party that would seal its victory at Nicaea and Chalcedon."[4] For Ehrman, thus, we have a distorted text of the New Testament as "corrupted," to use his own term, and this "corruption" took place by the ancient fathers and scribes of the New Testament.

Now for the Orthodox it is very clear that we are not the Church of a book. We are the Church of Jesus Christ. When we speak of the Bible and the Gospel, we speak about the message of salvation of Jesus Christ, born of the Virgin Mary, crucified, buried, risen and ascended, for our personal and collective salvation. Where there is no Christ, there is no salvation. On the other hand, the Gospel of Jesus Christ must been seen and lived through the experience of the Church of Christ. The Gospel did not flourish in a spiritual, historical, or cultural void. It was through the Apostles and their successors that the Gospel of Jesus Christ remained *and still remains* an absolute and living reality.

In that connection, the Fathers of the Church are the carriers, the interpreters, the living paradigms, the torchbearers, and the transmitters of Christ's gospel of salvation. The Fathers were biblical, really biblical. This we can claim, that without the Fathers, the message of the gospel would be elusive, even restricted to a limited people and with a limited scope. If one reads the *Didache*, St. Ignatius' letters, St. Irenaeus' books, or St. Athanasius' letter in which he lists the canonical books of the Old and New Testament, we see just a few examples of the importance of the Fathers' contribution to the study, the acceptance, the spreading, and the interpretation of the New Testament.

This is why the famous American patristic scholar Robert Grant writes, "The Bible contained the revelation recorded by prophets, apostles, and apostolic men; the writings of the Fathers contained the inspired reflections of the mind of the Church."[5] As T.J. Towers stated so succinctly, "The Fathers are our interpreters in Scripture. That Scripture needs interpreting, no doubt; the Bible is not a book which surrenders all its meaning at first sight. That it is the Church which must interpret seems no less obvious. God gave the Holy Scriptures in and through the Church; the Canon of what is truly Holy Scripture was drawn up by the Spirit in the Church..." The Fathers are "the eyes" of the Church, Towers concludes.[6] Or to put in the words of our own well-known theologian, Rev. George Mastrantonis, "The Fathers of the Church, as exponents of the Bible, shaped and molded the doctrines of the Church both in faith and morals by which the Christian finds salvation in the Person and the Redemptive Truth and Work of Jesus Christ." Thus the Fathers, Fr. Mastrantonis concludes, are the "Guardians of the Faith."[7]

The relationship of the Bible and the Fathers is not an easy theme to be discussed without paying reverence to the inspired Word of God and to the inspired teaching of the Fathers. We must approach, in other words, both the Bible and the Fathers as instruments of the same unwritten and written tradition, as St. Basil the Great writes in chapter 27 of *On the Holy Spirit*. Both are the fruits of the Holy Spirit. This is the view of the famous and much-respected Serbian Bishop Athanasios: "The Holy Scripture is a book, a text, a revealed book, an inspiring book, but a book. The Church is the atmosphere, the climate, the life, the pulse for the understanding of the Scriptures. It is not enough to say, as St. Augustine said, that the Church is the guarantee of the Bible thus the Scripture as the book of the community in the context of a worshiping liturgical atmosphere."[8] The late professor of the School of Theology of the University of Athens, John Panagopoulos, one of the finest biblical scholars of the Greek Orthodox Church in the twentieth century, presented seven important points or characteristics of the Patristic contribution in addition to the exegesis of the Bible.

They emphasized the unity of both the Old and the New Testaments.

The Fathers were Christocentric in interpreting the Bible.

In the Fathers, we find the unity of theology with biblical interpretation. There is a unity of the biblical message and the life of the Christians. They interpreted the Bible in the perspective of Christ's life.

The Fathers organically combined and unified the biblical message within the parameters of the liturgical and the sacramental life of the Church.

The Fathers do not restrict themselves to any specific methodology of interpretation. The mystery and the mind of the Bible were the major concern of their approach, not any specific method.

We cannot compare the interpretation of the Fathers always with our contemporary, or modern, and technological means. Some of the approaches of contemporary theologians are not always appropriate. The main thing, for the Fathers, however, was the message of the salvation in Christ, thus they are carriers of a special "ethos" and special approach and vision.[9]

Conclusion

I have made this large circle, in order to prove that the teaching of the Fathers both in academic as well as the parish level is not easy. It encompasses the problematic of historical, hermeneutic, cultural and biblical issues. Students at the seminary level, as well in catechetical or lay educational level, will ask these basic questions in regards to the Fathers, their approach and vision towards the Bible and their message to our own problems and to our own times. In that respect, we all should realize that the Bible and the Fathers stand on the same pedestal. They stand on the rock which is none other than Jesus Christ Himself.

NOTES

[1] See George S. Bebis, *The Mind of the Fathers* (Brookline, MA: Holy Cross Orthodox Press, 1994), p. 2ff.

[2] Bart D. Ehrman, *The Orthodox Corruption of Scripture, The Effect of Early Christological Controversies in the Text of the New Testament* (New York: Oxford University Press, 1993).

[3] Ehrman, p. 12.

[4] Ehrman, p. 275.

[5] Robert Grant, "The Appeal to the Early Fathers," *Journal of Theological Studies*, 11(1960), p. 13

[6] T. J. Towers, "The Value of the Fathers," *The Church Quarterly Review* 166 (July – Sept. 1965), pp. 294-298.

[7] George Mastrantonis, *The Fathers of the Church*, O Logos, p. 23.

[8] Athanasios, "How the Fathers saw the Holy Scripture," *Synaxis* 33 (1990), p. 37ff.

[9] John Panagopoulos, *The Patristic Exegetical Tradition and the Future of the Greek Biblical Scholarship*, p. 232ff.

THE INTERNET AND DISTANCE LEARNING: PLUMBING THE WELL OF CYBERSPACE FOR RELIGIOUS EDUCATION

FRANK MARANGOS

Preface

The theme of this conference suggests that we are concerned with what might happen to Orthodox faith in the new millennium. While there is a great deal of frantic conversation in the media about the twenty-first century and how it will most certainly pose more stunning, disorienting and complex problems than those faced by society in the previous century, the conference theme suggests that Orthodox theologians, educators and church leaders should soberly examine the opportunities and liabilities of the new millennium with clarity of purpose and loyalty to our past.

We are living in an age of enormous technological change. It is estimated that currently there are nearly 40 million households in the United States that have access to the Internet. It is believed that by the year 2005 that number will rise to over 50 million users! According to a recent study compiled by TBWA International (a subsidiary of the Omnicom Corporation), the fifteenth-largest advertising agency in the world, over 12.8 million households - that is thirty-eight percent of all families with children – own desktop computers.[1] Ninety percent of these families say that their children actively use their computers an average of five and one-half hours per week – with most of this time at the expense of television. Statistics complied by Teenage Research Unlimited (TRU) show that the Internet is coming into American homes as fast as television did.[2] Two-thirds of these teenagers say that they know how to use a computer to log on to the World Wide Web. In 1994, fifty percent of teens told TRU that it is 'in' to be online. Today, the figure has risen to a staggering eighty-eight percent!

From what has briefly been cited it is obvious that the Orthodox Church should be concerned with the societal effects of technology on religious faith. Technology, and for the purposes of this presentation, more specifically, the educational benefits that result from the emerging communication technologies of the Internet and World Wide Web, should be carefully measured upon the precarious balance of fanciful wonder on the one hand

241

and Faustian passivity on the other. While culture always pays a price for technology, the Church should fashion a means to utilize the monumental advances of the electronic communications tools of the Internet in a sacred way.

This presentation, entitled *The Internet and Distance Learning: Plumbing the Well of cyberspace*, will: (a) examine several theories associated with Distance Learning and online education, (b) evaluate the opportunities and threats created by these communication technologies, and (c) suggest ways that the Orthodox Church in America may thoughtfully take advantage of the tremendous benefits that these educational strategies afford the local parish. Finally, the scriptural pericope of the Samaritan woman at the well of Jacob (Jn 4) will provide the backdrop for my analysis.

PART ONE

The well of cyberspace

An icon miniature from an illuminated Gospel Lectionary at the Monastery of Saint Dionysiou on Mt. Athos depicts Jesus engaged in serious conversation with a woman. Both have outstretched their right hands to the other. Beside each of them the iconographer has painted a series of jagged mountain peaks behind which two groups of onlookers are respectively murmuring among themselves. While Jesus is clutching his robe, the woman is tightly holding a long rope that appears to be tied to an earthen jar. At the center of the icon is a well, the Well of Jacob.

The story of the Samaritan woman is described in detail in John 4. It recounts an unusual yet theologically focused conversation between Jesus and a Samaritan woman who came to draw water from the famous well of Jacob. Apparently, due to her questionable moral character, the woman was not allowed to come in the morning to draw water with the other women of the village. As such, she approaches alone at the sixth hour (about noon).

It is not the scope of this presentation to elaborate on the theological or scriptural implications of Jesus' conversation with the Samaritan woman. What is important and pivotal to our brief discussion concerning the Internet and Distance Learning is the paradigm that this New Testament passage provides. In brief, I would suggest that the Well of Jacob be understood as a metaphor for the Internet or what has been often referred to as cyberspace, the ever-deepening well of information and knowledge from which technology invites us to drink.

As we enter a new millennium, the Orthodox Church has the opportunity to utilize the opportunities that technology affords as effective tools for its educational needs. The dynamic of online technology should be employed as a water pitcher that may help those who thirst for religious instruction to plum the depths of the Sacred Well of Orthodoxy and thereby begin to quench their thirst. In this fashion the Orthodox Church may utilize the Internet as an effective tool for learning and a medium for religious edification that establishes the unifying presence of the sacred within an otherwise disordered environment.

The information revolution

Whether it is described as the information, digital, or technological revolution, the "Information Age" is characterized by structural changes that have profound implications for both the public and the private policies that frame lifelong learning. These changes include industrial and occupational changes, globalization, the changing nature of competition, and the very idea of community. They place a premium on knowledge, skills, training and education.

Information technology is changing the access to knowledge, the process of learning, and the delivery of education and training. Teaching and learning can now take place outside the traditional institutional and workplace-based venues for education and training that are anchored in accreditation and certification and tied to defined skills, jobs and career paths. The 1993 issue of *Peterson's College Guide* lists ninety-three "cyberschools" in America. Today, the same publication outlines more than 762 schools involved in Distance Learning or what has also been called "cyberlearning."

Brown and Brown describe that the concluding decade of the 20th century was a time of change from institutional-based learning structures of the past few centuries to open architecture education. According to Brown and Brown, open-architecture learning, cyber, or Distance Learning occurs at a time, a place, and in a configuration suitable to the learner rather than to the teacher or administration.[3] As such, they insist that Distance Learning and its variants have the potential to provide equity of access on a world basis.

From the preceding data it is safe to say that technology should be employed as a major driver of religious education initiatives in the twenty-first century – a century that ushered in the information revolution. In many ways technology has always produced revolutions within education. The first transformation took place over 2,500 years ago when both scholars and students moved beyond the Socratic paradigm of simple oral exchange to the more complex practice of reading and writing. Although the rich technology of the written word could not provide certainty that the reader had properly understood the intent of the author it nonetheless enabled teachers to reach more students and gave learners more time to critique complex arguments. Consequently, the technological advance of the written word ushered in a pedagogical revolution that heralded a wider access to education.

The second revolution concerns the advent of resident scholarship, which organized independent scholars and students into a pedagogical community. Campuses allowed students greater access to more sources and models of inquiry. The technologies of library science and laboratories provide possibilities that no single faculty member could have created alone. As such, the entire learning community of teachers, students, administrators, publishers and trustees was fortunate to gather the collective wisdom of generations of organized study, which fostered qualitative changes in the academic enterprise!

Like the previous paradigm shift, the adoption of campus technology resulted in negative as well as positive outcomes. The shift towards specialization fostered isolation and a passive learning posture wherein students waited in anticipation for experts to bestow knowledge upon them. While some students thrived in the lecture halls and libraries, others surely had trouble.

Futurists and expert observers of the social context tell us that we are currently in the throes of yet another paradigm shift in education. Once again, the revolution is being driven by technological advances that are providing opportunities as well as threats to the pedagogical enterprise. The landscape of education is changing. I would suggest that it would be wise, therefore, for those of us engaged in theological and catechetical education to reflect on the scope, direction and degree of change that technology affords our educational agendas.

The third revolution in education is made possible by current technologies such as computers, multimedia, virtual reality, compressed video, and the entire spectrum of advances in the telecommunications industry. Like the revolution that preceded it, the boundaries of the existing learning environment are being redrawn. The duration, pace and quality of interaction between students and teachers, students and students, faculty and faculty are changing. Once again, both scholars and learners are given opportunities for greater access to even wider ranges of experiences, expert opinions and academic resources.

Internet statistics

Oldenburg describes how people use coffee shops, community centers, beauty parlors, general stores, bars and other 'hangouts' to help them get through the day. He refers to these locations that are an integral part of social life but distinct from home and work as "third places."[4] We might consider the Internet as such a third place, a virtual hangout, town hall, or town common.

Survey data suggests that the Internet has become a growing sphere of interaction. Much like the Well of Jacob, the Well of Cyberspace has become a specific environment for discussion, relationship, commerce, education, and even prayer. According to a recent survey conducted by Cyber Dialogue for the Disney Company (2001), more than fifty-three percent of those polled said that the Internet has actually brought their families closer together.[5] Ninety-two percent call the Web a great educational tool. The study suggests that the Web has essentially become a family hearth, a focal point in the American home by providing new ways to communicate, interact, imagine and learn.

The number of worldwide Internet users has increased dramatically, from eighteen million in 1995 to 166.7 million in March 2001. In the United States, 41.8 million people had Internet access at work as of March 18, 2001 and 82.1% of them, four million, were active users.[6] At the same time, 166.7 million people had Internet access at home.

The Barna Research Group reports that eight percent of adults and twelve percent of teenagers use the Internet for religious or spiritual experiences. Listening to archived religious teaching was among the most appealing net-based religious activities.[7] The report suggests that listening to religious teaching online would likely draw more than 100 million adults.

According to the Pew Internet and American Life Project summary of findings, the Internet has become a vital force in many faith communities. The survey reveals that eighty-three percent of those responding to the survey indicated that their use of the Internet has helped congregational life. Twenty-five percent believe it has helped a great deal.

Data collected suggests that the Internet is being used by Christian congregations to strengthen the faith and spiritual growth of their members, evangelize and perform missions around the world, and perform a wide variety of pious and practical activities.[8]

The Pew survey further reports that seventy-two percent of clergymen have gathered information for educational programs. Twenty-one percent of Internet users (about nineteen to twenty million people) have used the Internet to seek spiritual and religious information. On a typical day more than two million people are obtaining such information. The report concludes that there is a healthy audience for religious and spiritual material online.

The Pew survey reports that on a typical day fifty-five million Americans log on to the Internet, forty-eight million send or read e-mail, and forty-eight million perform at least one activity on the Web. In all, forty-five percent (thirty million children) of those under eighteen years of age are connected to the Internet.

According to a survey conducted by the education technology nonprofit company, NetDay, more than eight out of ten teachers (eighty-four percent) believe that computers and access to the Internet improve the quality of education. Seventy-five percent of teachers agree that teachers without Internet access in the classroom are at a disadvantage.[9]

A survey conducted by the Opinion Research Corporation reveals that fifty-four percent of working adults believe that college courses offered via the Internet are the future of higher education. Nearly two-thirds of respondents said that they are interested in continuing their education. However, forty-eight percent also said that a busy schedule is the biggest barrier to continuing their education.[10]

According to the Online Distance Learning in Higher Education Report conducted by the International Data Corporation (IDC), the number of college students enrolled in Distance Learning courses will reach 2.2 million in 2002, up from 710,000 in 1998. This number represents fifteen percent of all higher education students, up from five percent in 1998.

IDC reports that the number of institutions of higher education offering Distance Learning programs is also growing dramatically. By 2002, eighty-five percent of all two-year colleges in America will be offering Distance Learning courses. This figure is up from fifty-eight percent in 1998. Eighty-four percent of all four-year colleges will be offering Distance Learning courses in 2002, up from sixty-two percent in 1998. The report concludes by affirming that Distance Learning via the internet has become a serious alternative to standard classroom environments providing enormous opportunities to providers of education in America.[11]

In the year 2000, home access to the Net grew from ten to forty-six percent. In 1983 only seven percent of all households owned a computer. In 1996 only fifteen percent of all households in America had access to the World Wide Web. By 1997 the number had grown to forty-four percent and to sixty percent for households with children. It is estimated that over two-thirds of all children use a personal computer. Eighty percent of parents believe computers help their children do better in school.[12]

The fastest growing group on the Internet is comprised of individuals between the ages of eighteen and twenty-four. Tapscott refers to this group as the new navigators.[13] They are more knowledgeable than previous generations. In a 1997 Wall Street Journal study, computer sales constituted 1.3% of the total consumer spending rate, or twelve times the percentage spent seven years prior.[14]

The use of electronic mail (e-mail) began in 1994. In 1995, 35 million individuals communicated via e-mail. By 1997 the number had risen to eighty million.[15]

Research suggests that in the year 2000 America children watched approximately 100 hours less television than in 1996. The reason given for this decline is the simultaneous growth of computer use.[16]

The first web browser was introduced in 1993. There were fifty known web services at the time. By the end of 1994 that number had increased to 5,000. By 1997, there were 1.5 million web services. For more information and statistics concerning computer use please refer to the Cyber Atlas Site (www.cyberatlas.com).

Definition of terms

Cyberspace, the World Wide Web and the Internet are terms that are currently receiving a great deal of media attention. But what exactly is the Internet or the World Wide Web and how might we as Orthodox religious educators use the new technology of multimedia telecommunication to design instruction for the purpose of pursuing catechetical literacy among the faithful?

Cyberspace is a generic term used to describe a virtual electronic well from which a variety of interconnected network tributaries and program streams deliver information. The Internet is a global computer network that links government institutions, commercial organizations, schools and people together to share information. The Internet, which should not be confused with the World Wide Web, has been in existence in one form or another for more than two decades, providing services such as electronic mail and file exchanges to computer scientists and researchers around the world.

The World Wide Web, on the other hand, is merely an Internet service, like e-mail or FTP (file transfer protocol) that sit atop the infrastructure of the Internet much like different television stations sit atop the cable that brings entertainment and news to our home television sets. As such, the World Wide Web is the multimedia portion of the Internet, the place where we find text, pictures, sounds and videos on a stunning array of topics.

According to M. Benedikt, "Cyberspace is a world created and sustained by the world's computers and communication lines, a world in which the global traffic of knowledge, secrets, measurements, indicators, entertainments and alter-human agency takes on form ... a common metal geography, built in turn by consensus and revolution, canon and experiment ... whose corridors form wherever electricity runs with intelligence."[17] The Internet has the capability of simultaneously conveying text, graphics, sound, video and data in cyberspace. This multimedia potential can also be carried in real-time interaction between numerous people over long distances. It is relatively inexpensive and is therefore being used by instructional designers as a fantastic delivery system.

There are numerous programs that can be classified under the general Internet name. These include Internet Relay Chat (IRC), which allows for real-time discussion, the World Wide Web (WWW), which acts as hyper-textual, multimedia interface; the Usenet, which allows for asynchronous discussion and transfer of multimedia and data; Multiple User Domains (MUDs) and Multiple User, Object-oriented (MOOs), which are text-based virtual worlds which allow for real-time interaction, and e-mail, which allows for asynchronous personal communication.

I believe the Church is called to use Her creativity and imagination to develop and apply systematic knowledge to solve problems encountered in using and enjoying God's world. The technology of cyberspace, therefore, is instrumental. It is not an end in itself but a tool that must be guided with ethical direction and constraints. Technology must not be viewed by the Church with suspicion and hostility. On the contrary, it can be employed by Orthodox Christians to restore an understanding of God and of His Holy Church.

The recent shift in educational theory from a traditional teacher-centered philosophy to a learner-centered philosophy combined with unceasing demands for flexible institutions have resulted in innovative approaches to education. According to Shale and Garrison, this increasing need for education, for those who cannot obtain it in the traditional way, has "led to institutional interest in distance education where previously there may have been little or none."[18]

If Distance Learning is to be employed by the Greek Orthodox Church in its theological institutions of higher learning, however, a new philosophical perspective towards education must be considered. Such a framework must therefore be based upon a clear understanding of the educational transaction sustained by Distance Learning and its ancillary technologically-based delivery systems.

The manner in which our contemporary world has approached the electronic well of cyberspace provides ample evidence that mankind still thirsts for living water. Like the Samaritan woman, people approach the electronic well of cyberspace still yearning for lasting refreshment. Like the Samaritan woman, whose five husbands should conjure up images of ever-changing spiritual apostasy, the new paradigm of electronic commerce and communication reveals the most recent courtship of mankind's idolatrous desires. Like the Samaritan woman who approached the Well of Jacob with a rope-tied earthen bucket, today's thirsty are tethered to cable-tied computer mouse pads. Their need to continually plumb the bottomless well of cyberspace illustrates the degree of our contemporary global thirst for community, knowledge, and truth! Unfortunately, while society may indeed be surfing upon the waves of a technological tsunami it is, nonetheless, in danger of drowning in a sea of information. Mankind's inner thirst for absolutes can only be quenched by Divine Truth and not by diffuse data-bits!

Theories of Distance Learning

There are as many approaches to Distance Learning as there are theorists and practitioners in the field. According to Moods, however, most theorists of Distance Learning agree on a basic approach to the field. This theory includes the following characteristics: (a) leader and learner must be separated for most of the learning process, (b) the course or program must be influenced or controlled by an organized educational institution, (c) some form of media must be used, both to overcome the physical separation of teacher and learner and to carry the course content, (d) two-way communication in some form must be provided between leader and learner.[19]

Maxwell considers Distance Learning as "a mode of delivering a course of study in which the majority of communication between teachers and students occurs non-contiguously, and the two-way communication between teacher and student necessary for the educational process is technologically mediated."[20] Like Maxwell, Cheng, Lehman and Reynolds define Distance Learning as "the application of telecommunications, computer, and other electronic devices to enable learners to use instruction that originates from a distant location."[21] The computer-based method for Distance Learning can either be individual or group-based.

Cheng, et al., insist that the "asynchronous group-based method provides both instructional efficiency and the benefits of group interaction." They argue that while synchronous group-based instruction refers to the participation of all class members at one time, asynchronous group-based instruction refers to the participation of class members at different times.[22]

Distance Learning is typically viewed as an evolutionary development of correspondence education. Pre-produced courses are self-instructional and consist of print-based material, and are often supplemented by recorded audio or video presentations. Non-contiguous courses can be conducted via voice, writing, telephone, audio tape and/or computers. As such, Distance Learning can also be defined as the transmission of interactive educational programming to geographically-dispersed individuals and groups.

Moods suggests that the roots of Distance Learning finds its roots in correspondence education, which used the postal service to carry the lessons and the student's responses. Radio and television were used by Distance Learning providers who were determined to employ the newest methods of technology to their instructional advantage.

Traditionally, Distance Learning consisted of correspondence courses taught to distant learners through a variety of media formats. Most programs were implemented with text-based materials, workbooks, and some form of adjunct support material from radio, television broadcasts, student tutors, or other types of instructive assistance. These systems, however, tended to lack significant interaction between instructor and students. Today, however, Distance Learning "has expanded to include newer applications of technology, such as interactive video and personal computers."[23]

Adding to Moods' list of new instructional technologies, Kaye outlines a variety of different ways that Distance Education courses at the university level are offered: (a) campus-based student correspondence via telephone and e-mail, (b) distance-based innovations, and (c) mixed model-based institutions which support both campus-based and external students .[24]

Advantages and benefits of Distance Learning

Kaye outlined three benefits of Distance Learning: (a) pedagogical, (b) economic, and (c) structural.[25] The pedagogical argument centers around two primary issues. First, Distance Education is essentially a medium of written discourse that shares spontaneity and flexibility of the spoken word. Second, Distance Education can be used for group communication and cooperative learning.

According to Kaye, "the discipline of being obliged to formulate ideas, thoughts, reactions and opinions in writing in such a way that their meaning is clear to other people who are not physically present is of key importance in the majority of educational purposes."[26] Educational theorists and practitioners who emphasize the importance of debate, discussion and group work in promoting meaningful learning will argue strongly for Distance Learning because it provides opportunities for collaborative experiences which may otherwise be completely lacking in more formal classroom settings.

Kaye's second argument for Distance Learning relates to the technological characteristics of the computer-mediated learning process and the way they match the nature of the distance educational environment. Finally, the economic argument centers on the need for small colleges and universities to reach out to a larger student market which includes: (a) older learners, (b) continuing skill-based learners, (c) learners with jobs, (d) geographically-isolated learners, and (e) students with low self-esteem.

Like Kaye, Cheng et al. outline nine advantages of Computer-Based Distance Learning (CBDL): (a) eliminates travel time and expense, (b) permits flexible scheduling, (c) provides convenient access to course materials and the instructor, (d) provides access to distant expert instructors, (e) provides lone learner access to group knowledge and support, (f) enhances opportunities for class interaction, (g) provides for an egalitarian atmosphere, (h) stores communications for convenient access, reflection and responses, and (i) provides instruction inexpensively once instructional hardware and software have been acquired.[27]

As we have observed thus far, Distance Learning has the potential to create communities of great dialogical encounter. However, the greatest motivation for developing successful Distance Learning strategies for parishes as well as for Orthodox institutions of higher learning appears to be in providing educational access to those who were previously denied learning opportunities. Obstacles, on the other hand, include: (a) reliability of the delivery system, (b) time delay, (c) funding, and (d) the attitude that Distance Learning is inferior to traditional campus-based education.

According to Blackwood and White, time and place are the two most frequently expressed barriers to participation in adult education. As such, if improvements in educational opportunities and access are primary goals, delivery systems should be designed to allow: (a) learning to become an integral part of the learners' activities in the home and the workplace, and (b) the learner to have control over the how, where and why of the learning.[28]

Moods outlines five groups of learners that are served by Distance Learning: (a) geographically-isolated learners, (b) women, (c) industry, (d) the physically disabled, and (e) learners isolated by socioeconomic factors.[29] Cheng et al., (1991) suggest that, in practice, traditional class discussion usually includes a small number of students. As such, the possible risk of embarrassment can discourage less-advanced students from presenting an oral report. "Instruction for Distance Learning appears to be effective only if there is active two-way interaction between teacher and student. In CBDL the computer becomes the interface between the teacher and the learner creating an active learning environment that supports ample human inter-active comments."[30]

Jevons narrows the preceding list of categories to six types of educational advantages for learners. According to Jevons, Distance Learning: (a) provides easier access for many people, (b) approaches the ideal of the autonomous learner, (c) provides better instructional quality, (d) creates less disjunction between the context of work and study, (e) provides the opportunity for cumulative improvement in pedagogic control, and (f) promotes staff development. [31]

Finally, like Jevons, Kelly considers five benefits to Distance Learning: (a) the broad range and orientation of student participation, (b) the positive effect of interactive skills on teachers, (c) the flexibility of the system permitting teachers to accommodate specific learner needs, (d) the establishment of a more personal relationship between teachers and learners, and (e) the provision of courses to be offered to small groups without a heavy initial investment in preparation of resource materials.[32]

Limitations and concerns

One of the first objections raised by educators and students alike to the acceptance of information and instructional technology into the educational context is the perceived loss of interpersonal interaction. "Interpersonal interaction," they correctly insist, "is a chief ingredient for helping students learn." As such, they warn that technology "will disrupt community and destroy the relationship between the teacher and students!"

It is important to note at the outset of this discussion that the debate concerning the interpersonal relationship between the teacher and the student is as old as Socrates and Plato. This debate did not begin with the invention of the computer or the advent of the World Wide Web. On the contrary, it began with the technological advent of the written word and has continued with each successive innovation such as the book, the campus, the library, the lecture hall, and even the blackboard!

While the current revolution in education runs the risk of disrupting interpersonal interaction, instructional technology and the prudent and strategic use of technology has been proven to have the reverse effect! Instructional technology has the capability of effectively encouraging greater community interaction between a larger diversity of members, which may draw from outside experts as well.

Information technology provides the opportunity for a moderate pedagogical pace and a safer 'place' for thoughtful and unbiased conversation to emerge. The thirsty do not have to approach the well alone at midday anymore! Technologies such as e-mail, computer video and audio conferencing, synchronous and asynchronous chat, and web page instruction make it possible to approach the well of information at any time and from any location. It has the power to draw together more diverse students and faculty and create the opportunities for a greater mix of learning styles. Teachers can take advantage of these new technologies to better serve and dialogue with students of diverse backgrounds, values and academic desires.

PART TWO

Distance Learning strategies

What are the most effective online Distance Learning strategies and how can the Orthodox Church utilize them to provide instructional opportunities to its parish faithful? Distance learning technology facilitates the sending and receiving of electronic messages, images and sounds by computer over phone lines or via satellite which tap into vast stores of text and data. Online learning strategies can be classified into nine general models: (a) interpersonal exchanges, (b) partnering, (c) electronic appearances, (d) online expeditions, (e) information collection and exchange, (f) problem-solving, (g) online simulations, (h) environmental action, and (i) distance learning. The following is a sampling of online projects that provide exciting possibilities for Orthodox distance learning.

At the simplest level, *interpersonal exchange* describes the sharing of ideas and information between two individuals. Although this type of personal interaction can relieve isolation by establishing regular correspondence, it can also produce opportunities for collaborative work. As such, interpersonal exchange may be described as a virtual water-cooler, a global Jacob's Well – if you will – that transcends geography, nationality, gender and time zones.

Another strategy of online interpersonal exchange is called *partnering*. Entire classes or groups can take advantage of this technique by co-reporting on similar environmental studies. For example, the International Education and Resource Network (I*LEARN) affords teachers the opportunity to link their classes as they study environmental issues. While one class is observing a local freshwater pond, another group of students can be studying the water quality of a saltwater estuary in another part of the globe.

Interpersonal exchange strategy may also include the *online appearance* of noteworthy individuals such as scientists, explorers, religious and political leaders and theologians. All may be invited to participate temporarily online via electronic mail or synchronous chat. *Electronic mentoring* may also be classified as an online interpersonal exchange strategy for Orthodox Distance Learning initiatives to the parish. Subject specialists are connected with students for co-exploration of specific topics. Such interpersonal exchanges often enrich both students and mentors. An Orthodox network of religious and political leaders, theologians and environmental experts may be created and given the responsibility of matching subject matter volunteers with interested students.

Another interpersonal online instructional exchange strategy that has recently become popular is the *electronic expedition* or field trip. The now famous JASON project links students with scientists and explorers via elaborate computer networks. In this fashion, classes may experience the exploration of ocean reefs or the study of rain forests as if they are really there. Electronic expeditions to significant Christian locations such as monasteries, libraries, theological schools and churches may be developed to further enhance the impact that such sites have and still contribute to Christian history. Such projects will indeed corroborate the collective potential for online interpersonal exchange strategies.

Information collection and exchanges is yet another online instructional strategy that should be seriously considered by religious educators developing Distance Learning strategies to enhance Orthodox catechetical literacy. These online educational initiatives range from newsletters jointly produced via e-mail and computer conferencing to the development of extensive patristic, theological and scriptural data-bases. The Web site for the Greek Orthodox Archdiocese of America (www.goarch.org) for example, regularly posts educational articles, communiqués, liturgical music and iconography. Dr. Paul Ferris of Bethel Seminary Minneapolis, Minnesota, offers Old Testament courses that include vectored maps of the Holy Lands with audio and video streaming media (see Appendix A).

These and other databases can be visited by individuals or by classes of students who in turn can begin to develop their own collection of specialized lists of data gathered from multiple electronic sites on the Internet. A sampling of pertinent Distance Learning websites have been included in the Appendix of this paper. The listing includes: (a) general Distance Learning issues and examples, (b) examples of courses offered by various theological schools, (c) hardware and software vendors, and (d) resources for developing Distance Learning strategies.

The idea of scientists and teachers co-designing *environmental field education* is currently one of the most popular themes in environmental education. The former Vice President, Al Gore, proposed in his book *Earth in the Balance* that scientists and teachers should collaborate in just such a fashion. His challenge has led to the creation of the GLOBE project (Global Learning and Observations to Benefit the Environment) whose goal is the creation of an international science and educational partnership in which K-12 students will collect environmental data and share it with each other and with the international community of environmental scientists.[33] We can only imagine the success that similar Orthodox environmental projects may have when combined with Orthodox theologians and students throughout the globe.

Problem Solving or Problem-Based Learning (PBL) is the most exciting and perhaps the most promising classification of online Distance Learning instructional models that parish religious educators may consider. In this category of electronic learning initiatives, groups and individuals can collaborate on projects that achieve authentic learning. By combining religious thought with scientific knowledge to resolve real-world, local, political and environmental problems, students can begin to learn how their Orthodox Faith can influence society.

Problem-Based Learning (PBL) is a pedagogical strategy for posing significant, contextualized, real-world situations, and providing resources, guidance and instruction to learners as they develop content knowledge and problem-solving skills. In online problem-solving scenarios, students collaborate to study issues associated with a societal problem as they strive to discover viable religious solutions.

Unlike traditional instruction, which is often conducted in a lecture format, online problem-solving activities normally occur as groups and individuals collaborate on projects. This is accomplished by applying knowledge to resolve real-world problems on the local level. These networks of virtual learners can reinforce and strengthen each other over time, building sustainable online Orthodox action-based communities in cyberspace! An example of such an online community is the National Geographic Kids' Network which involves hundreds of classrooms on acid rain monitoring and assessment methods that allow students to produce scientifically valid problem-based learning results with low-cost technology.

While online *simulations and gaming* strategies create opportunities for participants to try their hands at a number of fictional scenarios such as acting as delegates negotiating treaties on issues like chloro-fluorocarbon or oil pollution in the Black Sea, *environmental action projects* focus on the real thing. Computer networks are used in this online strategy to mobilize action in many different ways from working to change public policy to personal environmental responsibility.

Schools have used e-mail and online conferencing to coordinate fund-raising efforts and to learn how their own personal, small efforts can, in fact, collectively make a meaningful difference in the quality of life for other people as well as in the environment. The Orthodox Church should have an environmental presence in cyberspace. Apart from providing catechetical resources, religious educators can and should be encouraged to develop strategies that can instantly tap into a vast pool of environmental information. In this fashion, dialogue between theology and science may be enhanced. From environmental film footage to specialized data on ozone depletion or food shortages throughout the globe, students can utilize online strategies to learn at their own pace in their own style. Remote, environmental material and resources can be accessed via local electronic bulletin boards or interactive computer networks such as the Internet.

Pedagogical implications

Apart from the other benefits it may provide, information technology has the potential to positively effect the pedagogical enterprise itself. If nothing else, the advent of current instructional technologies invites teachers to reflect on the most important issue of all ... our methods of teaching! Similar to what must have taken place during the previous historical revolutions in education, questions arise that should be intelligently addressed. While passion and opinion will undoubtedly have their place in the discussion, care should be taken to deliberate the important issues created by the emergence of information and instructional technologies to campuses and classrooms with the objective rigors of academic research and evaluation.

The paradigm shift that is currently taking place in education has important consequences for theologians and Orthodox Christian religious educators. The challenge is to avoid adopting isolationist agendas based on quick judgment and personal assumptions and to proceed with a mature and critical eye focused on opportunity and growth. Instead of debating between only two options, like Mt. Gerizm and Jerusalem (Jn 4: 20), our task will be to seek the Truth in alternative ways. Here, we should recall the response Jesus gave to the Samaritan woman when asked to choose between Gerizm and Jerusalem. "The hour will come," He insists, "and now is, that neither on this mountain (Gerizm) nor in Jerusalem will they worship God. True worshipers will seek Him in Spirit and Truth" (Jn 4: 21-24). Accordingly, the contemporary well of information can and should be utilized as a means for such boundary-less inquiry. Reaction to change is almost always more important than the change agent itself. As with earlier changes, the way in which we, as theologians, educators and Church leaders respond to the contemporary phenomena will, to a great extent, affect the outcome for religious education.

If the Orthodox Church in America is honestly concerned with providing effective ongoing religious education to parish clergy, community leaders, adults and youth, it will focus on developing effective online initiatives for overcoming the barriers that, for one reason or another, separate its parish constituents from one another and from its theological institutions.

In this context, Distance Learning (DL) or what has also been referred to as Distance Education (DE) affords the Greek Orthodox Church in America the opportunity of establishing an educational delivery system that is capable of: (a) promoting student/teacher interaction, (b) sustaining the effective development of theological understanding, (c) supplying valuable opportunities for the professional development of its clergy and lay-leaders, and (d) providing unprecedented educational access to a large number of potential candidates for the priesthood. Consequently, since Distance Learning has the ability to overcome numerous physical, economic and educational barriers, its implementation should be vigorously pursued by the Orthodox Church and most especially by its educational organizations and theological institutions of higher learning.

According to Milheim, many established institutions are now considering implementing Distance Learning in order to increase: (a) course offerings, (b) number of students, and (c) types of students enrolled in their current courses.[34] As we have observed in the preceding section, however, education at a distance is more than information transfer or the electronic packaging of information. As such, this section is interested in examining the educational transaction and the importance of understanding various modes of communication when designing education at a distance.

As we have observed, online Distance Learning strategies utilize computer technology to create virtual courses and symposia, which might include traditional lecture and seminar formats via the Internet. It is argued that because every student can have individualized attention of the instructor via e-mail, this online strategy offers opportunities to improve student access and sustainable dialogue. The lack of face-to-face interaction, while a drawback to online courses, can be overcome by using video broadcast or tape to complement online communication.

The Public Broadcasting Service (PBS) has launched a new online communication and information delivery service called PBS Online that merges public television programming with computers. The service is taking advantage of new satellite technology to build a two-way interactive data network through local public television stations. Such Distance Learning initiatives should be seriously considered by Christian universities, seminaries and monasteries as well.

As we have seen from a brief review of nine online instructional strategies, using a computer is not the same as learning with a computer. As Religious Educators we must remain vigilant and guard against allowing our exuberance for new technologies to lure us into a false sense of productivity. Computer-aided instruction must be firmly linked to critical thinking and a robust theology on technology.

The proper use of computers can encourage online instructional strategies that encourage critical thinking rather than merely supplying the answers. We must not allow ourselves to get enamored with technological advances at the expense of solid time-tested instructional strategies. Online Distance Learning can be a cost-effective, time-saving instructional strategy, which has as two of its consequences interdisciplinary content and the development of critical thinking.

Good teaching has often been hampered by customary instructional strategies, which ignore divergent student learning styles. Online technology provides numerous ways of creating the instructional environment that utilizes proven teaching methods that accommodate learner needs.

Access to theological, scriptural, liturgical and other religious resources is currently being augmented by the emergence of easily-activated fiber-optic pathways and wireless digital satellite transmissions. Catechetical resources and instructional materials can be electronically accessed and viewed by students in the classroom, in the field, at home and in the parish. Strategies that afford students to interact with virtual encyclopedic and archeological resources can stimulate exploration rather than static transmission of content. Such techniques afford the religious educator the opportunity to integrate theological thought, Christian ethics and critical thinking, disciplines that have in the past often been truncated from serious online inquiry.

According to Shale and Garrison, "in its most fundamental form, education is an interaction between teacher, student and subject content... a transaction dependent upon sustained two-way communication which provides for the transformation of raw information into knowledge."[35] Distance Learning must avoid the temptation of overly attending to the isolated learner. For Distance Learning programming to succeed, its implementation should be based upon interdependence and not only upon the glamour of technological advancements for their own sake! Rather, as Shale and Garrison insist, it should focus on the educational transaction and the interdependence of teacher and student.[36]

Together with multimedia technology software tools, the Internet provides the Orthodox Church great promise for a new model of teaching and learning. Such a design could be based on discovery and participation, which would transcend the confines of the traditional classroom. Distance learning strategies have the ability to create an environment where life-long learning about Orthodoxy can be advanced. Rather than a generation of intellectual competitors, the Net has the potential of developing more collaborative and critical thinkers.

Historically, the field of education was oriented towards pedagogical models that focused on instruction as broadcast learning. In these systems, the teacher was considered the expert who had control over the information transmitted (pushed) to the students. Through repetition, rehearsal and practice, facts and information could be stored in long-term memory of the student, which could then be integrated to form large knowledge structures. The result of such teaching paradigms was made evident in certain outcomes or behaviors, which could be measured during testing. The lecture, text-book, homework and school environment itself are examples of a predominately one-way, centralized and predefined structure of broadcast teaching/learning model. It is based on an authoritarian, top-down, teacher-centered approach to education.

While much of Distance Learning employs examples of the broadcast-based learning model (one size fits all), the delivery system can be designed around another model that promotes more interaction. Such an educational paradigm would stress a 'pull' rather than 'push' epistemology.

In light of the previous information, the old approach to education is ill-suited for the new generation of Orthodox families and parishes. Society is shifting from the broadcast, analog models of learning to those that support more digital interactivity.[37] Consequently, the Orthodox Church should begin to adopt the new interactive model of education, which is easily supported by the multimedia computer tools of the Internet. Research shows that when appropriately integrated into the curriculum, the new technologies improve student performance and develop better motivated, collaborative and communication skills.

According to Tapscott, digital technology affords educators and students eight shifts in the learning paradigm: (a) from liner to hyper-media learning, (b) from instruction to construction and discovery, (c) from teacher-centered to learner-centered education, (d) from absorbing material to learning how to navigate and how to learn, (e) from school to lifelong learning, (f) from one-size-fits-all to customized learning, (g) from learning as torture to learning that is fun, and (h) from teacher as transmitter to the teacher as facilitator.[38] While it is beyond the scope of this introductory article to examine each of these eight potential shifts in the educational praxis it is important to agree on at least one point. When properly fused with multi-media technology, Distance Learning has the potential of affording the Orthodox Church in America a pedagogical framework and digital delivery system that can better serve its parish-based faithful.

As we have seen, technology's intersection with learning is not a simple trend of replacing old approaches. New hybrid forms of learning and delivering content are emerging. Such strategies include many combinations of traditional classes and teaching combined with technology-based methods for finding content and learning.

PART THREE

Issues of implementation

The Greek Orthodox Church of America is interested in providing catechetical opportunities to its parish faithful. What principles will determine and guide the selection and arrangements of educational strategies that will provide parishes the best access to such instruction? As we have discussed in the previous section, the usual perspective of Distance Learning has, unfortunately, been to view it as the evolutionary development of correspondence education. It would be a mistake to approach the implementation of Distance Learning as merely a hybrid or industrialization of correspondence materials.

Shale and Garrison insist that Distance Learning should be distinguished from correspondence study techniques by three essential criteria: (1) the noncontiguous educational communication between teacher(s) and student(s); (2) two-way communication between teacher(s) and student(s) for the purpose of facilitating and supporting the educational process, and (3) the use of technology to mediate the necessary two-way communication.[39]

According to Shale and Garrison, when one regards Distance Learning as an industrialized form of education, this leads to a regard of education "as a commodity to be packaged and distributed."[40] They also state: "Instruction reduced to packaging knowledge literally reduces teaching to telling, and learning is reduced to the largely solitary consumption of such packaged knowledge on the part of the learner."[41]

A number of problems arise from implementing Distance Learning or, for that matter, any other instructional strategy in this fashion. First, education becomes so amorphous and non-differentiated as to hinder any general definition of education being established. As a result, discussion will inevitably occur at cross-purposes!

A second problem that occurs when Distance Learning is implemented as packaged knowledge is the separation of subject matter from methods of instruction. Consequently, Distance Learning becomes, at best, the competitor or, at worst, the alternative to mainstream education!

Fortunately, during the last few years, Distance Learning systems have undergone radical changes in the methods employed for the design and implementation of instruction. This is the result of new technologies and satellite delivery systems through which interactivity is effectively sustainable. According to Milheim, regardless of the media choice, five guidelines should be observed to manage cost as well as other potential problems that might result from the implementation of DL programming: (a) budget for short- and long-term needs, (b) plan for teacher and support staff training, (c) use instructional design principles for the development of the material, and (e) deliver materials to students in an accurate and timely manner.[42]

Economic decisions comprise the first phase of Distance Learning implementation. As such, budgetary consideration should include: (a) cost associated with initial start-up, (b) program development, (c) staff training, and (d) equipment maintenance. After the budget has been properly prepared, issues concerning personal needs, staffing, instructor training and tutors must be addressed.

The choice of appropriate delivery systems should be made after budgetary and personal issues are addressed. As such, the third step of Milheim's (1991) guidelines for implementing Distance Learning should include separate decisions concerning: (a) delivery system, (b) instructional materials, (c) audience, and (d) the amount of interactivity between student, instructor, and material.

The fourth step entails making a decision concerning the actual design of the instructional material. This decision should made after an analysis of: (a) audience (b) course content, (c) instructional strategies that are appropriate to distance educational environments, (d) and appropriate evaluation strategies. Finally, the type of delivery system that will be selected to communicate materials to students should be determined by the: (a) amount of time delay, (b) form of material duplication, (c) revisions, (d) alteration, and (e) equipment maintenance schedule.

Television is a passive experience. Content is 'pushed' unto the viewer according to the political, religious and ethical values, timetables and agendas of the broadcasters. Simply put, rather than the viewer seeking it, content is pushed to the screen. In contrast, the Internet affords the viewer the ability to 'pull' information. In asynchronous access (archived), the user chooses to view previously stored content in the form of music, video, or news whenever it is convenient to do so. In synchronous access (real-time), the viewer accesses information as it is occurring.

Such interactivity allows users the opportunity to better investigate the content or information they desire according to schedule and need. It is significant that in a study conducted by America Online (AOL), families with Internet access spend fifteen percent less time watching television than those without computer access.[43] When asked to choose which technology is more fun, ninety-two percent of those who use the Internet prefer it over television.

The Orthodox Church should address the constellations of disorganized raw data on the Internet by helping users define, organize and synthesize it in an intelligible fashion. The Church should pursue initiatives that would help individuals to develop the critical-thinking skills that are necessary for tomorrow's viewer. The Church should develop the heuristics that may help viewers 'surf' the Net according to an Orthodox world-view which is based on implicit Orthodox Christian values and theology. In this fashion, we can help avoid 'cyber-drowning' in the ever- growing swell of information about information. We should strive to help individuals and families to develop the skills necessary for selecting trustworthy and appropriate information.

An example of how information technology can promote serious Orthodox religious inquiry is the Internet School of Orthodox Studies. The Internet School of Orthodox Studies (ISOS) was originally developed in 1998 by this author. It was created as a program of the Department of Religious Education of the Greek Orthodox Archdiocese of America in conjunction with the Department of Internet Ministries as a Distance Learning program for parish religious educators.

Currently, the program serves the educational needs of clergy, religious educators, university students, monastics and Orthodox parishioners from around the globe. Each week, on a two-semester basis, the Internet School of Orthodox Studies broadcasts a ninety-minute educational class intended to assist Orthodox Christians to more fully understand an element of Orthodox thought.

Apart from those who physically attend the Boston-based lectures on the campus of Holy Cross Greek Orthodox School of Theology, the classes can be heard by anyone with a computer and Internet access. The classes are broadcast in real time through the Greek Orthodox Archdiocese Web Server. PowerPoint presentations, video and audio streaming are used to enrich the Distance Learning environment. The syllabus, bibliography and class notes can be downloaded from the ISOS site (www.goarch.org/webcasts/religioused.html). The presentations are archived so that clergy, teachers and students can return and re-listen to the classes when their schedule permits.

Previously broadcast theological classes have been archived on the ISOS web page of the Department of Religious Education. Examples include: (a) an Examination of the *Triodion*, (b) an Examination of the Christmas Fast, (c) a Theological Examination of the Hymns of the Eight Tones (*Parakleteke*), (d) an Examination of the Orthodox Liturgical Year, and (e) an Introduction to the Church Fathers. Interested adults may access the page and listen to these presentations at their leisure.

During the 2000 Winter Semester, ISOS marked the first Distance Learning collaborative use of instructional technology between Saint Vladimir's Seminary and the Greek Orthodox Archdiocese. Physically, the classes took place on Tuesday evenings on the campus of Saint Vladimir's Seminary in New York and were taught by the Rev. Dr. Thomas Hopko, Dean of the Seminary. The theme of the 2000 Winter Semester was: "Mary: Icon of Human Perfection." The series of five ninety-minute educational classes were intended to assist Orthodox Christians to more fully understand the position of the Mother of God in Orthodox Tradition by reflecting on Mary as the model of human perfection. Apart from the theological students actually present at Saint Vladimir's and those who simultaneously attended the Boston location, the enrollees included virtual participants from around the globe! The cyber-class examined the scriptural, liturgical and theological aspects of the Theotokos in a casual yet systematic fashion.

The Department of Religious Education of the Greek Orthodox Archdiocese provides a certificate of educational recognition to students participating in the ISOS classes and who write a theological paper on a pertinent aspect of the semester theme. The DRE plans similar collaborative programs with theologians and faculty members from other theological schools in the future. The certificate of participation may be used as continuing education credit towards the Teacher Certification Program of the Greek Orthodox Archdiocese.

Numerous Greek Orthodox parishes have organized Distance Learning study groups that gather in homes or in community classrooms and view real-time ISOS presentations together. The parish clergyman and/or adult educator serves as the moderator and facilitator. Questions and comments from remote sites can easily be e-mailed to the ISOS broadcast site. In this fashion the ISOS faculty member can easily respond to the queries of distant students. Such information technologies have helped the ISOS project develop into a virtual educational classroom with students and subject-matter experts sharing their information and knowledge in a collaborative atmosphere. The Internet School of Orthodox Studies has been approached by representatives of the Institute of Orthodox Studies in Cambridge, England under the direction of Bishop Kallistos Ware and is currently discussing the possibility of linking their respective Distance Learning initiatives.

Recommendations
   This presentation has examined the theories and benefits that information and Distance Learning strategies may provide for the Greek Orthodox Church of America. Important guidelines and principles were outlined to facilitate the development and implementation of such Distance Learning instructional strategies. Consequently, the following recommendations are provided as a starting point for further conversation.
   As it enters a new millennium, the Greek Orthodox Archdiocese of America should: (a) establish an educational task force to explore new ways of thinking about the use of Distance Learning technologies for its various departments and institutions; (b) emphasize the learning and teaching transaction sustained by Distance Learning rather than on the latest technologies; (c) purchase basic, yet high-quality and versatile computer hardware and be imaginative in its use; (d) purchase and develop high-quality and appropriate instructional software for Distance Learning environments; (e) develop a theological framework to support the selection and use of Distance Learning technologies, and (f) develop formative and summative evaluative devices for determining the effectiveness of Distance Learning strategies.
   The Greek Orthodox Church of America is also concerned with increasing the number of men who may be interested in studying for the Holy Priesthood but for one reason or another their current situations prohibit them from full-time seminary attendance. As such, Orthodox Church leaders should focus on developing effective procedures for overcoming the barriers that may separate potential clergymen from each other and from its theological institutions.
   In this context, Distance Learning affords the Greek Orthodox Church of America the opportunity of establishing an educational delivery system that is capable of providing: (a) unprecedented educational access to a large number of potential candidates for the priesthood, and (b) effective continuing education opportunities for its parish-based clergy. Consequently, since distance education has the ability of overcoming numerous educational barriers, its implementation should be vigorously pursued.
   Finally, I would be remiss if I did not take a moment to suggest that future conferences and theological symposia include a Distance Learning component. One can only imagine how much more inclusive and theologically rich our present deliberations concerning the parish in the new

millennium would have been if the host committee included a simulcast of each and every presentation with the opportunity for participants at a distance to share their views.

If we are truly interested in serving the needs of our parishes as the Orthodox Church enters a new millennium, then future conferences should arrange for actual community representatives who cannot physically attend the symposium to be given the opportunity to participate via Web-enhanced online technologies. Our discussions will be much more diverse if we arrange for other experts and faculty members from other theological schools to be linked via the Internet and be given the opportunity to express their opinions. In the future these Distance Learning strategies will be a powerful way of more faithfully providing access to the Well!

Garrison predicted that of any other educational sector, education for adults will experience the greatest growth and change during the next two decades. Garrison further suggested that the role of educational technology, primarily that of Distance Learning, would greatly influence this change.[44] While numerous examples can be cited in military, industry, health care and secular institutions of higher learning to support Garrison's prediction, the Greek Orthodox Church of America has yet to experience this unprecedented development. Perhaps, by implementing the aforementioned recommendations, the Orthodox Church may quickly join the ranks of those who are enjoying the benefits of such boundary-less online learning.

The manner in which our contemporary world has approached the electronic well of information provides ample evidence that mankind still thirsts for living water. The story of Jacob's Well illustrates that society still yearns for lasting refreshment. However, like the Samaritan woman, whose five husbands should conjure up images of our society's ever-changing spiritual apostasy, the educational paradigm that technology invites must be tempered against mankind's courtship with post-modern relativism. Like the Samaritan woman who approached the Well of Jacob with a rope-tied earthen bucket, today's thirsty are tethered to cable-tied computer mouse pads. Their need to continually plumb the bottomless well of cyberspace illustrates the degree of our contemporary global thirst for community, knowledge and Eternal Truth!

Conclusion

As you may recall, the icon with which I began this examination on Distance Learning included two jagged mountain peaks, one behind Jesus and the other behind the Samaritan woman. If one is to look carefully at the icon, a group of murmuring onlookers can be seen hiding behind each mountain. From a review of the scriptural passage it is safe to surmise that one group represents the disciples while the other, citizens from the local Samaritan town of Sychar. Each group is distraught with the conversation that is taking place at the well.

The Jewish-Samaritan quarrel was more than 400 years old when Jesus spoke to the woman at the well. It had created a smoldering, resentful, bitter division between what was once the chosen people of God. By speaking and offering water to a woman – and a Samaritan woman at that – Jesus was in fact breaking down the arrogant barriers of nationalism, gender, custom, theology and ignorance. Here at the Well of Jacob is the beginning of the universality of the Gospel – not in theory – but in action!

Jacob's well was not a spring-fed oasis. One needed a bucket tied to a long rope over a hundred feet long to draw water out of it. It was a well into which rainwater was gathered. It is against this backdrop that one should understand Jesus' invitation to the Samaritan woman. "If you wish," he asks, "I can give you living water." To a Jew, the phrase "living water" is "running water." That is, water from a moving stream as opposed to a stagnant cistern or rain-pool. Our Lord's message to her was obvious: "Come to me, and I will give you the kind of water that provides true life!" Consequently, having spiritually tasted of Christ's water, the woman runs back to her own town – anxious to share her discovery!

According to a fourth-century hymn written by Saint Ephraim the Syrian in honor of this controversial meeting at the Well of Jacob, the Samaritan woman is characterized primarily as an apostle of the Lord! Throughout his hymn, Ephraim praises her for her courage and readiness to share her newfound insight into Jesus' Messianic identity with her fellow Samaritan townspeople.

In her revelation to others of what she had experienced, the Samaritan woman offers a wonderful model of how the contemporary Church should likewise "carry the water" of Christ's love and His challenge for personal, ecological and social responsibility to those who, for one reason or another, are hiding behind the jagged, self-imposed barriers of selfishness, ignorance and distance. "Blessed are you O woman," writes Saint Ephraim, "for your love for Christ was zealous, and so you shared your treasure, your water, with your entire town! O Woman ... Blessed are your ears that drank from the Source that now gives Drink to the entire World!"

This, in the end, is the challenge of the contemporary Orthodox Church as it enters the new millennium. As educators, church leaders and parish faithful, our challenge is to link the aquifer of salvation, the fountain of the Holy Trinity's creative love, intellectual, environmental, political, scriptural and liturgical to the deep yet stagnant well of the Internet, and through its electronic communication technology, to all the world. This is what I mean by the "Well of Cyberspace"... to link the Creator, His grace and love, with His creation. I am certain that through the help of properly developed online religious education initiatives, the barriers of race, nationality, gender, greed, age and affluence can finally be overcome.

APPENDIX*

Issues & Examples

www.mncts.org/workshops/copyright.htm , Copyright issues

http://www.mncts.org/workshops/IfTechnology.htm , Training issues: "5 Interesting Things..."

http://ceo.cudenver.edu/~brent_wilson/WebLearning.html, Constructivist Learning on the Web from *Learning Technologies: Reflective and Strategic Thinking. Ed.: Liz Burge. Jossey-Bass. Available May 2001*

http://www.fishersnet.net/anchordesk/surf.htm, Resources for examining Teaching and Learning from Luther's *The Fisher's Net*

http://john.fishersnet.net/ot1110penta_fl99/OnlineDissGraphic.htm, Dr. Dick Nysse describes how threaded discussions should work

http://john.fishersnet.net/ot1110penta_fl99/Discussions/WarsAndConquest-2.htm , Look at the "War Prayer" in this unit

http://www.fishersnet.net/save/april299/playtolearn.htm , How to see computers as valuable Scripture teaching tools

http://www.mncts.org/workshops/computercamp2.htm , Computer Camp promo

http://www.mncts.org/workshops/techpromo1.jpg , Fall Technology gathering promo

Theological School Samples

http://www.mncts.org/spssod/1/echert/WEBPAGE.htm, Excellent example of online material

http://www.mncts.org/spssod/1/jenkins/PT709/index.htm, Dr. David Jenkins, online elements for Liturgical Presidency course (in process)

http://www.bibletutor.com, Luther Seminary Bible Tutor

http://www.luthersem.edu/ckoester/revelation/main.htm , Highly graphical treatment for Genesis to Revelation course

* Ed. note: Some of these websites may no longer be active.

http://www.luthersem.edu/ckoester/paul/main.htm , Same highly graphical treatment applied to Paul course

http://john.fishersnet.net/ot1110penta_fl99/SyllabusF00.htm, Sample seminary Online Class

http://www.bethel.edu/seminary_academics/gensem/pferris/, Bethel Seminary - Paul Ferris OT courses combine open access and WCB

http://www.bethel.edu/seminary_academics/gensem/pferris/ot103/, Vector maps of the Holy Land and video and audio streaming media

http://www.bethel.edu/~gbourgon/, wealth of reflective material on distributed learning with guides for training faculty

http://www.bethel.edu/~gbourgon/Workshop.html, Instructional Processes given to faculty Spring 2000

Interesting New Stuff

www.idrive.com, idrive web storage

www.fineprint.com, Fine print saves paper and makes print storage easier

www.htmleditor.com, Coffee Cup's new online editor scheduled for Sept. 2000

Great Resources

www.mncts.org/workshops/CormodeMSW6.pdf , Dr. Scott Cormode's *Using Computers in Theological Education: Rules of Thumb*. Excellent discussion of PowerPoint and teaching using technology

http://www.christianleaders.org/ , Dr. Cormode's Almond Springs Case Study site (GREAT)

http://info.med.yale.edu/caim/manual/, Dr. Patrick Lynch's Web Style Guide online

www.patricklynch.net, Excellent example

Final Note

www.growingupdigital.com, Web site for Don Tapscott's best selling book on the subject of technology

www.ericir.syr.edu/Projects/Campus_computing/1998/, 1998 Campus Computing Project

http://www.isos.goarch.org, Internet School of Orthodox Studies – DRE, Greek Orthodox Archdiocese

NOTES

[1] *Technology Advertising Report*, November 10, 1999. TBWA International website.
[2] "Teenage Research Unlimited Press Release" (January 1996). TRU website.

[3] Brown and Brown, "Distance Education around the World." In B. Willis ed., *Distance Education: Strategies and Tools* (Englewood: Educational Technologies, 1994) p. 3. For more information on this subject, see B. Brown, "Digital Classrooms: Some Myths About Developing New Educational Programs Using the Internet" available online: http://www.thejournal.com/magazine/98/dec/feat04.html (Dec. 17, 1999); D. Dimitroyannis, "The Virtual Classroom: A Case Study" available online http://cuiwww.unige.ch/eao/www/OpenDistLearning/paper/html (Jan. 17, 1999); and C.K. Green "When Wishes Come True: Colleges and the Convergence of Access, lifelong learning and technology" available online http://irsdb2.ed.uiuc.edu:591/FMPro?-db=tested.fp3&-lay=allGrades&format=/testdb/stars/stars.html (Jan. 7, 2000).

[4] R. Oldenburg, *The great good place* (New York: Paragon House, 1991).

[5] Cyber Dialogue American Internet User Survey (2001). www.shop.org/learn/stats or www.Disneyonline.org.

[6] www.netratings.com/globalinternettrends

[7] Barna Research Company, Internet Survey, 2001

[8] *PewInternet and AmericanLife Project: Online Life Report*, (Washington, DC: Pew Foundation, 2001), p. 2.

[9] NetDay 2001

[10] In L. Sherry "Issues in Distance Learning." International Journal of Educational Telecommunications 1(4), p. 338. For more information see: E. Plotnick, *Trends in Educational Technology 1995* (Eric Digest No ED398861) Washington, DC: Association for the Study of Higher Education, 1996; K. McKinney, *Technology in Community Colleges* (Eric Digest No ED399992) Washington, DC: Association for the Study of Higher Education, 1996; G. C. Van Dusen, *The Virtual Campus: Technology Reform in Higher Education* (Eric Digest No ED412815).

[11] Online Distance Learning in Higher Education Report (2001) International Data Corporation

[12] D. Tapscott, *Growing Up Digital: The Rise of the Net Generation* (New York: McGraw-Hill, 1998), p. 22.

[13] Tapscott, p. 9.

[14] Tapscott, p. 27.

[15] Tapscott, p. 23.

[16] Tapscott, p. 29.

[17] M Benedikt, *Cyberspace First Steps* (Cambridge, MA: MIT Press, 1991), pp. 1-2.

[18] D. Shale and R. Garrison, *Education at a Distance: From Issues to Practice* (Malabar, FL: Krieger Publishing, 1990), p. 2.

[19] T. Moods, *Distance Education: An Annotated Bibliography* (Englewood, CO: Libraries Unlimited, 1995), p. 19.

[20] L. Maxwell, "Integrating Open Learning and Distance Education," *Educational Technology* 35:2 (1995), p. 43.

[21] H. Cheng, J. Lehman, and A. Reynolds, "What We Know about Asynchronous Group Computer-based Distance Learning," *Educational Technologies* 31:11 (1991), p. 16.

[22] Cheng, Lehman, and Reynolds, p. 16.

[23] Moods, p. 19.

[24] A. Kaye, "Computer-mediated Communication and Distance Education." In R. Manson, ed., *Mindweave: Communications, Computers, and Distance Education* (Oxford: Pergamon Press, 1989), p. 9.

[25] Kaye, pp. 10-13.

[26] Kaye, p. 10.

[27] Cheng, Lehman, and Reynolds, p. 17.

[28] C. Blackwood and B. White, "Technology for Teaching and Learning." In M. Galbraith, ed., *Facilitating* Learning (Malabar, FL: Krieger Publishing, 1991), p. 153.

[29] Moods, pp. 127-130.

[30] Cheng, Lehman, and Reynolds, pp. 16-17.

[31] F. Jevons, "Blurring the Boundaries: Parity and Convergence." In D. Garrison and D. Shale, eds., *Education at a Distance* (Malabar, FL: Krieger Publishing, 1990), p. 138.

[32] M. Kelly, "Course Creation Issues in Distance Education." In D. Garrison and D. Shale, eds., *Education at a Distance* (Malabar, FL: Krieger Publishing, 1990), p. 95.

[33] Al Gore, *Earth in the Balance* (New York: Penguin-Putnam 1992)

[34] W. Milheim, "Implementing Distance Education Programs: Suggestions for Potential Developers," Educational Technologies 31:4 (1991), p. 51

[35] Shale and Garrison, p. 4.

[36] Shale and Garrison, p. 5.

[37] Tapscott, p. 139.

[38] Tapscott, pp. 142-149.

[39] Shale and Garrison, p. 25.

[40] Shale and Garrison, p. 26.

[41] Shale and Garrison, p. 27.

[42] Milheim, pp. 51-53.

[43] Tapscott, p. 27.

[44] R. Garrison, "The Role of Technology in Continuing Education." In R. Brockett, ed., *Continuing Education in the Year 2000*, New Directions for Continuing Education, 36 (San Francisco: Jossey Bass, 1987). For more information see: J.L. Lemke, "Hypermedia and Higher Education." In T. Harrison and T. Stephen, eds., Computer Networking and Scholarly Communication (New York: State University Press, 1996); *Online Distance Learning in Higher Education Report*, International Data Corporation, 2001.

The Character and Life of a Local Parish: St. George Antiochian Orthodox Church, Boston

Michael Ellias

St. George Antiochian Orthodox Church of Boston just celebrated its one hundredth anniversary last year, and it ranks as the third-oldest parish in the archdiocese behind the mother church of St. Nicholas Cathedral in Brooklyn, New York, and St. Michael Church of Beaumont, Texas. The newly glorified St. Bishop Raphael of Brooklyn founded the parish among the "Syrian" immigrants who came to the New World at the turn of the century. These immigrants were fleeing Turkish oppression, seeking greater economic opportunities, and hoping for better futures for their children.

In addition to those original Levantine pilgrims whose offspring are now in their fourth generation, St. George has received succeeding tides of immigrants following World Wars I and II, and most recently incorporated an enormous inflow as a result of the fifteen-year "uncivil" war in Lebanon. This continuing immigration has created a situation where English is the predominant worship language, but there is a real need to minister in Arabic. Indeed the parish has experimented over the last two years with a second liturgy in Arabic at least once a month. There is, therefore, a strong ethnic identity to the parish that is both a strength and a weakness. While the *ethos* of the parish is thoroughly Orthodox, there is a creative tension between generations and between the established families and those more recently arrived. There are also divergent attitudes toward piety and polity in the so-called "American" and "Arabic" communities which present a question as to whether or not the parish should multiply into two or more still sizable communities.

St. George is far and away the largest church in the Antiochian Archdiocese of North America. The most recent census counted in excess of 1300 members in approximately 750-800 households; however, there are literally hundreds of other families who utilize St. George's services but are not officially registered with the parish. Despite the gaudy numbers, approximately only 250 households constitute the heart of the parish in terms of active

271

leadership, regular attendance and material support. The remaining families
are firmly rooted in their own minds and often nurture their young organically in the faith, but these non-participating families also include many
who are simply there through ethnic identification or spiritual inertia.

St. George is an urban parish, but its membership lives in largely middle
class neighborhoods and, increasingly, suburban settings. Geographically
the bulk of this population is centered in the West Roxbury, Roslindale and
Hyde Park neighborhoods of Boston, along with the surrounding towns of
Dedham, Norwood and Walpole along the Route 1 South corridor. The
rest of the population, however, is literally scattered around New England.
Members call St. George home even though they may live as far north as
Maine or New Hampshire, as far west as Shrewsbury near Worcester, as far
south as Rhode Island and Connecticut, and well out onto Cape Cod.

This geographic dispersion presents multiple pastoral challenges. On the
one hand, many parishioners live at great distances and are unable, therefore, to participate in parish life on a regular basis. On the other hand, these
parishioners in *diaspora*, so to speak, typically will not attend even other
Antiochian parishes nearer their homes, not to mention parishes of other
Orthodox jurisdictions, because of a powerful attachment to and identification with their parents' or grandparents' church. In other words, these
distant members would prefer not to go to church at all rather than attend
a "foreign" parish. As a non-Bostonian and a person who has lived in at
least five other cities and shared parish life fruitfully in each setting, this
puzzling perspective looks to me like a kind of ancestor worship. Although
this phenomenon is probably observable in other parts of the country or
even the world, here in New England the attitude seems to be shaped by a
certain "Yankee Congregationalism."

The parochial pastoral staff includes myself, an archpriest with fourteen
years of service, a newly arrived Arabic-speaking assistant archpriest, a truly
pious and holy attached archimandrite, a full-time youth director, and a
part-time deacon. The church's administrative staff includes a full-time
secretary and a full-time sexton. While this amount of staff may exceed
most parishes, it is still strained literally to the limit. This need forces us,
thankfully, to rely on significant lay ministries to fill the void. The parish
has adopted the "Parish Ministry Team" model pioneered by the Fellowship of St. John the Divine in the archdiocese. Ministry teams include outreach to seniors, the sick and shut-ins, the lapsed, and new members. There
are other teams dedicated to mundane but necessary tasks such as bread
baking, grounds beautification and building maintenance.

A constitution and by-laws govern the parish in a standard parish council format. A general parish meeting elects parochial officers as well as members of the parish council. Each parochial fellowship group or organization also designates a representative to the council as a voting member. These groups include an Adult Fellowship (over-50 crowd), a Sunday church school, Parents' Guild (in support of the church school), a Ladies' Society, Teen SOYO (Syrian Orthodox Youth Organization), Choir and Chanters, and a newly formed Young Adult Fellowship. While the parish is attempting to move toward a stewardship system, the traditionalists cling to a pledge system supplemented by an annual parish festival and other fundraising events. The last two years have seen the establishment of an endowment fund to provide the resources for additional ministries, especially to youth and young adults, as a complement to the operating budget.

The parish is now in its third location. After an initial phase near Tyler and Hudson Street in what is now Chinatown, the parish moved to the South End of Boston. At one point St. George Church was located on St. George Street where Fr. George R. George was the pastor! The current physical plant is located on the grounds of the former Arnold estate, the same family that established the Arnold Arboretum. The church, with its newly-replaced roof, was built in 1979 and is fully furnished with excellent iconography, stained glass, chandeliers and liturgical appointments. A small office and conference area connects a social hall that comfortably seats four hundred and a church school area of nine classrooms and office.

The absolute center of parish life, however, is the liturgical cycle. In addition to Great Vespers on Saturday evening with Orthros and the Divine Liturgy on Sunday morning, there is also a mid-week service, usually small vespers on Wednesday, followed by Bible Study or continuing Adult Education, and seasonally appropriate services. During Great Lent there is a Divine Liturgy of the Presanctified Gifts on Wednesday evenings and Small Compline with Akathist Hymn on Friday evenings. Holy Week actually begins with the Great Vespers for the Saturday of Lazarus, includes three Presanctified Liturgies, the Sacrament of Holy Unction and all traditionally prescribed services. In a typical year we celebrate as many as sixty-five baptisms and chrismations, fifteen marriages, and approximately twelve funerals.

In a marvelous recent development and as a counterbalance to New England's notorious parochialism, the parish has sponsored a new mission in Hingham on the South Shore. The mission started three years ago with a small group of former Protestants and their pastor and now numbers more than sixty members. The oldest member is the pastor himself at fifty-three, and half the membership is under eighteen years of age. The potential is enormous, but the challenges are legion. Since Pentecost there has also been discussion about starting yet another mission in the Fall River–New Bedford area of Southeastern Massachusetts. May God bless those endeavors.

As one of the oldest parishes in the Antiochian Archdiocese, and certainly one of the largest, St. George Church is a complex and challenging parish that has historically taken a leadership role in archdiocesan and inter-Orthodox affairs. While facing the challenges of a multi-ethnic and multilingual membership, a broad geographic dispersion, and a certain staid mentality, the clergy and laity of the parish cooperate at worship, work and play in a way hopefully pleasing to God with the hope of bearing witness to the Gospel of Christ in a dark and fallen world.

CONTRIBUTORS

George S. Bebis is Professor of Patrology *Emeritus* at Holy Cross Greek Orthodox School of Theology, Brookline, Massachusetts.

Peter L. Berger is Director of the Institute on Religion and World Affairs at Boston University.

Rev. Alkiviadis Calivas is Professor of Liturgics at Holy Cross Greek Orthodox School of Theology, Brookline, Massachusetts.

Rev. John Chakos serves on the Orthodox Christian Mission Center Board and has done foreign mission work in Galilee, Africa, and Guatemala. He is the Pastor of Holy Cross Greek Orthodox Church, Pittsburgh, Pennsylvania.

Rev. William Chiganos is Pastor of the Holy Apostles Greek Orthodox Church, Westchester, Illinois.

Rev. Michael Ellias is Pastor of the St. George Orthodox Church (Antiochian Archdiocese), Boston, Massachusetts.

John H. Erickson is Dean and the Peter N. Gramowich Professor of Church History at St. Vladimir's Orthodox Theological Seminary, Crestwood, New York, where he also teaches in the area of Canon Law.

Rev. Thomas FitzGerald is Professor of Church History and Historical Theology at Holy Cross Greek Orthodox School of Theology, Brookline, Massachusetts.

Robert Haddad is Sophia Smith Professor of History and Professor of Religion *Emeritus* at Smith College. He is a member of the Antiochian Orthodox Church.

275

Rev. Stanley S. Harakas is the Archbishop Iakovos Professor of Orthodox Theology *Emeritus* at Holy Cross Greek Orthodox School of Theology, Brookline, Massachusetts.

Rev. Thomas Hopko, who served in three different parishes, is Emeritus Professor of Dogmatic and Practical Theology and Dean of St. Vladimir's Orthodox Theological Seminary, Crestwood, New York.

Rev. Charles Joanides, LMFT is the Director of the Interfaith Marriage Research Project for the Greek Orthodox Archdiocese of America. He is also the pastor of the St. Nicholas Greek Orthodox Church in Newburgh, New York and has a private practice specializing in reclaiming marriages.

Steven Karidoyanes is an orchestra conductor and a composer. He has been both a church musician and professional musician for over twenty-five years. Among other institutions of higher education, he served on the faculty of Hellenic College from 1979 to 1983. He served as President of the New England Federation of Greek Orthodox Choirs from 1999-2001.

John Klentos is Assistant Professor of Orthodox Theology at the Graduate Theological Union, Berkeley, California.

Thomas C. Lelon is Professor of Management at Nicholas College, Dudley, Massachusetts. He is a former president of Hellenic College and Holy Cross Greek Orthodox School of Theology, and Central New England Colleges.

Rev. Frank Marangos is Director of the Department of Religious Education of the Greek Orthodox Archdiocese of America.

Paul Meyendorff is the Alexander Schmemann Professor of Liturgical Theology at St. Vladimir's Orthodox Theological Seminary, Crestwood, New York, where he is also Associate Dean for Academic Affairs.

Rev. George Papademetriou is Associate Professor at Hellenic College and Holy Cross Greek Orthodox School of Theology, Brookline, Massachusetts.

Jaroslav Pelikan is the Sterling Professor of History *Emeritus* at Yale University, is currently the John W. Kluge Scholar at the Library of Congress.

Rev. Theodore Stylianopoulos is the Archbishop Iakovos Professor of Orthodox Theology at Holy Cross Greek Orthodox School of Theology, Brookline, Massachusetts.

Rev. Patrick Viscuso is a priest of the Greek Orthodox Archdiocese and a canonist specializing in marriage and gender issues.

Anton C. Vrame is Director of the Patriarch Athenagoras Orthodox Institute in Berkeley, California.

Printed in the United States
17005LVS00004B/55-153